'Kirdar's *Saving Iraq* brings clear insight and valuable substance into the complex issues of restoring Iraq to the stable, prosperous and civil society it once was'

Dr Henry Kissinger, former Secretary of State and
National Security Advisor

'Nemir Kirdar has used his deep personal knowledge of Iraq and the Middle East to outline carefully thought-out proposals to enable a new Iraq to become a force for stability and prosperity in the region'   Lt General Brent Scowcroft, National Security Adviser under
Presidents Ford and Bush

'A bold vision of how that potentially wealthy country can be put back on its feet. His is an Iraqi voice that should be heard ... and widely read!'

Dr Zbigniew Brzezinski, US National Security Adviser under
President Carter

'What struck and moved me is Nemir Kirdar's passion, which shines through every page. A lucid and courageous commentary'
Alain Juppé, Former Prime Minister of France & now Mayor of Bordeaux

'Nemir Kirdar describes old Iraq as a country of enormous potential . . . on course for positive economic development and a bright future'   Dr Wolfgang Schussel, Former Federal Chancellor of Austria

'The future of Iraq will affect every human being. Kirdar's book provides the signposts for a more peaceful and prosperous future of a tormented country'

Professor Klaus Schwab, Founder, President and Executive Chairman,
World Economic Forum, Geneva

'Kirdar's insights help make sense of recent history and headlines. He lays out a vision for a future worthy of the next generation of Iraqis – one that only they can make for themselves'

Strobe Talbott, President, The Brookings Institution

Nemir Kirdar is the founder, executive chairman and CEO of the global investment group Investcorp, which operates out of New York, London and Bahrain. Now a British citizen, he was born in Iraq but left the country after the military coup of 1958.

Mr Kirdar began his banking career in New York in 1969. After covering South East Asia and Japan for Allied Bank International, he joined Chase Manhattan Bank, New York, in 1974. Between 1976 and 1981 he managed and directed Chase's banking network in the Arabian Gulf. He founded Investcorp in 1982.

Investcorp's mission is to act as a bridge between surplus funds in the Gulf and alternative, non-traditional investment opportunities in the USA and Western Europe. Its investment products include private equity, hedge funds, real estate, technology investments and Gulf growth capital. The firm's 400 staff are drawn from 38 nationalities.

Mr Kirdar graduated in Economics from the University of the Pacific in California, obtained an MBA from Fordham University in New York and completed Harvard Business School's Senior Management Program. He has since been awarded an honorary doctorate in Humane Letters from Georgetown University; an honorary doctorate in Laws from the University of the Pacific; and an honorary doctorate in Economics from Richmond, the American International University in London. He is an Honorary Fellow of St Antony's College, Oxford.

Mr Kirdar serves as director, trustee, councillor or adviser to numerous institutions in the USA and UK. These include George-town University, the Brookings Institution and the Center for Strategic and International Studies in Washington DC; the Eisenhower Exchange Fellowship in Philadelphia; the School of International and Public Affairs at New York's Columbia University; John F. Kennedy School of Government at Harvard University; Chatham House in London and the Judge Business School at Cambridge University. He is a founding member of the International Business Council of the World Economic Forum in Geneva and serves on the Board of the United Nations Pension Fund.

SAVING IRAQ

Rebuilding a Broken Nation

Nemir Kirdar

PHOENIX

A PHOENIX PAPERBACK

First published in Great Britain in 2009
by Weidenfeld & Nicolson
This paperback edition published in 2010
by Phoenix,
an imprint of Orion Books Ltd,
Orion House, 5 Upper St Martin's Lane,
London WC2H 9EA

An Hachette UK company

1 3 5 7 9 10 8 6 4 2

A CIP catalogue record for this book
is available from the British Library.

ISBN 978-0-7538-2704-8

Typeset by Input Data Services Ltd,
Bridgwater, Somerset

Printed and bound in Great Britain by
CPI Mackays, Chatham ME5 8TD

The Orion Publishing Group's policy is to use papers that
are natural, renewable and recyclable products and
made from wood grown in sustainable forests. The logging
and manufacturing processes are expected to conform to
the environmental regulations of the country of origin.

www.orionbooks.co.uk

To Nada, my wife and life partner

We met and married in Baghdad. When the time came
to begin our lives all over again in New York in 1969,
it was she who gave me the strength. From that day
to this, she has been the rock upon which I have relied –
for which I am profoundly grateful.

Contents

Map   x

Introduction   xiii

Part One – Iraq past: Prosperous Hashemite monarchy to brutal dictatorship, 1921–1990

   1   A road of hope becomes a tunnel of despair   3

   2   Lessons and examples from the past   31

Part Two – Iraq present: The build-up to war, occupation and disintegration, 1990–2008

   3   A road to a new Iraq not taken   63

   4   The neo-conservative recipe for disaster   89

   5   Giant steps backward   111

Part Three – Iraq future: A blueprint for prosperity and peace

   6   Making a new political start   149

   7   Fuelling progress with oil   164

   8   Building a vibrant economy   185

   9   Developing the greatest resource   217

   10 Awaiting visionary leaders   238

   Conclusion   258

   Endnotes   273

   Acknowledgements   277

   Index   281

   About the author   295

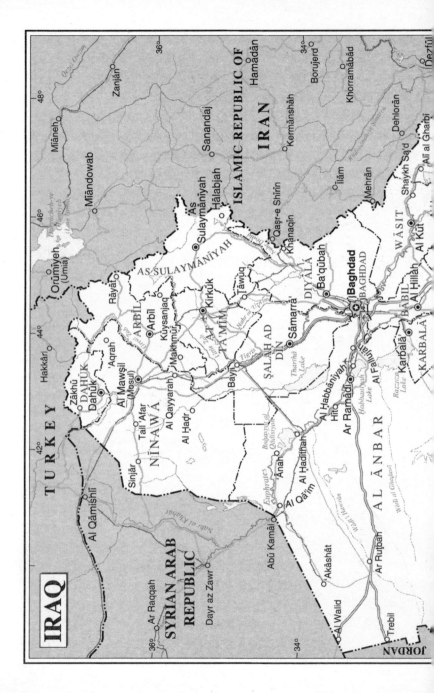

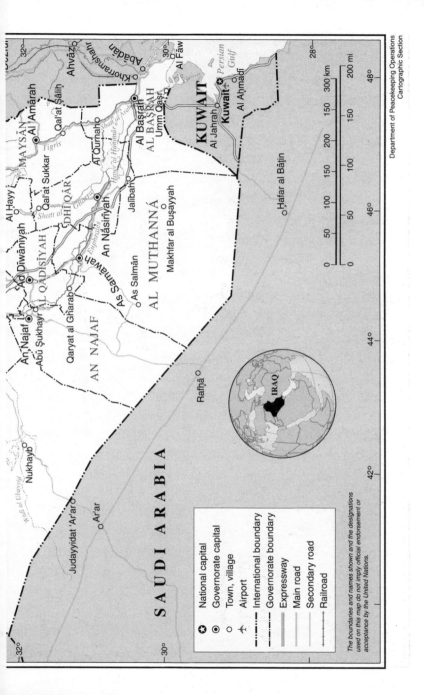

SAUDI ARABIA

IRAQ

KUWAIT

MAYSĀN

DHĪ QĀR

AL MUTHANNÁ

AN NAJAF

AL QĀDISĪYAH

AL BAŞRAH

Persian Gulf

Al 'Amārah
Qal'at Şāliḥ
Al Ḩayy
Qal'at Sukkar
Al Qurnah
Al Başrah
Umm Qaşr
Al Fāw
Khorramshahr
Ahvāz
Abādān

Tigris
Shatt al Gharrāf
Shaṭṭ al 'Arab
Nahr al Ḩammār al Arab

An Nāṣirīyah
As Samāwah
Ad Dīwānīyah
An Najaf
Abū Şukhayr
Qaryat al Gharab
As Salmān
Makhfar al Buşayyah
Jalībah
Ḩafar al Bāṭin

Euphrates
Shaṭṭ al Gharrāf

Nukhayb
Wādī al Ubayyiḑ
Rafḩā
Ar'ar
Judayyidat 'Ar'ar

KUWAIT
Al Jahrah
Kuwait
Al Aḩmadi

Legend

- ✪ National capital
- ◉ Governorate capital
- ○ Town, village
- ✈ Airport
- ·–·–· International boundary
- –·–·– Governorate boundary
- ═══ Expressway
- ——— Main road
- ——— Secondary road
- +++ Railroad

The boundaries and names shown and the designations used on this map do not imply official endorsement or acceptance by the United Nations.

0   50   100   150   200   300 km
0   50   100   150   200 mi

32°   30°   28°
42°   44°   46°   48°

Introduction

This is a very personal book about an old Iraq and a new Iraq.

The old Iraq is but a sweet and inspiring memory from my days as a child and young man. It was a country that was on the path to unity and prosperity under moderate, wise and patriotic leaders until a violent *coup d'état* in July 1958 set it on a course of dictatorship, oppression and denial of the population's rights and potential.

The new Iraq is a country I believe can still emerge from the broken Iraq of today. It is an Iraq of my dreams, and the dreams of many other Iraqis. This Iraq of tomorrow can be the country it was always meant to be if its leaders and people reassert the cherished values and principles of their country's promising early years: national pride, good governance, tolerance, openness and economic freedom.

Before I present my vision for a new Iraq, I feel it is necessary to dispel a number of myths and misconceptions that stand in the way of properly assessing the current situation and realizing the potential that is waiting to be unleashed in the country's rebirth. The most recent myths revolve around the claimed success of the US occupation's 'surge' policy and the outlook for future democracy and prosperity under current political arrangements. The occupation has done Iraq untold material damage. It has set back the cause of unity and democracy by promoting short-term solutions such as fostering the politics of division. I shall deal in more detail with the 'surge' policy's failures, but will note for the moment only that they have papered over deep-seated political and social problems that are bound to emerge before long.

Another myth is that political reform is on track and will lead the country towards democracy and prosperity. This is far from the truth. The current constitution has worsened the situation by giving rise to leaders whose main interests are personal gain rather than national unity and well-being. In short, the chaotic, divisive violence of the worst years of the insurgency have given way to a period of fewer casualties but no less uncertainty, no greater security, and no more ultimate hope for the future. Iraq is still a broken country, with dim prospects if current trends continue.

All the same, I believe that it is still possible to make the positive changes outlined in the following pages. I am a person whose optimism is based on the hard truths I have seen and experienced. When I was growing up, for example, I lived in the united, prosperous and promising Iraq of the pre-1958 era. I therefore feel confident that this nation can be put together again by dedicated leaders who share a clear vision for a new Iraq based on the best examples from its own remembered past as well as on other political and economic success stories around the world.

When the tyrannical and corrupt dictatorship of Saddam Hussein came to an end in the spring of 2003, I felt that the people of Iraq faced a unique opportunity. Unshackled from the terror and oppression of a widely despised regime, Iraqis at last had a chance to build for themselves a prosperous economy, establish an open and tolerant political system, and unleash a vibrant cultural reawakening that would fulfil their ambitions, inspire their neighbours and exert a stabilizing influence over a troubled region.

Unfortunately, it is clear that the situation in Iraq deteriorated gravely during the years of American occupation. It is my belief that a wholesale and lasting reversal of the country's fortunes is possible only if bold changes are set in motion. Given the proper conditions, I am convinced that a new and better Iraq can emerge from the ashes of the old. Because of my Iraqi heritage, experience in international business and interest in world affairs, many people have sought me out since 2003, asking for my opinions and insights regarding Iraq – its complex past, troubled present and uncertain future. In this book I elaborate on some of the views I have offered, in private and public venues, in recent years.

While the key role played by President George W. Bush in toppling the tyrant will be recognized by history, the declared intention of the US administration to create a stable, prosperous and democratic nation has not been achieved. By pointing out the misguided policies that led to this and other failures, and lamenting the immense harm done to Iraqi society and the cause of democracy and prosperity, I am in no way disparaging the United States and the great values upon which it stands.

On the contrary, I have the highest respect and admiration for the US and its history of freedom, democracy and economic opportunity. Indeed, I have been a beneficiary of these values in my own life, and I continue to admire them. I was educated at a US college and received my professional training at a US bank. I have many close American friends and colleagues whom I trust and respect. Of my two daughters, one was born in New York and the other grew up there. Both of my granddaughters were born in the US. The bulk of my non-profit work is for US institutions – Georgetown, Columbia and Harvard Universities, The Brookings Institution, Eisenhower Exchange Fellowships, and others.

In short, I am grateful for all the chances I have had in the US. I respect America's values and ideals, its optimism, its strong sense of individual liberty, its willingness to offer a home and, more importantly, hope to the world's immigrants, and its contribution to human advancement. If I criticize certain decisions of the US administration, it is a criticism born out of disappointment for what could have been, coupled with concern as an internationalist who wants to build a better world of peace and prosperity.

Part One of this book deals with Iraq before its occupation in 2003 and draws mainly upon my recollections and observations from before and after my emigration. This account of life in Iraq is a reflection of my personal views rather than an academic analysis. My family and friends lived Iraq's history; their experiences as well as my own have shaped my perspective. I treasure many fond memories of the Iraq of my youth, a land of great promise, and these memories have inspired and motivated me. Growing up, I saw around me a society that had considerable freedom and was progressing towards democracy and prosperity. Iraq was stable, vibrant and pro-Western and had enormous potential. But hopes for a bright future were suddenly dashed on 14 July 1958 when a handful of army conspirators staged a brutal coup, seized power and drove the nation into a long, dark tunnel of terror and destruction.

Although I was out of Iraq when the coup took place,

I returned in 1962 following my college education in the US. However, because the political and economic prospects of the country continued to deteriorate, I left my homeland for good in 1969, heavy of heart. Iraq's path towards socialism, nationalization, dictatorship and a police state left no hope for a person like me who was, ideologically, of an opposite mindset.

In Part Two I analyse the period from the Iraqi invasion of Kuwait in August 1990 to the post-2003 occupation, drawing on my own trajectory of thinking. During this period I became more involved in foreign policy discussions, often with high officials, particularly with regard to the fate of Iraq. While I was among those who advocated the removal of Saddam Hussein in order to free the people of Iraq, I describe in this section how my prescription for a post-Saddam Iraq differed markedly from the views of those who eventually succeeded in implementing much of their unsuccessful and short-sighted agenda. I firmly believe that it was possible to overthrow the dictator without throwing the country into the state of chaos, violence and disintegration that eventually prevailed. I present a brief summary of the period since the fall of the Saddam regime and explain the causes of my deep disappointment and sorrow at the downward turn the country has taken. The occupation has inflamed and intensified ethnic and religious tensions, and this has divided the nation and encouraged the wrong leadership to emerge.

Some of those who celebrated the collapse of the evil regime in Iraq stated that, now the threat of Saddam had been removed, the country should be left to find its own way, irrespective of what might follow. However, there were others, myself among them, who hoped for much more than that. Recognizing Iraq's enormous potential, I thought the opportunity should be seized to build a prosperous, tolerant and peaceful nation with a vibrant civil society. Iraq has all the fundamental ingredients to become a world-class country.

Unfortunately, the developments that followed the collapse of Saddam's regime have been a catastrophic disappointment. Nevertheless, I am convinced that the current perilous course of events is not irreversible. It may take several years, but if at some point in time a critical mass of Iraqis choose to reconstruct their nation along modern lines, they should be able to achieve the success and prosperity that everyone desires.

Of course, the ultimate success of Iraq would have benefits far beyond its own borders. From a regional perspective, the vital importance of stability in Iraq cannot be overstated. A failed Iraq, on the other hand, could severely undermine its neighbours and endanger Gulf security. The lack of internal security has drawn foreign terrorists to Iraq, and political instability and discontent have given rise to radicalism and sectarianism among its citizens. Should this process continue, the neighbouring countries could become more involved in the violence, either to increase their influence or in sheer self-defence. Moreover, there is a real danger that the country will become permanently divided, which would have dire consequences.

Part Three contains the heart of the book. While it is important to highlight the great unrealized potential of pre-1958 Iraq, and to analyse the grievous shortcomings of the occupation, my main motivation in this endeavour has been to present my vision for saving Iraq. And so in this part I describe how Iraq can become a beacon of true democracy and prosperity if only its abundant human and material resources are wisely harnessed. In this comprehensive blueprint for a political, economic and social transformation, I draw on examples from the past, the present and my own personal experiences to show how the people of Iraq can build a better future. I believe the Iraq of tomorrow should have government institutions that promote unity, ensure justice for all, and honestly and efficiently carry out their responsibilities. The country's economy should be open, innovative and governed by the rule of law. And the most basic social needs of the people – health, housing and education, all long neglected – should be made a priority. Only in such an environment will the young Iraqis of today have a chance to live their dreams as adults.

The transition from totalitarian rule to democracy, and from a socialist economy to free enterprise, will be neither rapid nor easy. It will require decades of sustained effort and leaders who possess foresight and determination. The total realignment of the social, economic, political and cultural mindset of the population can only be carried out if strong, qualified, talented and courageous Iraqi leaders take up the banner of change. They must undo the damage of the past even before they build a new future. This includes eradicating the culture of corruption and putting an end to self-serving politicians exploiting for their own ends the political and economic climate that followed the occupation of Iraq in 2003.

During the first years of the occupation, the people of Iraq suffered horrific violence. While the number of incidents declined in 2008, the underlying causes remained, which means that future flare-ups of killing and destruction are inevitable. And on the political front, the dictatorships of the past have been replaced by sectarianism and warlord rule in the guise of 'democracy'. Therefore I am convinced that if the present course is not reversed, the people of Iraq will never be able to realize their potential. However, I also believe that it is still not too late to save the country. Iraq can re-emerge from this period of pain and peril and be restored to become a prosperous nation and world-class exemplar. The country has all the vital natural and human resources needed to make this rise to excellence possible.

In addition, the people of Iraq have one potent social asset that few countries in the world possess: a cultural memory of past greatness. Iraqis are descendants of the oldest civilized societies in the world. This land between the Tigris and Euphrates rivers, called for centuries *al-Iraq* in Arabic, was the cradle of some of the greatest urban civilizations of antiquity, including those of the Akkadians, Sumerians, Babylonians and Assyrians. The inhabitants of these city-states were able to prosper because agriculture, for the first time in human history, could provide large surpluses of food. For millennia, Meso-potamia was home to a diverse society living in cities, villages and arid steppe, bound together by ancient and complex social and economic interconnections. After the rise of Islam, the Baghdad of the Abbasid caliphate was not only the centre Islamic culture but the intellectual capital of the world while the people of Europe languished in their so-called Dark Ages.

These shining episodes of their history can help reunite and inspire the people of Iraq, providing an example of how past greatness was achieved even among a diverse population, and pointing the way towards a future that can be just as illustrious. But first, Iraqis must disengage the current corrupt and incompetent warlords who have been injected by the occupation to rule their country. They must replace the destructive 2005 constitution with a new political charter that ensures unity, integrity, fairness and tolerance. And the people of Iraq must have qualified leaders who will govern in an honourable and visionary manner.

This is a personal account and vision for a country I still care about, four decades after leaving it.

The Iraq I left behind for good in 1969 held prospects as dim as the Iraq of today. After completing my university studies and getting established in the world of banking in New York, I saw that the situation at home had not improved and so decided to permanently become a citizen of the world. I moved to London in 1982, the year Investcorp was established. It quickly emerged as a respected and successful global financial organization specializing in alternative investments, operating in the Gulf and on both sides of the Atlantic. My professional experience has developed my insights and instincts regarding the political and economic characteristics of successful countries around the world. I bring this background to bear in the pages that follow.

Twice in my life I crossed the Atlantic penniless but found an environment in the US that allowed me to learn, to earn and to compete. I have no plans to return to the land of my ancestors and, as I have said, the Iraq that I envision is not for me, but for the youth of tomorrow. It is my heartfelt hope that they will be able to grow up in an environment that allows them to achieve their full aspirations and to go as far as their energies and abilities can take them.

I was forced to leave my native country in order to find my fulfilment. My hope is that the children of the future Iraq need not emigrate but will be able to attain their dreams in a land reborn.

PART ONE

*Iraq past: Prosperous Hashemite
monarchy to brutal dictatorship, 1921–1990*

I

A road of hope becomes
a tunnel of despair

My hope for a better future for Iraq is based not on a fanciful dream but on the hard realities of what Iraq used to be: a country on the road to openness, tolerance and prosperity.

That road still lies open. It may be difficult for many to imagine an Iraq brimming with hope, for most Iraqis have lived their lives under an oppressive dictatorship, and outsiders have consumed a media diet heavily seasoned with reports of sectarianism, corruption and violent repression. Yet when I think of Iraq, and what its people are capable of accomplishing, my mind is drawn not to the dark days of its recent past, but to the brighter period before 1958.

During the country's formative years, its leaders were beginning to fashion a political and economic system that held great promise. Government was not repressive, demanding absolute obedience at the barrel of a gun. Instead there were political organizations of nearly every stripe engaging in debate about what was best for the country. There was a large degree of media freedom and cultural openness, unheard of after 1958. And in the economic sphere, ambitious and entrepreneurial Iraqis had an opportunity to make a good life for their families, while at the same time improving the fortunes of the country.

The government was encouraging free enterprise and fuelling this economic boom by investing in infrastructure and other large-scale improvements.

This Iraq did not emerge without difficulties. The inhabitants of the country had endured the violence and privations of the First World War and the collapse of the Ottoman empire and, like peoples around the world at this time, they yearned for self-government and independence. These dreams were blown away by a British occupation that put a priority on imperial interests in the region rather than local aspirations. Nonetheless, out of the struggle between these often conflicting Iraqi and British aims arose the country's constitutional monarchy, under which a sense of true Iraqi nationalism began to take root. In the end, the persistent efforts by Iraqis to win self-rule resulted over a number of years in a steady decline in British control and eventually in full independence. And the development of Iraq's oil industry resulted in economic advancement that began to take the country from poverty to prosperity.

In short, life was good in the country of my birth before it turned so very bad. After a violent *coup d'état* in 1958 did away with the constitutional monarchy, the political freedoms and institutions which had been gradually put in place since independence were dismantled by Iraq's new military dictators. Press restrictions increased, and the government's control of large segments of the economy ushered in a period of inefficiency and corruption.

In the following pages I will give the reader a brisk and personal tour of the formative years of the Iraqi state as the fortunes of the Iraqi people promisingly rose, then disappointingly declined.

The British mandate, 1920–1932

British officials took control of the former Ottoman provinces between Persia and Turkey after the First World War because these lands lay astride the strategically important imperial route to India. The British initially called their imperial spoils 'Mesopotamia', using the Greek-derived English name for 'the land between the rivers' – the Tigris and Euphrates. But this choice also implied an effort to unify formerly distinct but closely connected Ottoman provinces. For millennia the peoples of these lands had more in common with each other than with the people of neighbouring lands. A tight and complex web of social and economic connections bound the people of Mesopotamia to one another, and their shared history dating to the dawn of civilization provided another powerful force for unity.

. Britain's claim to the lands that would become modern Iraq was ratified by the League of Nations in a resolution dated 25 April taken at its 1920 meeting at San Remo, Italy. This resulted in the creation of an arrangement called a 'mandate', designed to be a temporary period of British rule until Iraqi leaders were deemed ready to take over an eventually independent state. There were many in Iraq, however, who were hoping for immediate independence. After all, for years there were educated, experienced and ambitious inhabitants of the Ottoman provinces of Mosul, Baghdad and Basra who had been making decisions on local policy, collecting taxes, regulating marketplaces and ensuring security with very little interference from Istanbul. My great-grandfather, for example, had served as an elected mayor of Kirkuk under the Ottomans. His son (my grandfather) served in the Ottoman and Iraqi parliaments,

5

involving my family in public service in an era that spanned Ottoman and British rule.

Once the Ottoman empire ceased to exist, many people in the lands of Iraq dreamed of a united and independent country. Despite the mandate's provisions to facilitate this end, British officials began to set up an administration in 1918 that featured a style of direct rule akin to that of her colony in India, replete with a system of administration that left almost no room for meaningful Iraqi leadership. This and other new policies naturally caused discontent across wide segments of the local population.

The ambitions of Iraqis would clash many times with Britain's during the course of the mandate era and beyond, but the largest disturbances came in 1920, when peaceful demonstrations, riots and fighting broke out in many parts of the country. This Iraqi revolt has been seen over the years by the country's nationalists as a milestone in their long struggle for independence. The motivations and goals of those participating in the revolt were varied, but one thing all Iraqis could agree on was the need to prevent complete and permanent British control of their country. There were some episodes during which Iraqis of different backgrounds acted in unison. On a number of occasions in Baghdad, for example, Sunni and Shia supporters of independence peacefully stood shoulder-to-shoulder listening to speeches and patriotic poems at each other's mosques. It was clear even at this early stage in the country's history that members of this diverse population could join together and support the idea of a united, independent Iraq.

The conflict was costly in lives and money, and the intensity of the Iraqi opposition taught British officials an important lesson: their mandate government must somehow pay greater heed to the maturity of the Iraqi political elite, and their determination to participate in a government that would lead to full independence sooner rather than later. And as far as Iraqi leaders were concerned, Britain's strong show of military power demonstrated that in order to work towards independence they had to make temporary accommodations with their great-power 'guest'.

At the Cairo Conference of March 1921, British officials decided that a constitutional monarchy should be established in Iraq, with Faisal ibn Hussain as the first king. During the war years the British had encouraged the regional political ambitions of the Sharif of Mecca, Hussain bin Ali, whose family had gained prestige and political status due to his descent from the prophet Muhammad. Hussain's son, Faisal, had worked closely with British officers, including T. E. Lawrence as leader of the 1916 Arab Revolt, to liberate Arab lands from the Ottomans during the First World War. This history of cooperation, as well as the prominence of the Hashemite family, persuaded the British to invite Faisal to assume the throne in Iraq. A referendum was held to ratify this choice, and on 23 August 1921 Faisal became the first king of Iraq. King Faisal I filled many government positions with Iraqis who had fought at his side or served under his command during the Arab Revolt. In addition, Arab nationalists from Syria, Palestine and other countries were invited to participate in this challenging state-building project.

Relations between the fledgling Iraqi state and Great Britain were codified in the 1922 Anglo-Iraqi Treaty which provided for Iraqi control over most of its domestic affairs. Britain retained control over finances, foreign affairs and defence, including two RAF bases. Although many Iraqis chafed at the broad areas of British control, this treaty offered more local autonomy than did many postwar arrangements elsewhere. This was due in large part to the strong calls for self-rule by Iraqi leaders. And Britain made good on its promise to gradually hand over full control. Over the course of the mandate period, for example, the number of British advisers gradually declined from 3,000 in 1920 to just 100 in 1932, the year of independence.

Iraq's monarchy evolved into a constitutional system, beginning in 1925. This embodied the stability, continuity and prestige of a Hashemite ruler who presided over a government that was representative of the country's population and which was limited in its power by an independent judiciary and a legislative branch with elected representatives. For example, the constitution provided for representation of all the people, no matter what their religion, tribe or ethnic identification, through delegates to a Chamber of Deputies. The other chamber of the bicameral parliament, the senate, was appointed by the king. The constitution adopted by the founding parliament in 1925 stated: 'All Iraqis are equal in rights, opportunities and responsibilities, irrespective of their differences in origin, religion or language.'

Although the king was constitutionally the head of state, he did not rule. He was given the power to dissolve parliament, choose the prime minister and appoint other ministers chosen by the prime minister. In practice, no one rose to become prime minister without substantial public service experience, outstanding personal qualities and a record of extraordinary achievement. For its part, the parliament had the power to draft laws and the chamber of deputies could dissolve the council of ministers with a simple majority vote of no confidence. This gave incentives for both the legislative and executive branches to work together, or at least to strive towards compromise.

The independent judiciary was a third branch of government, put in place to ensure the rule of law and to act as a check on the other branches. The civil service professionals working in the ministries were permanent employees. They were chosen on a non-political basis and supplied the efficient provision of government services and implementation of its policies. In financial affairs there was transparency and consultation. The parliament each year approved the national budget, which included the salaries for the king and crown prince, and the expenses of the royal court.

Like political systems everywhere, Iraq's fledgling constitutional monarchy may not always have been perfect, but it put the country on the right track. Under the energetic and wise leadership of King Faisal I and the prime ministers he appointed, important first steps in the country's social, political and economic development were taken. Under his able and visionary leadership, Iraq made gigantic strides from a past of ethnic, tribal and religious divisions towards a future of unity, prosperity and national pride. Faisal I's 12–year rule laid the foundations for free enterprise, social welfare and a modern infrastructure. Needless to say, the system in place in the Iraq of yesterday stands in stark contrast to the dictatorships that followed.

Another important landmark of the mandate period was the establishment of Iraq's international frontiers. These were finalized in 1926 after a League of Nations commission recommended that the disputed province of Mosul be permanently part of Iraq rather than Turkey.

During Faisal I's 12 years of leadership, Iraq made

extraordinary progress towards building a modern, secular state. Illiteracy was reduced through the long-overdue development of the educational system. Leaders from the various segments of Iraqi society were encouraged to participate in local and national government, building an Iraqi national ethos among a people who for years had been influenced mainly by tribal, religious, ethnic and family identities. The economic well-being of the people benefited from improvements in transportation, agriculture and the business sector. The king nurtured the growth of Iraqi nationalism while respecting the diversity of Iraq's population, seeing it as a source of strength and inspiration. He considered all Iraq to be one, protected by the constitution and governed by the rule of law. In addition, he worked tirelessly to promote Iraq's full independence, pressing Britain to live up to its mandatory obligation. The historian Charles Tripp says that King Faisal I's views were based on two main ideas: the gradual achievement of real independence from British control and the integration of the existing communities of Iraq into a unitary structure in which they could feel that their identities and interests were fully respected.[1]

During the 1920s, Faisal astutely used the patronage powers of the state as a nation-building device. For example, he instituted land reforms that helped to bring tribal leaders and urban notables into the national political structures, thus giving these and other key members of society a strong stake in the future of Iraq. This was crucial in a period when challenges to the legitimacy of the new state were common. In 1923, for example, some tribal leaders from the mid-Euphrates area, supported by Shiite clerics, encouraged resistance to the mandate government. One such act was to issue a decree prohibiting their followers from serving in government positions.

The efforts failed and the clerics were forced to flee the country, heralding a period of relative stability.

In this period, Faisal I and the British laid the foundations of a constitutional order and institutions of state. This was a crucial factor in the formation of the Iraqi state, because these structures were durable enough to withstand a number of other attacks. By 1929 British officials were in the process of making recommendations that Iraq should become the first independent Arab nation and join the League of Nations.

Building an independent nation, 1932–1941

Iraq became the first Arab nation to achieve independence and join the League of Nations in 1932, in large part because Faisal I was able to maintain order and oversee the steady development of government by Iraqis. Although I will go into greater detail later about the positive legacy of the Hashemite monarchy, I would now like to touch on just a few high points of the period.

Faisal I's rule established the roadmap for free enterprise, social welfare and a modern infrastructure. He made education a priority, opening schools and sending successful high school graduates to the best Western institutions for university and postgraduate studies.

During the monarchy, government policies were geared towards building a sense of Iraqi identity and loyalty to the nation. For example, tribal affiliations, sectarian differences and cultural diversity did not prevent members of the younger generation from looking forward and identifying themselves as Iraqi nationals, equal citizens of one united country. Indeed,

I was part of this new generation, and we were proud to see ourselves as Iraqis rather than as members of any sectarian or ethnic group. No official document (passport or birth certificate, for example) made reference to ethnic background or sect. In a major step towards modern statehood, the members of this diverse community of Kurds, Christians, Arabs, Turkomans, Jews, Sunni and Shia began proudly to call themselves Iraqis for the first time.

The period immediately after independence was to prove extremely difficult for the new country. In preparation for independence, Iraq had signed a new treaty with Britain which ensured that Britain would retain military basing rights during wars, as well as some of her economic interests. When Iraq was declared formally independent in 1932, a power vacuum was created with the departure of British officials. This problem was compounded by the sudden death of Faisal in 1933, and the rise to the throne of his son Ghazi, who was less able even if more popular (at least among the youth).

What Ghazi possessed in energy, he lacked in the good judgement that is usually born of experience and maturity. He collected cars, loved to drive them fast and surrounded himself with a similarly inclined crowd of young army officers. In short, Ghazi was a pale shadow of his father.

There were two important effects. First, as the Iraq scholar Phebe Marr comments, this was 'an era of communal and tribal rebellion' – one might say the period in which opposition was now able to organize against the government rather than the British.[2] Second, the army emerged as a major political force for the first time.

Rashid Ali al-Gailani was chief of the royal court. In March 1940 the regent, Prince Abdul Ilah, chose him to be the next prime minister of Iraq while Nuri al-Said (to whom I shall return later) was appointed mister of foreign affairs. The Second World War was at its height and Iraq was aligned by treaty with Great Britain. Poland, Holland and Belgium had been overrun by Nazi Germany and France faced a similar threat. The German embassy in Baghdad (later operating through the Italian embassy when the formal relationship with Germany was severed) conducted an active propaganda war to expand its influence among Iraqi military officers, opposition politicians and students.

When the new government was unable to function as a result of divisions within Iraq and deteriorating world conditions, the regent accepted the prime minister's resignation and wanted to pass the responsibility of heading the government to Taha al-Hashimi. However, four leading military officers protested at the regent's choice and insisted that Rashid Ali al-Gailani be reappointed to lead the government.

Furious that the military should be allowed to interfere and, more dangerously, to dictate politics, Nuri al-Said left for Jordan to take refuge under Prince Abdullah (later King Abdullah I). Later the regent also had to escape to Jordan. Queen Aliyah remained in Iraq with her child son, King Faisal II, and played a courageous role in not allowing the conspirators to force the abdication of the young king.

Rashid Ali al-Gailani and his military supporters had received a promise that Nazi Germany would provide weaponry for the Iraqi army to attack the existing British base in Iraq. However, after Field Marshal Erwin Rommel's withdrawal from North Africa and changes in the course of the war, the arms never arrived.

At this point, Prince Abdullah of Jordan, encouraged by his

Iraqi guests, sent the Jordanian army (then known as the Arab army and headed by the British general best known as Glubb Pasha) to liberate Iraq and return the legitimate regent and his government to power. Iraqis were jubilant to see an end to this catastrophic upheaval.

Rashid Ali al-Gailani's attempted coup and its overthrow resulted in Britain once again dominating Iraqi policy – a development that seriously set back, for a few years more, the country's efforts to maintain full independence.

Building a modern Iraq, 1941–1958

After the Second World War, Iraq had another opportunity to make a fresh start. This is the period from which we can draw the most positive lessons for the current problems of the country. It began with the restoration of the legitimate government in 1941. Given a second chance at state-building, members of the old guard tried to learn from their experiences in the earlier period. Experiments in political liberalization were attempted. In 1946, for example, under the assertive tenure of the Sorbonne-educated prime minister, Tawfiq al-Suwaidi, martial law and press restrictions were lifted and, most significantly, opposition parties were licensed. The National Democratic Party and Istiqlal Party captured important currents of opinion among urban-educated opponents of the government. Even the Iraqi Communist Party (ICP) was allowed to operate more or less openly at this time, despite the hostility of senior government officials to their ideology.

Following that phase, Nuri al-Said played a more dominant role in Iraqi politics. Under Nuri, who was to remain prime minister in title or spirit until 1958, Iraq embarked on a nation-building programme that focused on national security and economic development. Nonetheless, external events were creating dangerous forces that threatened to tear the state apart. For example, Iraq sent its forces to fight against the new state of Israel, and the defeat suffered in this war galvanized Arab nationalists in Iraq, especially in the army, and increased pressure against Iraq's relationship with Britain. This was a problem for Iraq's leaders, who attempted to achieve a further diminution of British control with the 1948 Treaty of Portsmouth. While this treaty handed back the remaining British bases to Iraq, it continued to allow Britain some access during wartime, institutionalized a defence supply relationship and extended other benefits to Iraq, such as officer training at the prestigious Royal Military Academy, Sandhurst. Nevertheless, the treaty was widely condemned throughout Iraq, and could not be ratified due to the protests known as the *wathba*, or uprising. In the face of overwhelming public opposition, the government resigned. The new prime minister, Muhammad al-Sadr, did not present the treaty to parliament for ratification and it became null and void.

Another external factor that hindered the nation-building project during this period was the Cold War. Iraq was just one of many small nations caught between the aggressive efforts of the Soviet Union to expand its influence around the world and the equally vigorous attempts by the West to counter these moves.

Nuri's economic development programme proceeded against this backdrop of menacing political forces at home and abroad. However, he believed that these challenges could be overcome by investing government funds in Iraq's long-term economic development: if the economic condition of the people improved, the political situation would stabilize. The key driver of economic expansion was an agreement with the IPC which shifted payments to the government from a royalty system to one of 50/50 profit-sharing. This agreement was negotiated in 1950, and was ratified by the Iraqi parliament in 1952. The effect, along with rising oil prices and expanding production, was a massive increase in Iraqi oil revenues. The Iraqi Development Board was set up to invest 70 per cent of these funds for Iraq's future, and to prioritize spending on large-scale infrastructure, agricultural and communications projects. Iraq's economic future prosperity seemed assured.

Iraq was being built into a modern nation-state, with notable improvements in its infrastructure, economy and national institutions. For example, its increased income was channelled into an ambitious industrialization and infrastructure development programme. Modern roads and highways connected distant villages, towns and cities. Dams, hospitals, schools and housing developments sprang up everywhere, and Iraq in the early 1950s looked like a massive construction site. National institutions such as the bureaucracy represented a clearly centralized structure of authority. Iraqis were taking full control of their own fate, and economic progress was accelerating.

But all of this came to a sudden end with the violent events of July 1958, when a handful of army officers drove their troops into Baghdad and overthrew the monarchy. The new regimes consisted of a series of unstable juntas which stunted Iraq's political and economic development, and eventually led to the rise of Saddam Hussein, who was to continue the destruction of Iraq.

Before 1958, Iraq had seemed set for a stable and prosperous future, with many factors in its favour – remarkable natural resources, unique archaeological sites, a strategy for full economic development, a benevolent monarchy vested in an ancient royal house, an honest and functioning government system and the determined efforts of its own people to achieve sophisticated modern standards by using Western technology.

I well remember Iraq on the eve of the 1958 coup, and I can affirm that it was a country of incredible potential. But I am not alone in that view. The British official Lord Salter commented in the opening remarks of his 1955 report on the development of Iraq: 'Iraq has an altogether exceptional opportunity of achieving a development which within a few years would substantially increase her economic resources and raise her general standard of living. For she now has advantages which are rarely found in combination.'[3]

I will offer a detailed account of pre-1958 Iraq in the chapters that follow.

The lead-up to the coup

For all the progress that was under way in Iraq, and despite all its promise of a prosperous future, dangerous political tides were sweeping across the Arab world that would inundate the Hashemite monarchy. These tides were in large part an effect of the global confrontation and conflict unleashed by the Cold War. It is not difficult to see, therefore, why some of the drastic changes that overtook Iraq were neither anticipated nor easily preventable.

As I have noted, the Iraqi government had focused on internal economic development in the years following the Second World War, and in its foreign policy had maintained a pro-Western stance. At the height of the Cold War in the 1950s, this placed it at odds with the ambitions of the leaders of the Soviet Union, who sought to expand their influence in this energy-exporting region.

The Soviets had already obtained a partial foothold in the Middle East when a charismatic and ambitious young army officer named Gamal Abdel Nasser and his allies overthrew the Egyptian monarchy in 1952. Nasser's magnetic persona, anti-Western rhetoric and mass-oriented political propaganda won him ardent support among young people across the Arab world from Oman to Morocco. And his desire to shift Egypt's historically pro-Western foreign policy opened the door to ties with the Soviet Union.

Such inroads in the region posed a threat in the eyes of the leaders of Iraq, who responded in 1955 by signing the Baghdad Pact, an alliance with Turkey, Iran, Pakistan and the UK, supported by the US. This gave Iraq access to modern Western weapons and technology, and provided a defensive shield strong enough to enable precious national resources to be marshalled for internal economic development. But its alliance with the West made Iraq a target for the Soviet Union, whose leaders saw the Middle East as a prime battleground against Western interests. They therefore unleashed a determined campaign of subversion and underground revolution to overturn the existing order. This effort worked hand-in-hand with the activities of Nasser and his allies in the Arab world.

The political movements outside Egypt inspired by Nasser grew on fertile ground. For years the political destinies of many Arab countries were heavily influenced by foreigners, and this had created a great deal of resentment, mainly towards Britain's role in the region. I have already mentioned opposition to Britain's takeover of Iraq after the First World War. Britain had also presided over the Palestine Mandate in the same period. The mishandling of the mandate and the tragic displacement of the Palestinians in 1948 were among the chief grievances that Arabs everywhere felt against Britain, causing social and political fractures throughout the region.

One of these fractures was the creation or intensification of discord based on religion, resulting in the breaking of centuries-old bonds between communities that had lived side by side in productive peace. For example, there had been more than 100,000 Jews in Iraq. They were respected and trusted, and many played leading economic and political roles. The troubles in Palestine during Britain's watch aroused a great deal of sympathy among many Iraqis for the Arabs of Palestine. In the wake of Israel's creation in 1948 and the resulting Palestinian refugee crisis, these sentiments as well as violent outbursts of anti-Semitism drove away almost all of Iraq's Jews – a truly regrettable loss.

Part of Nasser's appeal derived from his strong advocacy of his brand of Arab nationalism and criticism of foreign intervention. His popularity soared in 1956 when he was able to retain control of the Suez Canal after a surprise attack by British, French and Israeli forces. Arabs everywhere were buoyed by this political triumph, and pro-Nasser army officers in Iraq became so motivated that they made plans for their own rise to power. Other segments of Iraqi society were influenced by Nasserism as well. The intelligentsia took the country's economic progress for granted and adopted the anti-Western cause, embracing Nasserism and denouncing the monarchy. The youth of Iraq, too, were swept up by the anti-Western, pro-Soviet tide of passion that was sweeping the country.

The avalanche of propaganda against Iraq's government from Egypt and elsewhere held irresistible appeal, because it was able to criticize from the outside without accountability. Nasser and his allies in the Arab world promised the moon to the people of Iraq, if only they staged their own revolution. And despite their dedication to making Iraq a thriving economic powerhouse, Iraq's leaders under the monarchy could not counter the Nasser-inspired propaganda. They thought they had time on their side because of the gigantic development projects that were under way: surely the prosperity that was certain to flow from these projects would convince Iraqis that the policies of the monarchy had been judicious all along. One of the tragedies of the monarchy's downfall was that its leaders believed they could prevail in the face of Nasserite propaganda through perseverance and honest hard work. Events would prove them wrong.

The political threat posed by the spread of Nasserism reached the very borders of Iraq when Egypt and Syria announced on 1 February 1958 the formation of the United Arab Republic. Egypt's hostile intentions had been clear for some time in the tide of Nasserite propaganda directed against the Nuri al-Said government in Iraq as well as the government of the Hashemite Kingdom of Jordan. The threat from Egypt, coupled with the fact that Syria borders Iraq and Jordan and could pose a danger to both, prompted the governments in Baghdad and Amman to take steps to defend themselves.

In February 1958 the constitutional monarchies of Iraq and Jordan agreed to unite in a federation known as the Arab Union. Each country would retain its parliament and continue to run its own internal affairs, but the two would operate as one government in areas such as defence, national security, monetary policy and foreign affairs. Given Iraq's size and prominence, King Faisal II of Iraq became the head of the union and his cousin, King Hussein of Jordan, was elected as his deputy. The Iraqi and Jordanian parliaments endorsed the new federation and issued the supporting legislation. The Arab Union was recognized around the world.

Within the Iraqi army, however, a small number of officers in contact with Nasser were plotting a coup. On 14 July 1958 the government instructed one of its military units to move to Jordan to support its sister nation. Instead of obeying this order, Colonel Abd al-Salam Arif directed his unit to boldly attack the royal palace in Baghdad, and then take control of the radio station. The Communist Party, as well as pro-Nasser elements, had been alerted in advance and confirmed the night before that, should the adventure succeed, they would proceed to the heart of Baghdad to cause chaos and spread terror so as to discourage any resistance to the coup.

The coup of 14 July 1958 took Iraq off the road to hope and into a long, dark tunnel of despair. It was not the first coup in Iraqi history. The army had been used by Bakr Sidqi to take power in 1936 and again by Rashid Ali al-Gailani in 1941. But events following the 1958 coup made this change in government more durable than previous ones because the constitutional monarchy was not able to return to power.

For Iraq, 14 July 1958 was disastrous and devastating. It was the beginning of the end. For me personally, it was a horrific emotional blow.

On that 'black Monday', I was in Istanbul's international airport at Yesilkoy waiting to welcome His Majesty King Faisal II, who was expected to arrive from Baghdad to attend a meeting of heads of state of the Baghdad Pact nations. A festive atmosphere was created for this special occasion, with colourful flags waving around the terminal building, and a Turkish armed forces band playing marches. It was a beautiful day, cloudless and with bright sunshine. But the excitement and cheerful mood did not last. The royal flight from Baghdad did not arrive. The crowd was led to believe that there was an indefinite delay. Initially, some people concluded that the weather conditions in Baghdad might have been unfavourable – it was not unusual for Baghdad, in midsummer, to experience heavy sandstorms that could prevent flights from landing or taking off. No other possibility for the delay occurred to anyone who had been eagerly awaiting the arrival of Iraq's king that day.

That summer I completed my third year at university. I was a student at Robert College in Istanbul, the American college that had been in existence since 1863. I had known King Faisal since my early childhood. My mother used to visit the Queen Mother about two or three times a year as a courtesy and to pay her respects. Given the long and extended relationship my family had with the Hashemite royal family, I used to accompany my mother on those visits to play with the young king, who was a year older than me. Later on, as a teenager, the king moved to England to continue his education at Harrow and I did not see him for an extended period.

We met again several years later when, upon reaching the age of majority, he returned to Iraq in 1953 to assume his official responsibilities as the monarch. His uncle, who ruled as regent until this point, stepped down.

During the day, the king would meet with members of his government in order to carry out his duties as head of state.

In the evenings, if he had no official duties, he liked to pass the time with a few friends whom he would invite to play chess or tennis, discuss books, listen to music or watch the latest Hollywood films.

I was still in high school, attending Baghdad College, the American Jesuit institution. About twice a year I would be invited to visit His Majesty. Sometimes I would be the only guest and on other occasions there could be one or two others.

After I left Iraq in 1955 to go to college in Istanbul I made it a practice to visit His Majesty whenever I was back home on vacation. My last visit was in April 1958, when I was back in Baghdad for the Easter holidays. Unlike other times in the past when our meetings were at his residence, this time the appointment was set for the morning and was to take place at his official headquarters. This was the first and only time when I visited his office and, tragically, it was the last time that I saw His Majesty. As I was leaving to go, his final words to me were that he looked forward to seeing me in Istanbul in the summer. That was not to be.

The sunny day in Istanbul that had begun for me with anticipation and high hopes among the airport crowds ended with shock and utter sadness as I listened to Baghdad Radio shouting the announcement of a bloody coup. On 14 July 1958 the military coup leaders, Arif and Abd al-Karim Qasim, first murdered the members of the royal family and the leading politician of the day, Nuri al-Said. This was possible because the leaders of government under King Faisal II, though competent in many areas, paid too little attention to their own security or that of vital government institutions. The palace had minimal protection and the Arab Union prime minister, Nuri al-Said, almost none at all. The weapons of the guards at the central government radio station were no match for those of the invading army unit.

This coup was quickly consolidated by the popular support of Iraq's organized Nasserites, Baathists and Communists. The victory of this sort of 'mass politics' in Iraq had many dark aspects. For example, as soon as word of the coup spread through Baghdad, the streets were taken over by organized and violent demonstrations. Not only were the mass political parties encouraging their supporters to take to the streets in support of the new rulers, but armed thugs were dispatched to intimidate or kill those attempting to voice opposition to the coup. The club, the knife and the gun would increasingly become the political tools of choice under the regimes that followed.

The announcement on official Iraqi radio that the king, the crown prince and all their family members had been massacred at dawn, and that Iraq was now a pro-Nasser republic, came as a shock to many Iraqis. But the socialist-leaning youth celebrated. And since all top leaders of the constitutional monarchy had been killed, their supporters did not know who would lead them even if they chose to mount a counter-attack.

The Iraqi military organization in 1958 consisted of four divisions. Those responsible for the coup, Qasim and Arif, were middle-ranking officers in one of those four divisions. They were able to arrest their commander and move on to take over the government in Baghdad. Separately, the commander of one of the other three divisions – headquartered in Diwaniyah, 100 miles south of Baghdad – stood out against the coup and tried to mobilize his forces to move to Baghdad in the hope of saving the regime. This was Omar Ali, a formidable and distinguished general. Unfortunately, his attempt failed. The

sudden collapse of the government in Baghdad deterred his
followers from obeying their leader. General Omar Ali was
later imprisoned and sentenced to death. However, given his
stature and widespread respect in the army, the sentence was
not carried out and he was subsequently released, only to be
killed later in a mysterious car crash officially explained as a
tragic accident.

External intervention to reverse the coup was not the option
it had been in the past, because this was the peak of the Cold
War. The Western powers were locking horns with the Soviet
Union and its allies, and could scarcely afford to risk a large-
scale conflagration in the Middle East. Immediately after the
coup, Nasser flew to Moscow and stood alongside his supporter,
Nikita Khrushchev, who threatened that if the West interfered
in Iraq it would lead to World War Three. The US, under
President Dwight D. Eisenhower, chose not to interfere. British
prime minister Harold Macmillan and other politicians, along
with Jordanian officials, did consider military action to restore
the monarchy, but quickly ruled out the idea. Macmillan wrote
in his memoirs that 'it was impossible to restore the old regime,
whose chief representatives had been so brutally murdered'.[4]

The new dictatorship in Iraq acted at once to exchange
ambassadors with the Soviet Union, abolish the Development
Board, withdraw from the Baghdad Pact, cancel the federation
with Jordan and stage public executions. Iraq's downward spiral
had begun. Between 1958 and 1968, the grand promises of
greater popular participation in politics were not kept. Instead,
Arif and his successors presided over a transformation of
the Iraqi political landscape into one of increasing secrecy,
conspiracy, intimidation and the centralization of power.
Political parties were tolerated only until they outlived their

usefulness to the regime. And rather than nourishing the nascent electoral process of the constitutional monarchy, Iraq's new leaders began to rely on cronyism, corruption and coercion in order to keep power and reward their followers. Instead of the ballot box, power was transferred through the thuggish violence of military officers.

The Baath Party, which seized power in February 1963 and executed Abd al-Karim Qasim, ruled brutally for nine months before being overthrown by Colonel Arif. It was in this dictatorial milieu that Saddam Hussein began his political education, and the coup of 1968 brought the Baath Party back to the centre of Iraqi political power.

The year 1968 began a new dictatorial rule that eventually evolved in 1979 into a one-man, one-family rule. Saddam Hussein eliminated any possible differing or opposing views within the Baath Party and surrounded himself by yes-men of dubious character and little capability. A new era of pure dictatorship, violence and international misadventures ensued. The beginning of Saddam's evil reign in 1968 thus raises the curtain on the darkest, most violent era in Iraq's history. The contrast could not be starker between the hope and tolerance of the Hashemite monarchy and the corrupt, reckless and murderous period of the Saddam era – the years when the people of Iraq were forced into a dark tunnel of despair, intimidation and fear.

Iraq suffers under Saddam

There is wide agreement that the Saddam era ushered in terrible times for the people of Iraq. However, one aspect of his reign is often misunderstood. Many people have characterized his regime as 'Sunni-dominated'. This is a radical mistake. Saddam was a tyrant who tortured and persecuted *all* Iraqis irrespective of their identity. Although he happened to be of Sunni extraction, this fact had no bearing on his criminal behaviour. He came to power with the backing of tanks and no Iraqi faction had a choice in the matter. It was obedience that mattered to Saddam, not religion or ethnicity. Just as he welcomed Shias and Kurds into his fold if they promised loyalty to his person, he did not hesitate to imprison, torture or kill anyone, Sunnis or otherwise, if he felt he could not trust them.

Under Saddam, the criteria for achieving a position of influence in government were altogether different from those that had existed under the constitutional monarchy. Advancement was based on a single measure – loyalty and obedience to Saddam – and he alone made that judgement. Those he considered loyal enjoyed the benefits his corrupt regime offered. As soon as that loyalty was doubted by Saddam, the next step was not an investigation of the suspicion but the quick, physical elimination of the individual.

In his relations with the Kurds, Saddam reversed the policy of continuing to build Iraqi national integration and identity – a process that had been in place since the 1920s. Indeed, he was the first Iraqi leader to offer privileged autonomy to the Kurds in the north of Iraq in the early 1970s. Then, when he changed his mind and sought to reverse his own initiative, he went to the other extreme. He bombed the Kurds, burned their villages and destroyed their homes, using chemical weapons in a horrific campaign to wipe out an entire community.

As for the Shias, Saddam attacked them brutally in 1977 and 1991. On the first occasion, he responded savagely and disproportionately to disturbances and demonstrations against his regime. Later, following the 1991 Gulf War ceasefire, the Shias counted on the signal they received from the US-led coalition and rose up against Saddam. Their one-month rebellion ended in disaster. Thousands of Shias were massacred by Saddam's forces and buried in mass graves.

Kurds and Shias alike – along with the whole of Iraq – could reasonably be labelled victims of Saddam's rule. But that should not entitle any group to a political reward based on their ethnicity or religion. Rather, all Iraqis should enjoy a constitution that guarantees them individual rights, irrespective of colour, creed, religion or gender. In the purges that Saddam periodically carried out at the higher levels of power, it was Sunnis who were most affected as power was centralized on Saddam and his immediate coterie.

Many Shias joined the Baath Party as a pathway to social mobility. As a matter of fact, their numbers in the rank and file of the party exceeded those of Sunnis. The post-invasion emphasis on demographic statistics and sectarian and ethnic divisions has encouraged people to ignore the fact that many Iraqis shared a sense of Iraqi national identity rather than primarily defining themselves in sectarian, ethnic or tribal terms. There was total mixing of the sectarian and ethnic groups in geography, society and marriage. Kurds, Shias and Sunni Arabs were not tidily divided among three specific geographical areas in the way recently portrayed. In the war with Iran, Iraqi Shia soldiers fought Iranian Shias for Iraq.

At the same time, there are divisions within the main ethnic and sectarian groups. They are certainly not monolithic blocs. Democratically-minded, forward-looking Iraqis of different religions might find more in common with each other than with many members of their own sect or ethnic origin.

Saddam did play on sectarian differences, especially after the 1991 Gulf War and the subsequent uprisings. Different sectarian, ethnic and tribal factions struck deals with Saddam at various times for their own interests and in order to survive. But the loss of security and stability following the 2003 invasion and occupation have forced people to identify more with their sectarian and tribal leaders as a reaction and a source of protection in a chaotic situation. It was the new leaders of Iraq who inflamed and exploited differences in an attempt to fulfil their own political interests by forming their own support bases, constituencies and militias.

Iraq's history shows the stark differences between the periods before and after the coup of 1958. Under the constitutional monarchy, the essential institutions of the modern state were established with policies generally aimed at ensuring that Iraqis of diverse origins would have similar opportunities to participate as equal citizens in the economic, political and cultural life of the country. Before 1958, people could enjoy open political and cultural expression, with a number of newspapers free to publish a broad spectrum of opposing opinions. The kaleidoscope of Iraq's multi-ethnic, multi-religious population began to see themselves first as Iraqis. This all changed after 1958, with political life and free expression withering away under the gathering oppression of a dictatorial one-party state. This deterioration intensified greatly following the American occupation.

In this chapter I have dealt only briefly with some of the exemplary policies of the pre-1958 period. I will turn now to a fuller tour of the Iraq I remember, an Iraq that had been on the right path.

2

Lessons and examples from the past

Many people erroneously view the Iraq of today as a state destined to fail because it was born with permanent fatal defects. First among these, supposedly, is the unalterably fractious nature of Iraqi society, divided along numerous religious, ethnic and tribal fault lines. Related to this is the prevailing assumption that Iraq has always been a Sunni-dominated state with a dysfunctional economy and authoritarian political institutions. This is simply untrue. As I have mentioned already, under the monarchy Iraq made enormous progress towards solving the structural problems she inherited from her founders. And even under Saddam's dictatorship, loyalty to the regime was the ultimate measure of political survival, not ethnicity or religion.

Rather than wring our hands over the supposedly intractable nature of the current situation, I believe we should draw inspiration from some of the overlooked positive policies and personalities of the monarchy period. The sight of the country's past from this new perspective can dispel a number of defeatist myths about its supposed shortcomings, and offer important lessons for the future. The historian Martin Bunton is among those to argue against the notion that the Iraqi state is 'artificial'.

Instead, he insists that 'the end of the nation-state' in Iraq would be a result of the policies of the US and British sponsored regime, rather than inherent faults in Iraq.[1]

It is important to note that the vast majority of Iraqis themselves are now openly expressing the view that the years of the Hashemite monarchy were crucial in the project of state-formation.

The myth of a fractious society

Much of what is written in the West about today's Iraq stresses the composition of the population, with the endlessly repeated formula that the Shias make up about 60 per cent, Sunni Arabs 20 per cent, the Kurds 17 per cent and Turkomans, Christians and others 3 per cent. Even though no census has been taken for decades, this breakdown of the population may possibly correspond to reality, but it does not tell the whole story of Iraqi society. In fact, it too often leads to entirely false assumptions. Most powerful of these misconceptions is that, throughout Iraq's history, ethnicity, language and religion have been the deciding factors in political life. Moreover, according to this line of thought, since the formation of modern Iraq in 1921 the minority Sunnis have ruled while the Shias and Kurds have been excluded. This is quite false.

Under the Hashemite monarchy, members of the Iraqi parliament were represented on a geographical basis, with delegates from every corner of the country. So the legislative body included Shias, Sunnis, Kurds, Turkomans, Christians and Jews. Diversity also existed at the highest level of government, the ministerial cabinet. This body was headed by a prime minister, and no member of the royal family served in the cabinet or assumed any senior governing post. The selection of ministers was based on merit. At different times during the monarchy, ministerial positions were held by Jews, Christians, Sunnis, Shias, Kurds and Turkomans. Several self-made Shias rose from humble backgrounds to serve as prime minister, including Salih Jabir, Fadhil al-Jamali, Abd al-Wahhab Mirjan and Muhammad al-Sadr. Indeed, no government was formed during the period of the monarchy that did not include several Shias, Sunnis and Kurds. They were chosen not because of their ethnic or religious backgrounds, but because they were deemed the best candidates at the time.

While some Shias chose to go into public service, most preferred to make their fortunes as traders and entrepreneurs in the marketplace. As a result, they dominated the country's business and commercial activity. What is most obvious on carefully re-examining the role of religion in politics is that there was not one monolithic Shia population following a single political agenda. Some Shias did indeed play important roles in the government led by Faisal I, while others expressed varying degrees of opposition. (A similar range of responses could be found among other groups, including Sunnis.) Shia religious leaders, in particular, expressed opposition, in part because they saw the modern Iraqi government removing some of their traditional sources of income and reducing their influence among their followers. Thus some Shia religious leaders not only urged rebellion against the British during 1920, but later expressed opposition in a variety of ways against the secularizing policies of the monarchy governments. As in many Islamic societies, the advent of modern education in Iraq was perceived as a threat to traditional schools operated by the religious establishment, and was opposed. In a way this was the sort of 'culture war' between traditional groups and modernizing forces that has been occurring around the world over for many decades.

The leaders of Iraq's constitutional monarchy saw the secularization of public life as an important way to draw members of the diverse population together in the nation-building project. And so they attempted to prevent religion and ethnicity from becoming the deciding factor in government policy. In this way, any Iraqi in theory could go as far as his or her qualifications allowed, irrespective of ethnic or religious background. One measure of the effectiveness of this policy is the fact that on that catastrophic day in July 1958 when the Hashemite kingdom of Iraq was extinguished, the two highest and most powerful government positions were held by Kurds: Ahmed Mukhtar Baban was prime minister, and Said Qazaz was interior minister. Another Kurdish prime minister who served earlier was Nureddin Mahmud. These men were shining examples of the monarchy's policies which sought to create equal opportunities for all. Baban, Qazaz and Mahmud had reached these positions by rising through the ranks and providing distinguished public service over a period of more than thirty years each.

The myth of Sunni dominance

The founders of independent Iraq, it is true, inherited a state that was biased in favour of the Sunni Arabs, who had dominated the leading administrative positions during the late Ottoman era. The British perpetuated this pattern by failing to bring any Shias into senior government positions. This policy was based in part on expediency, since those Sunnis tended to be more experienced in government work. But politics played a part too: the British were concerned about Shia loyalty to the state after the 1920 revolt, and many Kurds were openly hostile to inclusion in Iraq. Given this biased inheritance, it is hardly surprising that several of the leading positions over the next years went to the available Sunnis.

Despite this tendency, however, once British influence in Iraq's affairs diminished after independence in 1932, the monarchy was able to make significant progress in diversifying political participation and leadership. As I have mentioned already, by the final years of the monarchy there was no mention of inequality in ministerial appointments.

Unfortunately, not every aspect of government made equal progress. In the armed forces the integration of non-Sunni Iraqis was much slower, and this was to have a decisively negative effect in 1958. At the inception of Iraq's armed forces, the leadership was mostly Sunni, due to this group's greater training and experience of serving in the Ottoman army. In addition, at the start of his reign Faisal I had consciously brought into the army those Iraqi officers who had served under him during the Arab Revolt in 1916. This same pattern did not hold for enlisted men, who entered from a wide range of ethnic backgrounds. It is ironic that the army had served for a time as an important if bloody tool of nation-building by crushing the Assyrian revolt in 1933 and helping to quell other challenges to the state. But the control of the army by mostly Sunni officers made it appear biased, especially in the years after the Second World War when it became a hotbed of Nasserite opposition. In retrospect, the failure of Iraq's leaders to keep politics out of the officer corps of the armed forces was an unfortunate mistake.

The myth of a crippled economy

There is a well-justified perception of today's Iraqi economy as inefficient and corrupt, based on the terrible policies and practices of the series of dictatorial rulers ending with the Saddam era. However, it is often forgotten that things were on the right path during the Hashemite monarchy.

One of the most positive changes under the monarchy was the development of a large-scale oil industry in Iraq, which was to transform the economy. It took some time, however, for the regime to gain its fair share from the country's oil revenues. As happened elsewhere in the developing world, the balance of power between struggling new states and the major world powers played itself out in Iraq in the quest for oil. The early years of oil exploration and production were dominated by foreign, mainly British, companies. The Turkish Petroleum Company had majority participation by British interests, and was awarded the concession to exploit Iraq's oil in 1925 on terms that were highly unfavourable to Iraq. For example, a promise in the mandate agreement that the Iraqi government would be given a 20 per cent share in any future oil development was not kept. In 1927 the large Kirkuk oil field was discovered, and two years later the company was renamed the Iraq Petroleum Company (IPC). This was despite the fact that it had no Iraqi ownership, its shares being held instead by British, Dutch, French and American companies.

With the prospect of Iraqi independence looming, and desiring to expand its concession area from the north of the country, the IPC renegotiated its agreement with the government in 1931, offering an increase in payments into the treasury. Iraq's oil exports to world markets began in 1934, marking an important economic turning point. In 1952 another revision of the IPC concession was signed, this one providing for a 50/50 sharing of profits. By 1954, Iraq's oil royalties had contributed so much to the national income that they provided all the investment capital required to pay for a number of projects. With revenues exceeding public expenditure, Iraq was able to use the surplus to invest substantially in its future. Between 1950 and 1958, for example, increased oil production translated into a nearly sixteen-fold increase in revenue for the government.

Oil Production and Revenue in Iraq, 1946–58

Year	Oil Production (Million Tons)	Revenue (Iraqi Dinar Million)
1946	4.6	2.3
1948	3.4	2.0
1950	6.5	5.3
1951	8.6	13.3
1953	28.0	49.9
1955	33.0	84.4
1958	35.8	79.9

Source: Y. Sayigh, *The Economies of the Arab World: Development since 1945*, Taylor & Francis, 1978, p. 37.

The expansion of the oil industry created a massive opportunity for Iraq. The strategy of Nuri al-Said was to funnel most of the new revenue into the long-term development of the country. He created the Iraqi Development Board (IDB) in 1950, a panel comprised partly of development experts, which was given 70 per cent of Iraqi oil revenues to invest in projects. This technocratic solution was, in the words of historian Charles

Tripp, 'intended to disburse funds and oversee development in an atmosphere relatively free of partisan and personalized politics'.[2]

Funding priority went to projects aimed at the development of the agricultural sector, which received 33–45 per cent of the funds. These projects were focused in particular on large-scale irrigation schemes such as the Tharthar Dam, opened in 1956. This major dam greatly improved the quality of life for many Iraqis, and it also prevented the frequent flooding which had previously plagued Baghdad. These government projects, in turn, served to enhance the effect of a boom in agricultural investment by the private sector. As a result, grain production rose by 56 per cent in the years following the Second World War, and the total area under cultivation by 50 per cent. Iraq was self-sufficient in wheat and rice by 1958.

The second priority was transport and communications, again with a focus on large-scale infrastructure schemes. By 1958, 2,000 kilometres of new roads had been built, along with a new airport in Baghdad and an expanded port at Basra.

The Development Board pursued a wide range of projects that were making massive progress and, in economic terms, were creating a country primed for a prolonged economic boom. It is also worth noting that the IDB financed schemes throughout the country, to benefit all Iraqis.

This huge expansion of state-sponsored economic activity in the 1950s was complemented, and in some accounts even surpassed, by an upsurge in private-sector investments. As the Iraq scholar Phebe Marr has noted of the agricultural sector, 'Most of the growth in this period ... took place in the private sector and was due to individual investments in pumps and tractors, not the development program.'[3] A new wave of entrepreneurship was sweeping the country.

This combination of private and public-sector growth swept Iraq into an economic boom. Stephen Longrigg, writing before the revolution, observed that '[Iraq's] curse had for centuries been poverty; it stood now at the threshold of an era of abundant wealth'.[4]

Iraq was destined for a stable and prosperous future, with many factors in its favour.

If so much progress was being made in developing Iraq's economy, why did the critics of the monarchy, including the supporters of the 1958 coup, stress economic grievances among their justifications for demanding drastic political change? One explanation is undoubtedly the fact that the massive expenditures on dams, irrigation and transportation took many years to complete and often more years to yield palpable benefits. In addition, it was likely that rurally-based large-scale development projects were not visible to the urban poor, who may have been expecting a more expedient and tangible share of the new oil wealth.

In fact, social spending was increasing considerably throughout the period of the monarchy. Education, for example, was being made available to more and more Iraqi children. Between 1930 and 1958, the number of secondary school pupils increased dramatically, from just 2,000 to around 74,000. William Polk wrote in 1958 that 'Iraqi society has changed radically in the last decades under the stimulus of Nuri's own reforms – investment of oil revenues by the Development Board which made possible better education for a whole generation of Iraqis. At a rate of 500 persons a year, the pick of the post-war generation of men and women have been sent to European and

American universities to acquire technical skills and advanced degrees.'[5]

While this was a welcome transformation that benefited most sectors of the population, other types of social change were harder to manage. In particular, a massive migration was occurring from the countryside to the cities, with many jobless or underemployed poor living in substandard conditions. Between 1922 and 1944, the population of Baghdad doubled. Between 1956 and 1958, there was a race between development and revolution. While massive social and economic advances were taking place, so too were the dislocations that resulted in popular unrest and political disadvantage. Clearly, different classes of society had diametrically opposed views regarding Iraq's future. However, the overwhelming priority for many Iraqis seemed to be not economic concerns, but their deeply held perception that the country's pro-Western stance was out of step with Arab nationalism, which was broadly embraced by the masses.

The myth of Britain's legacy

Iraq's relationship with Britain and the West lay at the centre of the debate about foreign policy. On the one side were the political leaders of the monarchy period, most of whom were convinced of the wisdom of Iraq's pro-Western foreign policy. Opponents, on the other hand, blamed Britain for much of the region's ills, and many embraced the left-wing ideologies or the non-aligned outlook of the Nasserites. They had a distorted view of British influence as entirely negative and pervasive, and advocated a total break in relations.

I did not agree with those views. Tracking the degree of

British influence since the creation of Iraq, we can see a clear pattern of rapid diminution. Furthermore, it is wrong to see British influence in Iraq as uniformly negative: from internal security to economic development, Britain often played a highly constructive role. Britain, after all, was the midwife of the modern Iraqi state, laying the foundations for its governmental institutions, instituting land reform and playing a major role in designing a constitutional order.

These institutions were necessary for Iraq foundations to become a modern state, and included a professional public administration, a constitution-based legal system and a national army. Britain's interventions during the 1920s held the state together – for example by controlling separatist movements in the Kurdish areas in 1924 and sponsoring Iraq's case at the League of Nations, which declared oil-rich Mosul to be part of Iraq. British help was also required in the mid-Euphrates revolt of 1935.

We should remember, however, that opposition to Britain was often mobilized and inflamed by British policies outside Iraq. Chief among these was Britain's failure to guarantee the national aspirations of the Palestinian Arabs by supporting the new state of Israel. This policy caused widespread protest and anger among Iraqis. Britain's attack on Egypt to reoccupy the Suez Canal in 1956 caused massive riots throughout the Arab world and empowered the opposition in Iraq, whose members claimed they were fighting the new Western imperialism.

Nevertheless, while the system of political representation set up in Iraq by the British may not have been perfect, it was more democratic, progressive and liberal than any other in the Middle East. Moreover, it was rapidly evolving towards ever greater democratization.

Under the Hashemite regime the rule of law was fully

enforced, and that made it resilient enough to overcome a number of fundamental challenges to its authority. The best evidence of the value of this political system is to observe the events in Iraq when it was removed. Whatever shortcomings it may have had before 1958, what followed was dramatically worse, with disastrous consequences for the Iraqi people and their nascent state.

Two great leaders

So far I have been discussing the policies that proved their worth during the Hashemite monarchy period. Now I would like to discuss two individuals whose dedication to building a modern Iraq may serve as examples for the leaders of tomorrow.

When I was a young boy, I had the privilege of meeting both these men, two of the most notable Iraqi leaders of their day – Nuri al-Said and Fadhil al-Jamali. Each of these men rose through the ranks of public service in Iraq by their hard work, integrity, talent and a burning desire to make an important contribution to their country. The memory of their exemplary lives inspires me still, and can serve as inspiration to those who dream of rebuilding the Iraqi state.

Nuri al-Said: a pragmatic visionary

Born in 1888, Nuri al-Said was the most prominent and influential statesman of Iraq pre-1958. Before entering politics, he distinguished himself as an extraordinarily promising young officer in the Ottoman army. After the First World War he was among the first to join Faisal I in building the new Iraq and remained one of his closest advisers. Active under every monarch from 1921 to 1958, he was the founder and the first chief of the armed forces of Iraq, repeatedly served as minister of defence or minister of foreign affairs after 1926, and was prime minister 14 times up to 1958.

Among the key politicians of his day, Nuri was the strongest, the most visionary and the most pragmatic. His authoritative grasp of geopolitics helped him and like-minded leaders to bring about Iraq's peaceful transformation from colonial rule to political freedom. Just as impressive was his formidable drive in instituting a gigantic economic development programme to modernize his country. He was one of Iraq's – and indeed the region's – most far-sighted and respected leaders.

On the domestic front, Nuri successfully negotiated the increase to 50/50 revenue-sharing with foreign oil companies in 1952, as noted earlier. By pushing for the use of 70 per cent of Iraq's oil revenues for economic reconstruction through the Iraq Development Board, he hoped to turn the country into a showcase for economic, social and cultural development. He was an almost utopian visionary, foreseeing an Iraq that was free of poverty, ignorance, illiteracy, corruption, exploitation and discrimination. In his view, social justice and economic democracy were necessary foundations – and indeed a pre-requisite – for an enduring political democracy.

Nuri al-Said also left behind an important legacy in the conduct of foreign policy. In a world divided by the antagonisms of the Cold War, he courageously believed that Iraq's future interest would be best served by siding with the democratic West. He was a staunch believer in the market economy and free enterprise. In making that choice, he knew he was facing overwhelming popular opposition. He did not shrink from the threats that confronted him, nor hesitate in pursuing his vision with formidable resolve.

He fully understood and appreciated the difference between implementing pragmatic national security policies and conducting foreign relations. The first he regarded as the foundation, fundamental and constant. The second, in his view, was open to discretion and personal preference as long as it did not contradict the first. Foreign relations and diplomacy are fields in which political leaders may exercise their own style, pursue their own insights and alter direction in response to changing circumstances. National security and national interest, on the other hand, cannot be driven by ideology or the personal discretion of any leader. Instead, they must be based on a fundamental understanding of the make-up, location, realities and constraints facing the nation – factors beyond the control of any individual politician.

For Nuri al-Said, the underlying realities of Iraq's national interest and security were clear. Iraq, as an underdeveloped country, had to pursue a course that would ensure its survival and long-term development and prosperity. In so doing, it had to work with what it had in terms of the composition of its people, its social and religious fabric, its psychological and linguistic make-up, its history and geography, its neighbours, its natural resources and the source of its water supplies. If it wanted to prosper and advance, it could not afford to isolate itself from global technology and commerce. In its international relations, it had no choice but to form alliances with partners who could help Iraq to unlock its potential. In other words, long-term national security meant working with what was best available to achieve national interest.

He based his foreign policy on four pillars.

1 Iraq's position as an integral part of the Arab world

The ties between Iraq and the rest of the Arab world are insep-arable – geographic, historic, economic, emotional, social and psychological. National interest therefore required, among other things, an active role in the Arab League and, at that point in time, a commitment to supporting such causes as the freedom of Algeria and Tunisia and the defence of Palestinian rights.

2 Alliances with Iran and Turkey

Iraq's longest border is with Iran, extending over 1,200 kilo-metres. Furthermore, the Shia in Iraq and those in Iran share deep-rooted emotional, religious and historical ties. As for Turkey, Iraq could not survive without the two great rivers, the Tigris and the Euphrates, both of which flow into Iraq from Turkey. Iraq had also had a 500-year relationship with Turkey as part of the Ottoman empire – a fact that cannot be erased. These factors made it vital to maintain alliances with both countries.

3 The importance of oil

Oil was vital to the country's wealth, so it was essential to extract and market it and to use the proceeds to develop Iraq. This meant cooperating with the giant international oil industry which held the monopoly in those days. When neighbouring Iran, for example, tried to nationalize its oil industry and kick out the Western oil companies in 1951, its production came to a total standstill and the country faced bankruptcy. The Soviets could not help, as they themselves were energy producers and they had no marketing access to the Free World. Nuri al-Said, in contrast, was able to capitalize on Iraq's vast oil reserves. Instead of fighting the oil giants, he achieved an enormous increase in national revenues for Iraq through non-confrontational yet effective negotiation.

4   Access to the developed world

Finally, Iraq needed access to the developed world to gain education, knowledge, technology and commerce, and to be able to build its own productive capacity. At the time, the world was divided into East and West. The decision was whether to side with democracy and freedom for the sake of national advancement, or to try and meet the country's needs from behind the Iron Curtain. Nuri al-Said was far-sighted enough to choose to align Iraq with the West and its advanced technology.

Central to accomplishing Iraq's national security objectives was the establishment of the 1955 Baghdad Pact, an alliance that included Iraq, Turkey, Iran, Pakistan and Great Britain as formal members. The United States attended meetings informally as a supporter and observer. In terms of geopolitical advantage, the pact enabled Iraq to achieve the second, third and fourth of the objectives described above. Additionally, it provided security for Iraq against any Soviet aggression – a real threat at the height of the Cold War. It also supplied Iraq with armaments at no cost, along with state-of-the-art military training.

As a result of securing its borders in this way, Iraq was able to devote its available resources and human energy to realizing its ambitious economic development programmes. The Baghdad Pact therefore generated multiple benefits at a time when the country was totally devoted to transforming itself into a prosperous world-class economy.

The wisdom of Nuri's sophisticated grasp of Iraq's need to tie its foreign policy to national security interests becomes all the more evident when one compares his policies with the disastrous course followed by his successors. The Iraqi dictators who grabbed power in 1958 and in the coups that followed shared with Nasser an utter failure to recognize that certain realities had to be accepted. Instead, they were ideologues driven by the politics of division, blindly toeing the party line and, just as blindly, vilifying those who did not. Iraq's foreign relations during the post-1958 era of junta leaders and dictators, because it was so often divorced from its fundamental interests, resulted in a serious decline in Iraq's security and regional standing.

For example, when Iraq's leftists agitated to end the alliances with Turkey and Iran, to damage their relationships with the international oil companies, to expel the West and to turn to the Eastern Bloc, they were simply mouthing easy slogans – ones that met the Soviet national interest rather than Iraq's. Because Iraq's post-1958 leaders did not understand, and there-fore abandoned, the country's national security requirements, the links with Turkey, Iran, the West and the oil industry were allowed to disintegrate.

In response, Turkey started to build mammoth dams at the sources of both the Tigris and the Euphrates, drastically redu-cing the flow of water into Iraq. Relations with Iran were allowed to deteriorate to such a low ebb that a disastrous eight-year war with Iran from 1980 to 1988 caused more than one million deaths on both sides and cost hundreds of billions of US dollars. The funds for the war came from running up ruinous debts as well as from tapping internal reserves that could have been channelled into building greater prosperity. And the hostility shown by successive Iraqi governments towards foreign oil companies put an end to exploration, expansion and the modernization of the country's oil industry.

Basing Iraq's foreign relations on political whims rather than national security interests also led to some abrupt changes of direction. After 1958, for example, Iraq sided for a while with Nasser, cheering him on and promising to follow him blindly. A few months later, purely on the basis of personality and chemistry clashes, Iraq changed course and became 100 per cent opposed to Nasser. It even became a criminal offence to utter his name. Pro-Nasser Iraqis were tried and executed.

Another example occurred in May 1990 when the Arab summit met in Baghdad and Iraq's president, Saddam Hussein, was full of praise for the Emir of Kuwait. In August the same year, he decided to invade Kuwait and the Emir had to flee for his life.

The follies of these years show how far ahead of his time Nuri al-Said really was. As a statesman, he was able to ensure that Iraq's foreign policy was soundly based on its long-term national security interests. Rather than deciding for himself what those interests were, he took care to understand the unchangeable realities and was willing to shape his policies accordingly. He deserves to be studied and applauded for his pragmatic outlook.

Nuri al-Said was also highly respected for his personal qualities. For example, even his most vicious opponents could not cast doubt on his integrity. He had no assets other than an average-sized house which he was only able to build three years before he was tragically killed. And before this, for 13 of the 14 times that he was prime minister, and despite being the highest-ranking official in public service from 1921 to 1955, he resided in a modest government-owned house, in a compound built by the British in the 1920s for executives of the Railways Department.

He himself believed that personal integrity was a powerful defence against his political enemies. 'As everyone knows,' he once stated, 'I own no material assets which might make me fear communism and its principles, but I have the faith to resist it because I think it is dangerous to my country and to its freedom, sovereignty, independence, religion and traditions.' Iraqis of all political stripes, looking at his long career in public office, could come away with only one conclusion: that Nuri's view of leadership was not about power but about duty, mission and responsibility. In short, his vision, courage and dedication helped propel Iraq towards a bright and prosperous future.

In terms of principle, Nuri al-Said was driven by a strongly held philosophy:

> It is the duty of a responsible politician to seek, in the first place, to ensure the safety of his country and protect it from external aggression and to ensure the safety of its citizens and to ensure that they live their life with dignity. When a statesman believes in this and seeks to achieve it, his conscience will be clear and he will not pay much attention to whatever false

charges are levelled at him because lies do not last and truth will eventually prevail.[6]

Why, then, did the system that Nuri helped put together fall victim to the coup of 1958?

My answer is that two fatal handicaps contributed to this tragic downfall. While Iraq was still under British mandatory rule in the 1920s, Nuri chose peaceful engagement as a means of achieving pragmatic and realistic gains for his country. It was Nuri who initiated the process leading to Iraq's independence by negotiating the 1930 treaty with the UK, which was followed by Iraq's formal membership in the League of Nations in 1932 as an independent state. It was he who negotiated the increase in oil revenues and the subsequent establishment of the Iraq Development Board.

But when the Western powers, branded as imperialists, came under attack from Communist, Baathist and Nasserite propaganda, Nuri himself was targeted and his reputation was tarnished as a result of his cooperation with Britain and other Western nations over the years. In this volatile atmosphere, a new leader like Nasser who advocated socialism and was backed by the Soviets was able to present himself as a genuine nationalist, in contrast to those he accused of siding with the Western imperialists.

Nuri's second handicap was his inability to reach out and win the support of the Iraqi masses. His vision, principles and far-sightedness were not appreciated by most young Iraqis, whose passions at that time were being deliberately stirred up against the West. The avalanche of skilful propaganda from Cairo and Moscow was overwhelming. Nasser was a powerful communicator and a highly dangerous force. To advance his personal ambition, he used his power with fanatical determination to inflame public opinion throughout the Arab world, stoking discontent that had nothing to do with economics and everything to do with the politics of division. His propaganda consisted of non-factual yet powerful messages and lies that got repeated endlessly until the ordinary citizens of Iraq and other Arab countries began to accept them as truth.

Nuri al-Said failed to respond effectively to such political propaganda and accusations, preferring to concentrate on Iraq's stability, territorial integrity and economic prosperity. His pragmatic outlook in this highly charged and emotional atmosphere did not impress the youth of Iraq. Such is often the fate of quiet, dignified and honest statesmen in an era dominated by the inflammatory rhetoric and empty promises of demagogues.

On 15 July 1958 the life of this giant of modern Iraq came to a violent and undeserved end when Nuri al-Said was brutally murdered by Nasser-inspired revolutionaries and his corpse was mutilated and burned. He was survived by his wife and daughter-in-law, who lived out their lives in exile, supported by friends.

Also killed in the coup was Nuri al-Said's only son, Sabah, who had studied aeronautical engineering at Cambridge University. On his return to Iraq, Sabah was appointed a pilot in the air force. Young, dynamic and adventurous, he was not one to learn from previous mishaps, including a fall from an airplane in 1935. One summer's morning, he flew his plane under the bridge that connected the two sides of Baghdad across the river Tigris. Obviously he calculated the space beneath the bridge and the size of his airplane and the deed took only a few seconds. Nevertheless, it was a daredevil stunt.

The next day, Sabah received a call from his father who, in

a calm and decisive tone, asked him what his motive was in undertaking this immature and highly dangerous act. Nuri al-Said then said to his son: 'Let me warn you very seriously. You are free to risk your own life with such an imprudent action. But you are not allowed to expose a government asset – an air force plane or a national bridge – to any risk.'

This was clearly a rule that Nuri al-Said applied to his own life. As he once commented, 'It is the right of any politician to risk his money or his reputation or even his life, but it is not his right to expose to risk the safety of his nation and the integrity of his country.'

On that same day, Sabah al-Said was fired from the air force and appointed to an administrative job in the Iraqi Railways, where he worked for the rest of his life. Although he took no interest in politics, he was killed along with his father in the July 1958 coup.

Sabah had two sons – Falah, a chief pilot, who flew King Hussein's airplane in Jordan, and Issam, who studied architecture at Cambridge University. Both died prematurely.

In 1988, when I attended the annual World Bank meetings in Washington, DC, I ran into Mahmoud Othman, an old acquaintance from Iraq and a member of a respected family from Irbil. Mahmoud explained that he was a member of the Iraqi delegation headed by the then minister of finance, Hikmat al-Mukhailif, and that the minister had expressed an interest in meeting me. Apparently he had heard about Investcorp. After an initial hesitation, I agreed to meet the minister.

The meeting was cordial and the minister could not have been more complimentary. In response, I invited him to dinner in Washington, along with anyone else he chose to bring along. He accepted graciously, but indicated in a slightly lower tone of voice that he would not wish to include anyone from his team. I had the impression that he could not trust them and was afraid of being spied on. He did indicate, however, that Mahmoud Othman would be welcome.

In the evening, I booked a private room at a Chinese restaurant and invited my brother Fahir, who lives in Washington, and a dear old friend from Iraq, Nijyar Shemdin.

Around the table we were relaxed, and this led to discussions about Iraq pre-1958. I provoked him with a question. 'Mr Minister,' I said, 'do you really believe that Nuri al-Said was not a symbol of integrity, competence, vision and patriotism?' The minister did not respond directly, but he could not disguise his agreement either.

He then went further by offering his own experience of Nuri al-Said as prime minister of Iraq in 1956. At the time, he said, he was a college student in Baghdad and belonged to the Baath Party, whose members poured into the streets to protest against the government. When the police were sent to keep law and order, the Baath students moved forward to clash with them. Next they threw stones and rocks at the police who were trying to defuse the demonstration. Some policemen were badly injured, and more force was used to round up the protesters. Those who were caught, including Hikmat Al Mukhailif, were taken to prison at sunset.

At midnight, while the protesters were being held, the prime minister arrived to see them. Nuri al-Said entered the room and sat on the floor with the rebels. He told them that he understood their political motives and considered them to be political opponents who wanted to see him replaced. He emphasized that if they succeeded in assuming the responsibility of leading the nation, he would be on the opposite side protesting against them as they were doing now. That, he said, was perfectly legitimate and fair.

Nuri al-Said then explained that they were not taken to jail because of their opposition to him. They were being punished because they attacked a third party – the law-enforcing officers. Those policemen were simply doing their duty of keeping law and order. They were public servants, irrespective of who was in government. Nuri went on to inform them that they would now be set free, though he thought he should come personally to deliver this message as a lesson for the future for these hot-headed college students.

This incident, like many throughout Nuri al-Said's life, showed his foresightedness and dedication to advancing a country that has suffered much since his tragic death.

Fadhil al-Jamali: a paragon of integrity

Another example of a courageous, honest and able leader from Iraq's past was Dr Fadhil al-Jamali. Rising from an unprivileged background, born in 1903 into a Shia family, Mohammed Fadhil al-Jamali excelled both at primary and secondary school. He then won a government scholarship to pursue his education at the prestigious American University of Beirut. On graduating with outstanding results, he was told that his academic potential would be further developed not in Baghdad but in the West. His Iraqi government-sponsored scholarship was therefore extended so that he could pursue postgraduate studies at Columbia University in New York, where he earned Masters and Doctorate degrees.

On returning to Iraq, he was appointed to head the Board

of Higher Education in Baghdad. From there he shifted into foreign service and served in subsequent cabinets as minister of foreign affairs, becoming one of the signatories of the UN Charter. He was then elected speaker of the Iraqi parliament, following which he served as prime minister on two occasions.

Fadhil al-Jamali's integrity, vision and competence were internationally recognized, respected and admired. As a man of humble Shia origins in a country supposedly dominated by a closed Sunni elite, his impressive rise to power and fame is tangible evidence that, in pre-1958 Iraq, advancement was built on merit and available to anyone with the right skills and qualifications.

I myself had the privilege of meeting Fadhil al-Jamali in 1957, when my eldest brother Nezir – an engineer with an eye on politics – invited Dr al-Jamali to visit Kirkuk as our houseguest for two nights.

Part of Dr al-Jamali's purpose in coming to visit was to meet with up-and-coming young professionals, including doctors, engineers, lawyers and teachers. Following dinner, which I attended, the group gathered in our garden to exchange views and engage in town hall-like discussions with our guest of honour.

Dr al-Jamali provided a macro-perspective of world affairs, and then focused on Iraq's progress and foreign policy. This was followed by extensive questions and answers. I remember one young lawyer asking him why Iraq should not seek a revolution similar to Egypt's under its charismatic leader, Nasser.

Dr al-Jamali gave an eloquent response. He emphasized that Iraq was, indeed, in the midst of an extraordinary revolution of its own and on many fronts – education, healthcare and housing, for example – in addition to building massive infra-structure. He referred to progress and accomplishments in every corner of the nation and noted that the face of Iraq was being transformed by the Development Board.

He then considered the example of Egypt, advising patience to see whether Egyptian promises would be fulfilled and what the achievements would be. If the end-gains in Egypt proved the value of Nasser's policies, there was no reason not to consider emulating them. In short, he drew a contrast between ongoing, tangible results in Iraq and promises for the future being broadcast from Egypt.

Dr al-Jamali then argued that we should not be content just with physical progress in Iraq. Rather, we needed to develop our mindset and our outlook. He cited a hypothetical example of a tribal leader, perhaps 25 years ago, who might have thought that the way to obtain a favour from the government was to solicit the assistance of the British ambassador, whom he might have perceived as a source of power and influence. Today, Dr al-Jamali stressed, no one in his right mind in Iraq would entertain such a possibility. Iraq was a completely sovereign state and no foreign ambassador in Baghdad would dare to pretend that he could influence, or interfere in, the country's domestic affairs. In so saying, he refuted claims to the contrary contained in the avalanche of broadcasts from radio stations in Cairo and Moscow.

Finally, Dr al-Jamali's message was that in Iraq, at that time, capability was the only criterion for getting ahead. He stated that anyone in the audience, or any of their children, could aspire to the highest position in the country as long as they had the right qualifications. He cited himself as an example. He said that inspite of his modest background, he had risen up to serve in several cabinet positions and twice as prime minister. Success, he said, depended on integrity, competence, dedication and energy.

For me to hear such a powerful and eloquent message was most inspiring. It confirmed my faith and confidence in the prevailing system of government in Iraq. I will never forget the impact it made on me.

Had I written this book on 13 July 1958, immediately before the revolution, I probably would have been more critical of some of the policies of the Iraqi government than I am now. Undoubtedly there may have been some mistakes, and certainly not everything was perfect. One crucial error, for example, was to allow the lowest-achieving high school students – those unqualified for any other college – to join the armed forces. As a result, year after year, inferior people were promoted to high-ranking positions in the military. Low in self-esteem but with guns in their hands, they were all too easily persuaded to advance their own self-interest rather than guarding the national interest. That is exactly what happened in July 1958.

Nevertheless, 50 years later, I see an Iraq so badly damaged that I have to acknowledge the quality of its pre-1958 leaders. Comparing whatever mistakes they made with the deliberate crimes committed over the past half-century, I see them now as giants – honest, patriotic and devoted to the public good.

Today, it is easy to see the damage that the highly popular Nasser inflicted on Egypt and its economy. In contrast, the unpopular government of Iraq was steadily building a great economic future, but these efforts were violently ended before they could bear fruit. The bitter lesson that Iraqis have had to learn is that great leaders are not those who seek instant popularity. Tragically, the nation in the 1950s was not mature enough to realize that this is so.

Lessons for tomorrow's Iraq

My main purpose here is not to blindly defend the pre-1958 regime from the judgement of history. Just as in any great human endeavour, many mistakes were probably made by the leaders of Iraq under the monarchy. However, a better understanding of this period is crucial if we are to draw the appropriate lessons about how Iraq can best go forward today. The things that were right about the monarchy can best be understood in comparison with the period that followed – the chaos of coup and counter-coup from 1958 to 1968; the dreadful Baathist regime that lasted from 1968 to 2003; and, finally, the disastrous dismemberment of Iraq under the current US occupation.

Instead of living up to the many promises they made to improve the lives of the people of Iraq, the leaders in the post-1958 era have forced the country to take giant steps backward. For example, in the immediate aftermath of the 1958 coup the 'temporary' constitution of Qassim's first government replaced the nominally liberal democratic institutions of the monarchy with a very different model. There was no separation of powers between legislature and executive and no provision for elections to a representative body. In closing off channels for political action, the role of the army as a major political actor was ensured. Economically, the regime began to falter too. Desperate to shrug off the last vestiges of imperial control, Qassim picked a fight with the foreign-controlled IPC and eventually rescinded many of its oil concessions. The short-term result was a problematic shortfall in revenues. Simultaneously, Qassim disbanded the Iraq Development Board.

Under the Baath regime, internal divisions worsened. The Kurds launched a virtual war of independence, often cloaked by the rubric of 'autonomy'. The Baathists responded to this challenge using both carrots and sticks, by turns offering counter-productive concessions and cracking down militarily – the worst such episode was the terror of the Anfal campaign in 1987. The Shia regions of the country (such as the south around Basra) saw infrastructure collapse from lack of investment.

Saddam ruled through a tight-knit elite drawn from his Albu Nasir tribe and other allied tribes in the country's northwest. That said, it was Saddam's perception of an individual's loyalty, not his or her religion, that ensured a person's survival or otherwise in the regime. Sunnis were among the many who were killed by the dictator or on his orders. During Saddam's reign of terror, the political freedoms which had blossomed under the Hashemite monarchy were totally extinguished. Dissenters were cowed into submission by the threat of harsh punishment. Those opponents of the regime who ignored this threat faced torture and execution. The use of violence for political ends became the norm.

While the economy did recover somewhat in the earlier days of the Baath regime, this was mostly the result of an explosive rise in oil prices. Socio-economic development was hindered by Saddam's skimming of the country's oil revenues and his costly military posture and policies. Oil revenues were dispensed in a patronage network and public-sector employment soon choked the entrepreneurial culture that was developing under the monarchy. From 1958 to 1977 the number of state employees spiralled from 20,000 to 580,000, and by 1991, 40 per cent of the population were dependent on the state for their income.

Far worse, however, Saddam used his oil windfall to launch two bloody wars which destroyed the economy and left the country bankrupt. Prior to his attack on Iran in 1980, Iraq had an estimated $30 billion in foreign exchange reserves. After the conflict, the country owed more than $100 billion and could not meet its daily payments, let alone spend on reconstruction and development. Rather than concede power, Saddam launched his attack on neighbouring Kuwait to steal its assets, hoping to cover his financial deficits. These grotesque, megalomaniacal adventures extracted a terrible human toll. In Saddam's wars, more than one million people died and many more were injured.

The monarchy may not have been a utopia. Yet, when we compare it with what followed, the most striking difference is that the political system provided security and stability. On these foundations, Iraqis had begun to build a state and to manage challenges such as socio-economic development, independence and political freedom. The events of 1958 swept away these foundations. The era of military dictators and the Baath period that followed destroyed what was left of Iraqi society, sharpened sectarian differences and imprisoned the population in a corrupt and violent republic of fear. In answering the challenge of how to build a new Iraq, the country's future leaders should consider both the successes and the shortcomings of the monarchy.

PART TWO

Iraq present: The build-up to war, occupation and disintegration, 1990–2008

3

A road to a new Iraq not taken

In our lives we travel many roads. Often we have to choose between one road or another, and these choices can have lasting effects. The paths I chose in my life took me away from the land of my birth and focused most of my professional concerns on building a successful financial institution – an effort I will discuss later in more detail.

This changed in the 1990s when Saddam Hussein invaded Kuwait and, despite being expelled by a US-led military campaign, persisted in ruling Iraq with an iron hand and posing a regional threat. During this period I continued to guide my company towards success and growth, but I also embarked on an additional road, spending some time and energy on the question of Iraq's future. After all, the land of my birth, of my relatives and friends, continued to hold sway in my heart and to occupy my mind. And with opposition to Saddam increasing and the prospect of his eventual departure a distinct possibility, discussing a new Iraq went from being a wishful academic exercise to a practical imperative. It was during these turbulent years that I thought I should express my views to those who might be involved in US foreign policy initiatives in order to encourage, to whatever extent possible, the idea of a regime change in Iraq.

In the following pages I will describe my attempts as a private international citizen with no personal agenda to present to certain leaders my wish for a post-Saddam Iraq. My reasons for discussing these private meetings are threefold.

First, they provide readers with some background regarding my views on the future of Iraq. My track record in the world of business is fairly well known. However, an Iraqi interested in the future of his or her country, or a foreign policy specialist reading this book, might wonder about the credentials of the author. And while I am neither an academic nor a foreign policy professional, I have kept well informed about Iraq and the Middle East through my reading and regional contacts. I have also served on the boards of a number of foreign policy institutions and have had some contacts with world leaders and high officials.

My second reason for presenting these accounts is to contribute to the mounting record showing that American officials received a wide range of advice towards developing a workable plan in the wake of military victory in Iraq. When things began to go badly in the early days of the occupation, a number of officials threw up their hands and said, in effect: 'No one warned us this would happen!' In fact, there was sharp debate within the US administration and among its Western allies regarding the most effective way to go forward in the new Iraq. There were a number of good and viable ideas presented by people with long years of experience, and some of these other possibilities were discussed and then dismissed. As a result, the US occupation ended up on the wrong road.

Finally, an account of my efforts before the invasion and

occupation of Iraq will help the reader understand a principal motivation for this book's creation: frustration and disappointment that a workable post-invasion plan was not followed, yet hope that it is not too late to salvage the situation.

In short, my sorrow over the tragic course of events in Iraq after its occupation in 2003 is mingled with anger and frustration because much of the death, destruction and waste that have racked the country could have been avoided. Although I joined many others in supporting a US-led effort to liberate Iraq, my vision of how the country should be led during the post-Saddam transition differed markedly from the programme that was actually implemented. But before I describe how I attempted to place my concerns before leaders and policy-makers, I will explain how my road came to cross the path of US policy in Iraq.

Beginning to ponder a new Iraq

As noted in chapter 1, the 1958 coup was followed by a succession of governments as one regime was violently replaced by another. The Baathists seized power in February 1963, only to be overthrown nine months later by another faction loyal to Nasser. As one bad government followed another, Iraq grew progressively weaker and I allowed myself in 1968 to wonder whether now, after ten years of misrule, someone might strike a blow to restore the pre-1958 regime and get the country back on track.

A blow was indeed struck. Unfortunately, it came not from any monarchist group but from the Baathists who returned to power in a brutal counter-coup in July 1968. This time they were determined to stay in power whatever the cost, and were prepared to be ruthless in crushing any opposition. As an entrepreneur trying to build my own business in Baghdad, I now saw no prospect of winding the clock back to 1958 and left the country for the last time in 1969.

During the 1970s I was totally immersed in pursuing my banking career in New York and the Gulf, and gave little thought to Iraqi politics beyond holding on to a faint hope that democracy and freedom might one day prevail. The 1973 hike in oil prices gave little encouragement. As prices quadrupled, huge sums of money began pouring into the coffers of the oil-producing states, Iraq included. This removed any hope that the Baathist regime in Baghdad could ever be overthrown. Not only were they brutal, they were now also extremely rich.

In July 1979, Saddam Hussein replaced Ahmed Hassan al-Bakr as president and commenced his single-handed rule by executing all his rivals in the Baath Party leadership. The 1980s brought the Iran–Iraq War. Years later in the south of France, I met socially with Alexandre, Comte de Marenches, the retired head of the French foreign intelligence service and a man of enormous experience and stature in his country. He told me that he had called Saddam a week before Iraq's invasion of Iran in September 1980, warning him that he risked entering a quagmire and would have to face Iran's suicide-prone fanatics. Saddam told the French intelligence chief that the fighting would be over in two weeks. Instead, the bloody and costly conflict lasted eight years.

Although Iraq was weakened by this long war of its own choosing, there was still no serious prospect that Saddam Hussein could be dislodged. Saddam's fomenting of this regional catastrophe should have taught the world that the man was reckless with the lives of his victims, including his own citizens, but brilliant at self-preservation, even in the direst situations. And brute force was the only language he understood.

When I heard that Saddam had invaded Kuwait on 2 August 1990, I was on vacation and was torn by conflicting emotions. On the one hand my heart went out to the Kuwaiti victims of Iraqi violence and rapaciousness. I immediately called my Kuwaiti friends, Abdul Rahman Al Ateeqi, Mustafa Boodai and others, to express my sense of devastation and offer any support that I might be able to provide. But part of me saw a silver lining to this tragedy: at last the man had gone too far and instigated his final battle. He had aroused the hostility, not only of the Western powers but of most of his Arab neighbours. The whole world now wanted him out of Kuwait. Could this be an opportunity, I wondered, to liberate not just Kuwait but Iraq as well? I began on this dark day to think about how best to remove the blight of Saddam and to set Iraq back on the right path.

The diplomatic activities that followed the invasion of Kuwait gave me some cause to worry, however. King Hussein of Jordan, in particular, was trying to broker a solution that would have allowed Saddam to leave Kuwait without loss of face. If he succeeded, Saddam would claim a propaganda victory and be left in an even more powerful position. Much as I loved, admired and respected King Hussein, I was not sorry to see his attempts fail and the allies resorting to force to drive Saddam out of Kuwait.

After 1991, a number of Iraqis opposed to Saddam took advantage of his defeat in Kuwait and the international opposition to his regime by establishing opposition groups. From my point of view, the more I learned of these exiled opposition leaders, the more I was disgusted by their motives and doubtful about their calibre. By now there were millions of qualified, professional Iraqis permanently settled and working outside their home country. Those with any credibility, I thought, would surely have established new lives, be integrated into society and be unwilling to sacrifice their hard-won gains for the sake of political power back in Iraq. A professor at Stanford University, for example, or a successful dentist in Toronto, or an accomplished architect in Paris would have little reason to uproot his or her family and disrupt careers and schooling. It seemed to me that the opposition groups clamouring for support were people who had failed to make it in the West and were hungry for money or power – or both – in a post-Saddam Iraq.

During the 1960s, I had seen that simply changing the government in Iraq was no guarantee that things would improve. I saw the same danger in the 1990s. While removing Saddam was a worthy aim, it would backfire if it simply opened the door for dangerous and unqualified power-seekers with agendas of their own to grab positions and authority.

In order to prevent this sort of reversion to bad government by bad leaders, I believed it was necessary instead to fix Iraq in a comprehensive way. After decades of dictatorship, there would be much to do in terms of economic development, restoring the rule of law, raising the quality of education, tackling population growth, improving the lot of women and so forth. All this would require extraordinary leadership and dedication on the part of those seeking power. And the prize, if they succeeded, was a glittering one. Japan and Germany had both risen from the ruins of war to become economic powerhouses in their respective regions. If Iraq could be helped to do the same, it could become a beacon of freedom and prosperity and a powerful influence for good in the region and the wider world.

To squander the opportunity by installing another generation of worthless leaders would be a disaster, I believed. If the Western powers were intent on removing Saddam, the task should be a means to an end – restoring Iraq to free and prosperous nationhood – rather than an end in itself. The objective should be not just to remove the bad, but to replace the bad with the good. The first priority, then, for building a new Iraq was to ensure that highly qualified leaders who had the best interests of the country in mind took control once the Saddam regime had ended.

A growing campaign against the rogue regime

The liberation of Kuwait resulted in two important victories for the people of Iraq: Saddam was militarily weaker, and internationally he was much more isolated. Although he clung to power after the swift and total defeat of his Kuwait adventure, the bombing campaign that preceded the ground war had destroyed much of his military capability. More important, the question of how to prevent a recurrence of this catastrophe moved higher up the agenda of officials in the US, the UN and elsewhere. The world had seen the threat posed by Saddam and, as long as he ruled in Iraq, it was clear his fanatical dreams of power would not fade. When, after his defeat in Kuwait, armed opposition broke out in the north and south of Iraq, Saddam's forces were sent to smash the uprisings with characteristically swift brutality. In an effort to protect these vulnerable populations, US-led forces imposed no-fly zones over their territory. These were kept in place as a means of continuing to squeeze Iraq militarily after the war.

The world's effort to punish and contain this rogue regime commenced just days after the invasion of Kuwait with a UN resolution calling for stringent sanctions on Iraq. After Kuwait's liberation, these efforts intensified and expanded, with further UN resolutions calling for the dictator to destroy his weapons of mass destruction and for outside observers to verify progress on this front and ensure that the WMD disarmament was complete and durable. Saddam responded to the UN weapons inspection programme with obstruction, evasion and deception. Nonetheless, inspectors found and destroyed large quantities of WMD and missiles capable of delivering them.

On another front, not long after Kuwait's liberation the US undertook covert measures to weaken and unseat the dictator. These included providing assistance to opposition groups inside Iraq who were eager to topple the regime. Thus, while President George H. W. Bush saw the limits of overt military action against Saddam at this point, he was willing to begin a secret programme of regime change which continued under President Bill Clinton.

In the midst of the international condemnation of Saddam and close UN scrutiny, the dictator continued to act the brazen bully both at home and abroad. In 1993, for example, the authorities uncovered an Iraqi plot to assassinate former President George H. W. Bush during a visit to Kuwait in April. In October the following year, Saddam threatened the Kuwaiti frontier once again with a force of some 80,000 men. For each of these transgressions, US-led forces responded by attacking military and intelligence targets in Iraq.

Among his own people, Saddam stepped up his reign of terror and oppression. To punish populations in the south, for example, he drained the massive wetlands that for centuries had provided sustenance for the country's famous 'Marsh Arabs', not to mention all manner of wildlife. And when the UN brokered an agreement through which the Iraqi government could export oil if it used the profits for the basic human needs of the population in the infamous Oil for Food Programme, Saddam and his cronies made certain they benefited handsomely while common Iraqis, including countless infants and children, suffered and died for lack of food and medicines. Critics of the programme claimed that it was the sanctions regime that resulted in this terrible suffering and loss of life, but it was Saddam who was directly responsible.

Why not a 'Hashemite option'?

With Saddam seriously weakened and on the defensive after his defeat in Kuwait, and with the proponents of regime change steadily gaining influence, I was ready in the mid-1990s to express my hopes for Iraq in the debate on the country's post-Saddam future. In considering alternatives, I thought, all possibilities should be examined. My motivation was certainly not to get personally involved in implementing a solution: my commitment to Investcorp and my duties as its CEO were more than enough to keep me fully occupied, and I had no desire to get embroiled in Iraqi politics. As a person who cared about Iraq's future, however, I wanted to advance a concept that seemed to me to merit consideration. Whether or not anyone took it up, I at least wanted the decision-makers to know there were other desirable alternatives.

My prime motivation in hoping for regime change was to release the people of Iraq from their shackles. With political life in a straitjacket, the economy plundered by a tight-knit family kleptocracy, and social life stifled by a rigid Saddamist ideology, the people of Iraq were more and more impoverished and forcibly prevented from attaining the most basic human aspirations. Rid them of Saddam, and the people might thrive once again, at long last. I really hoped that the downfall of Saddam would bring Iraqis out of the dark tunnel into which they had been driven after 14 July 1958. As mentioned already, I saw in Iraq the potential to build a modern and prosperous state that could benefit its own people and be a beacon of peace and stability for the whole of the Middle East.

And once Saddam was ousted, rather than taking a chance with an untried and unworthy opposition group, I advocated going back to the last time Iraq had a legitimate government. In other words, I called for the reinstatement of the democratically approved federation of 1958. Given that Faisal II was no longer alive, the revived federation would logically be headed by his legitimate successor, King Hussein. The idea of a Hashemite federation between the two countries was not new. The founder of the Hashemite Kingdom of Jordan, King Abdullah, considered it towards the end of his reign in the early 1950s. As noted earlier, it came to fruition briefly in 1958.

For a number of reasons, I felt that a 'Hashemite option' for Iraq would be the best solution.

First, a convincing legal argument could be made to support this proposal, based on the country's constitutionally-based period of Hashemite rule and the short-lived federation agreement. Importantly, King Hussein's role as Faisal II's deputy during the federation had been approved by the Iraqi and Jordanian parliaments and thus provided additional legitimacy and legal justification for this proposal.

Second, I thought it made political sense to have a recognized, legitimate and moderate ruler with an established local history who enjoyed prestige and respect throughout the region. Despite serious internal and external threats, Jordan had remained stable and relatively peaceful throughout King Hussein's long reign. The king's record on economic development, education, democracy, civil liberties and human rights was exemplary. As a statesman he had always been a good friend of the West and was highly respected on the world stage. As a Hashemite monarch, he could still claim, in my opinion, enormous respect and affection within Iraq. (I should note also a personal connection: my family's relationship with the Hashemites goes back 100 years. Both King Hussein's grandfather, Abdallah bin Hussein, and my grandfather, Mohammed Ali Kirdar, were members of the Ottoman parliament in 1908.)

Finally, I had strong personal reasons for advocating the return of the Hashemites to Iraq. I had experienced at first hand the character and qualities of King Hussein and his top officials, and felt that the people of Iraq could greatly benefit from their guidance and leadership. His Majesty King Hussein, a giant of a leader and one with extraordinary vision, courage and stature, was committed not only to building a modern state in Jordan, but also to fulfilling his mission as a Hashemite leader by advancing the Arab cause.

Field Marshal Prince Zaid Bin Shakir was among the outstanding advisers who dedicated themselves to King Hussein's mission, and he was the closest to the monarch. I came to know Prince Zaid well and enjoyed a personal friendship with him. He was one of the most honourable, dignified and forward-looking personalities of our time. The untimely deaths of King Hussein, and of Prince Zaid shortly afterwards, were great losses, not only for Jordan but for anyone who had come to know these two exemplary leaders.

Prince Zaid's loyalty and devotion to his king and country were second to none. As a military officer, he advanced step by step to reach the highest rank in the Jordanian armed forces. On more than one occasion, he fought on the front line for the king against enemies attempting to overthrow the monarchy in Jordan. When he retired from the military, he was appointed head of the royal court and twice served as Jordan's prime minister.

Given my contact with Prince Zaid, it was only natural for me to discuss with him my deep concerns over the future of Iraq. As I have noted, my view was that the Lion of Jordan, King Hussein, was the best hope for saving Iraq, considering that he had been the legitimate next leader of the 1958 Arab Union which included Iraq and Jordan. Prince Zaid never discouraged me from expressing this opinion. He also appreciated that while I had strong views on the future of Iraq, I had no personal interest in returning to the country. Prince Zaid respected the fact that I was now an international citizen, focused on my responsibilities at Investcorp, and that my interest in Iraq was from a distance and simply out of concern for future generations of that nation. He also appreciated my view that a stable and prosperous Iraq would benefit not only its citizens, but the wider Middle East and the world at large.

In the presence of Prince Zaid, I also got to discuss the

concept with King Hussein directly. Again, I did not expect King Hussein to commit himself, and I was certainly not in a position to offer him any plan of action. But I wanted him to know that at least one private citizen was thinking along these lines. (There may also have been many others: the idea was certainly not original.) I also had an opportunity to discuss the proposal with Prince Hassan, who at that time was Jordan's crown prince.

As I have mentioned, to forcibly restore the Hashemites to power was clearly impossible following the coup of 1958 because of the dire consequences threatened by the Soviet Union. However, with the dissolution of the Soviet Union in 1991 there was no major power to stand in the way in 2003. But to my knowledge, this alternative solution was not on the table. It was certainly not being proposed by any of the opposition formations, each one pressing its own self-serving agenda which too often ignored the welfare of Iraqis as a whole.

In addition, the proposal had a recent precedent. In 1991, the first democratically elected leader of Haiti, Jean-Bertrand Aristide, had been overthrown in a military coup. Three years later, the US had intervened militarily to return him to power and restore constitutional rule. President Clinton's justification for this action was that a military coup could not undo the legitimacy of an elected government and that the US had therefore reinstated the legal status quo. Although the Iraqi coup had taken place nearly 40 years earlier, I did not see why the same principle should not apply, despite the passage of time.

Here was a proposal for Iraq that I believed to be honourable, defensible and legitimate. Intending no role for myself, and with no personal interest at stake, I wanted those in whose hands the solution lay to consider the possibility and see if it could be made to work – and whether it might hold the key to returning Iraq to stability and prosperity.

By the mid-1990s, my position at Investcorp and my broader access to international organizations had brought me into contact with a large number of influential people in the US and the Middle East. Aware, obviously, that I had no power myself to influence change, I decided to place the proposal in front of as many of the relevant people as I could.

One of the people with whom I discussed my hopes was President George H. W. Bush. I had first met him in 1989 when King Hussein invited me to join him at a fabulously glittering dinner party at the White House which President Bush was hosting in the king's honour. I later served under George Bush's chairmanship on the board of trustees of the Eisenhower Exchange Fellowships.

In the summer of 1993, shortly after the president left office, he invited me to a one-day conference at Walker's Point, his summer home in Kennebunkport, Maine. The purpose was to discuss world affairs in general, but I asked if I could talk to him privately about Iraq and he suggested we meet before the other guests arrived. Iraq was a sore topic for the president. Although he had successfully expelled Saddam Hussein from Kuwait in 1991, he had chosen not to press on to Baghdad but to pull back once the immediate task was accomplished. Now Saddam was testing the limits, stirring up trouble again, and President Bush was taking flak for not having finished him off.

I asked him why he'd made this decision. He replied that the coalition was created to liberate Kuwait and that it wouldn't have lasted if he'd changed the objectives of the mission. He then asked me what I would have recommended in those circumstances.

I said I agreed that he should not have continued to Baghdad: that would have been messy. I would, however, have recommended retaining control of the southern third of the country already under US occupation following the success in Kuwait. I believed US forces should have stayed there longer in order to continue destabilizing Saddam. I then moved on to talk about restoring the Hashemite federation and the possibilities for the region if Iraq could be turned into a powerful pro-Western economic force. He listened intently and conceded that the idea had merit – and that maybe some analysis should be done to see what the repercussions might be.

Of course, I did not expect the former president to take any action. My objective was to see if someone at his level and of his stature saw anything impractical about my proposal. At the Kennebunkport meeting that followed, however, he introduced me to Richard Haass, who had been his director of the National Security Council for the Middle East (he's now President of the Council on Foreign Relations). I passed on my views to him as well as to General Brent Scowcroft, the former president's National Security Advisor.

More contacts came about through my good friend Arnaud de Borchgrave, who currently serves as a senior specialist at the Center for Strategic and International Studies (CSIS) in Washington, DC. Before that he was the editor-in-chief of the *Washington Times*, and prior to that he was the senior international editor at *Newsweek* for 30 years and a legend in the world of journalism. Arnaud had interviewed every important leader of the last half-century, from Ho Chi Minh to Mullah Omar of the Taliban. His list of contacts was formidable, and he invited me to dinner at his home on several occasions with key Washington decision-makers. On one of those occasions, I discussed my idea with Jim Woolsey, who was then director of the CIA. Jim expressed an interest in following up with some analysis, but soon afterwards he was replaced.

Arnaud and I also had lunch with Zbigniew Brzezinski, who had served as National Security Advisor to President Jimmy Carter. I had got to know Brzezinski through CSIS, where I served on the International Advisory Board. Brzezinski, while he listened carefully to my proposal, was sceptical about the feasibility of imposing a Jordanian king on Iraq.

Another contact suggested by Arnaud was Alexandre, Comte de Marenches, whom I have mentioned previously. Arnaud and I flew by helicopter to visit the Comte at his home in Grasse. I explained my hope for Iraq over lunch and he listened with intense interest. He later called me back to follow up, but some time afterwards I heard that he had unfortunately died.

My links with CSIS also brought me into contact with Dr Henry Kissinger, whom I invited to my office in New York to discuss the Iraq proposal over lunch. As a pragmatic statesman, he wanted to focus on how to go about implementing such a concept. I responded that this was not for me to determine. Every enterprise has to start with a vision, I said. If the idea sounded feasible, its achievement could be planned by the experts and professionals in government whose task is to turn policy into action.

Suggesting a return to the status quo in Iraq to Clinton

Eventually, I was able to put my proposal to the president of the United States. The meeting came about after President Bill Clinton had helped to broker the 1995 peace agreement between King Hussein and Prime Minister Yitzhak Rabin of Israel. The entourage on President Clinton's Air Force One flight back from Jordan included a Jesuit priest, Father Leo J. O'Donovan, who was then president of Georgetown University. When President Clinton discussed his desire to engage more actively in the Middle East, Father O'Donovan had apparently mentioned me, perhaps among others, as someone the president might wish to meet. (Father O'Donovan and I had become acquainted while I served as chairman of the Center for Contemporary Arab Studies in the university's School of Foreign Service.) The result of his suggestion was a phone call shortly afterwards from the White House inviting me for a one-on-one meeting with the president.

When we met in the Oval Office at 5.30 pm on 25 July 1995, the president's intention was to talk broadly about the Middle East peace process. He was complimentary about my role at Georgetown University. I was determined, on the other hand, to use the opportunity to discuss Iraq, and began by congratulating him on his recent successful intervention in Haiti.

He was somewhat surprised and wanted to know why I'd mentioned Haiti. I went on to draw the parallels with Iraq in terms of a constitutional government overthrown by a military coup and the determination of the US to work towards a restoration of legality. Applying the Haiti principle to Iraq, I said, would involve getting rid of Saddam (which was US policy anyway), then reconvening the federation with Jordan and installing King Hussein as its legitimate head. The potential benefit would be a stable, prosperous and powerful ally at the heart of the Middle East – another major advance in bringing peace to the region. 'Forty years ago,' I added, 'an intervention by the US would have caused World War Three. Now there is nothing to stop you.'

I ended by thanking the president for his time and insisting that I myself had no personal agenda in this matter. My only motive was to find a solution that would best serve the interests of Iraq, the Middle East and the world at large. I simply asked that if he found the concept to be of interest, he should put me in touch with someone in a position to follow it up so that I could explain my ideas in more detail. He agreed to give it his consideration.

After the meeting, I summarized my proposal in a letter to President Clinton and flew to Jordan to meet with King Hussein. The king welcomed me with his customary warmth and courtesy and said he greatly appreciated my friendship and loyalty to the Hashemite family.

King Hussein's later years were plagued by ill health. He had surgery for cancer in 1992 and underwent chemotherapy in 1998. After his death in 1999, an elaborate memorial service was held at St Paul's Cathedral in London. It was the first time that a non-British royal had been honoured in such a way since before the First World War. The event provided a fitting setting for world leaders to pay their final respects to a king who was not only admired for his wisdom, generosity and moderation, but was held in great affection. According to Professor Avi Shlaim, King Hussein's 'personal qualities of charisma, courage, determination and far-sightedness' enabled him to deal with his severely limited political and economic options as ruler of a small and relatively poor state 'and to survive in the face of overwhelming odds'.[1]

With the departure of this notable leader from the world stage, I had to accept that my dream of a Jordanian–Iraqi federation had also passed. Had it been implemented while there was still time, I wonder if the subsequent history of Iraq might have been very different.

The US openly embraces regime change in Iraq

Through most of the 1990s Saddam employed thuggish resistance and bald deception in making a mockery of the world's attempts to verifiably disarm his forces. Because Saddam refused to cooperate with international inspection efforts, and continued to maintain a threatening posture, it was not difficult for the US to enlist other countries to stand guard against the dictator. There was international consensus that Saddam's actions continued to warrant close monitoring and sanctions. But in the US, the Iraqi threat was painted in even starker colours, especially by members of the neo-conservative movement who were pushing hard for a full-scale US invasion.

Saddam brought the situation to its most serious crisis in January 1998 when he completely blocked the work of the UN weapons inspection team. Although UN Secretary General Kofi Annan went to Baghdad and was able to negotiate a way out of the impasse, Saddam's intransigence quickly resumed and continued through the year, culminating in Iraq's complete shutting down of UN inspections and monitoring on 31 October.

That very day, President Clinton signed into law the Iraq

Liberation Act of 1998, which was aimed at removing Saddam from power and supporting a 'transition to democracy in Iraq'. In signing the bill, the president said: 'We look forward to new leadership in Iraq that has the support of the Iraqi people. The United States is providing support to opposition groups from all sectors of the Iraqi community that could lead to a popularly supported government.' The act allowed for the provision of up to $97 million in military assistance to Iraqi opposition groups, and $2 million for radio and TV broadcasts.

This was a major turning point in US policy towards Iraq. After the First Gulf War, there had developed a debate over how best to deal with Saddam. Many voices joined in, but two of the major groups disagreed on such fundamental questions as whether it was better to continue with the policy pursued by President Clinton, or to pursue the more forceful option put forward mainly by neo-conservatives.

The Clinton approach, which in large part continued the policies of his predecessor, was to contain Saddam using multilateral, mainly diplomatic methods that relied on the use of military force only to punish egregious Iraqi behaviour. The policies of the neo-conservatives were more unilateralist, calling for the use of US military power as an important option for removing Saddam. The Iraq Liberation Act, then, was a high point in the efforts spearheaded by key neo-conservatives and their political allies to embolden the US programme of regime change. In essence, it became the public face of regime change, while the multi-million-dollar covert programme continued as well.

An underlying assumption of the neo-conservatives and of this legislation was that the UN efforts to disarm and punish Saddam were ultimately fruitless, and that providing increased military assistance to opposition groups was an essential step, if only to prepare US public opinion for an eventual US invasion. (The neo-conservative tactics will be discussed in greater detail in the next chapter.)

With millions of dollars set aside for Iraqi opposition groups, and the president mandated to identify and fund them within 90 days of the passage of the Iraq Liberation Act, it was as if the dinner bell had been rung. Opposition figures living outside Iraq, with dubious backgrounds, hungrily sprang to the front of the line. While many of these so-called 'opposition leaders' claimed to be fighting to replace Saddam, they were even more eager to fulfil their own personal agendas and line their own pockets. With dissent all but impossible inside Iraq, these tended to be exiles operating outside the country and looking for a chance to seize power once Saddam was out of the way. Many of the groups that they mustered received a sympathetic hearing, especially by neo-conservatives pushing for armed force to topple Saddam, and were generously bankrolled by the US (and possibly by other Western governments), which saw them as useful agents for destabilizing Saddam.

Unfortunately, these political opportunists did much more harm than good. In the frenzied effort to win credibility and promote themselves, they presented a distorted picture of the situation in Iraq to their American handlers. They diverted attention and resources from those proponents of regime change who had the best interests of Iraq in mind. And their selfish and misguided priorities helped to influence those who created an occupation authority during the post-Saddam era that was broken from the start. The opposition leaders, as I shall describe in more detail, not only lacked competence but were motivated by ambition and greed rather than by principles of Iraqi unity, equality and reconciliation.

Post-invasion suggestions unheeded

After the death of King Hussein in 1999, I felt a key player was lost, and with him a chance to revive enlightened Hashemite leadership in a post-Saddam Iraq. However, I continued to pay close attention to events, speaking to various individuals and groups about my hopes for the country's future. After the terrorist attacks of 11 September 2001 it was clear that the US, supported by Britain, was even more determined to get rid of Saddam Hussein. As preparations were made for the Second Gulf War, I wrote both to President George W. Bush and to Prime Minister Tony Blair to support their policy and to express the hope that any liberation should be followed by a transition towards peace and stability in Iraq.

Three months after the invasion, in June 2003, I had another opportunity to talk to President George H. W. Bush. Brazilinvest, an organization that promotes investments in Brazil, had invited me to its annual gathering in Rome and George H. W. Bush was to be the guest of honour. The former president was staying at the US ambassador's residence in Rome, and we arranged to meet there before going together to the dinner.

The US-led invasion had toppled Saddam, but Baghdad was out of control: looting and violence went unchecked. I could see that former president Bush was still very concerned about Iraq, and he asked me outright what I thought the US should now be doing. Although the plan for a Hashemite federation had ceased to be relevant with the death of King Hussein, I had other proposals to help save Iraq from continuing anarchy and decline.

The first was that the US should remove Saddam, his two sons and no more than a handful of family members and key figures in the tyrannical hierarchy. (At that point Saddam was still in hiding and his sons had not yet been killed.) All other Baath Party members should be told to go back to their previous jobs. In other words, I said, do not dismantle the machine. Iraq needs the bureaucrats, the professionals, the doctors, engineers, army, police, border guards, civil servants and all other functionaries back in place to keep the country running. To ban them from working because they belong to the Baath Party overlooks the fact that they had to be members to get jobs in the first place. These people were simply obeying orders, I said. Give them different orders and they'll work equally well for a post-Saddam regime. Anyone who had committed specific crimes should be prosecuted in due course, but no one in the Baath Party should be punished purely on the basis of belonging to the party.

Second, I thought that no Iraqi should ever be identified or differentiated on the basis of his ethnic origin, religion or background. That would simply create factions. Under the new regime, all Iraqis should be treated as equal citizens and be part of civil society, protected by the rule of law irrespective of the different components of their individual identities. This had been the principle under the pre-1958 monarchy and Iraq had been remarkably united as a result. Under Saddam, many people throughout Iraq were brutally mistreated and suffered terribly. However, that should not entitle them to any preferential gains or status in the post-Saddam era.

My third word of advice doubled as a warning: that the US should not take the current batch of opposition leaders and preferentially inject them into the new government. They did not have the integrity, the competence or the credentials; their commitment to the greater good of Iraq was highly suspect; and, in any case, Iraq already had a functioning administrative machine in place that could perfectly well be allowed to continue.

As we then made our way to the Brazilinvest dinner, President Bush asked if I could summarize my views in a short paper and send it to him. I did so as soon as I got back to London.

Later that same year – after the US had done exactly what I advised it shouldn't and Iraq had tipped further into anarchy – I had the opportunity to meet the then US National Security Advisor, Dr Condoleezza Rice, when she attended a meeting of the International Institute of Strategic Studies in London. When I was introduced to her, I acknowledged that I knew her former boss, George H. W. Bush, and had recently sent him a paper on Iraq. It turned out that she had read the paper, and she asked me to arrange to see her the next time I was in Washington.

The meeting took place on 11 September 2003 in the West Wing of the White House. Also present was Assistant National Security Advisor Elliott Abrams. While Abrams said not a word, Dr Rice received me very courteously. She asked me, first of all, to explain the thinking behind my paper. By now the advice I'd given in Rome was mostly out of date (the Baath Party machine had recently been dismantled, for example), but I was able to express my concerns at the direction Iraq was taking and said I hoped the administration would keep to its declared objective of building a new, prosperous nation.

The conversation then turned to the new constitution. I told Dr Rice that the best contribution the US could make would be to ensure that the constitution was fair, secular and inclusive of all Iraqis. It should not refer to factions or minority groups, but should treat all citizens as equal under the law. I reminded her that a similar constitution had served the US extremely well for 200 years.

Dr Rice's response was that it was up to the Iraqis to frame their constitution. To which I replied, 'Which Iraqis? If you mean the ones you've placed in charge of the country, they'll write a constitution that suits their own agendas. If it's in their interests to divide the country along tribal, religious and ethnic lines, they'll use the constitution to achieve those ends.' It would be better, I suggested, to have the constitution drafted by independent Iraqi scholars with no vested political interests. If they happened to be people who had fled the country under duress, all the better: they would want to ensure that the next generation of Iraqis would not have to do the same and therefore would build in appropriate safeguards.

Having started the meeting with high hopes, I left with a huge sense of disappointment. Dr Rice was never less than polite, but I had the impression she was seeing me simply as a courtesy. Whatever the reason, nothing I said was likely to change her views. My comments certainly made no difference to the drafting of the constitution. The power in Iraq was already in the hands of those least worthy or competent to exercise it.

Before the US-led invasion to topple Saddam Hussein, I was firmly convinced that it was entirely possible to remove this criminal dictator and put in place a government that would help reunify the country, ensure its internal stability and work towards future prosperity. I still believe this end can be achieved, but the post-2003 occupation has thrown up all sorts of obstacles.

Even though my policy recommendations for Iraq were not taken up, I consider myself fortunate to have had a number of opportunities to present them to influential figures in the world of international relations. And despite the mistakes and misplaced priorities that have been the hallmark of occupation policies in Iraq, the preceding account of my efforts provides evidence that many of those in positions of authority were at least willing to listen to a number of voices. In the following chapter I will present an overview of steps leading to the invasion and occupation of Iraq and argue that the course chosen by the US was destined to fail.

4

The neo-conservative recipe for disaster

The neo-conservatives, who heavily influenced US policy towards Iraq through Vice President Dick Cheney, had many ideas, one of which was good. The success of this group in pushing the US to carry out regime change was laudable, but this has been overshadowed by their dishonest path towards war, and the destructive and corrupt occupation that flowed directly from their policies.

The long catalogue of neo-conservative mistakes, miscalculations and cynical manipulations should serve as a cautionary tale to future leaders, tempering their judgement, for example, on the best path towards a viable Middle East policy. In their cynical world view, in which ends dictated means, neo-conservatives manipulated or manufactured intelligence to support their goal. They promised the Iraqis freedom and democracy, but saddled them with selected, corrupt and incompetent opportunists. In a complex, interconnected world, they pushed simple unilateral solutions. When problems could be solved only by the flexible application of common sense, their dogmatic approach and detachment from the real world made things worse, not better.

The number of books and articles exposing the numerous

catastrophic results of the neo-conservative programme for Iraq is large and increasing, so I will not elaborate here about the subject. My aim will be mainly to show how their view of the world was bound to result in a debacle for the people of Iraq, and for the Iraqi nation. One need only see who came out ahead after the invasion of Iraq – the hand-picked, self-serving opposition leaders and the US contractors – to see where their priorities lay. One measure of the huge gap between the promise and the reality is to recognize how the optimistically named Iraq Liberation Act and other neo-conservative policies led directly to a country now that is divided, impoverished and vulnerable.

While it is true that I was among those supporting the US-led movement for regime change, the need to eliminate Saddam was the only point of agreement between me and the George W. Bush administration. I wanted a brighter future for the people of Iraq, hopeful that the country's new leadership, backed by the US, would employ common-sense solutions and just policies to create a unified, free and prosperous country. The neo-conservative movement, on the other hand, was straitjacketed by its ideology of US supremacy through the use of force. Iraq was not a country inhabited by living, breathing people, but a piece on the geopolitical chessboard. In this world view, the people of Iraq were unimportant, the country's disunity was expedient, and long-term freedom and prosperity were propaganda buzz words rather than a goal to be realized.

A flawed and dishonest march to war

The neo-conservative movement was neither monolithic nor all-powerful in the matter of regime change in Iraq and of fashioning a post-invasion strategy. However, it is clear that key figures in the movement were instrumental in laying down the framework for US policy towards Iraq and, at the crucial moment, were powerful enough to carry out their programme. As noted, calls for regime change from among this group began to intensify in the early 1990s, following the 1991 Gulf War. Some saw the need to remove Saddam as 'unfinished business' after President George H. W. Bush decided not to prosecute the war all the way to Baghdad.

The most ardent neo-conservative pundits, politicians and policymakers who wanted Saddam gone used the time-honoured method of the shady used-car salesman: promise anything to seal the deal. To be sure, there were any number of good reasons for regime change in Iraq, as I have already discussed. And these backers of military intervention used them all: the WMD threat; Saddam's aggression abroad and oppression at home; supposed links to terrorist groups; and the promise of a post-invasion Iraq that would be free and democratic. Unfortunately, Saddam was eventually removed for those reasons that were the most frightening to the American public, but the least supported by the evidence. As a result of the single-minded drive to oust Saddam at any cost, policies pushed by the Bush administration proved to be disastrous not only for US standing in the region and the world, but mainly for the people of Iraq, the supposed beneficiaries of the invasion.

The neo-conservative drive to depose Saddam gained momentum in the late 1990s as the Iraqi dictator's truculence and bluster increased. In 1996, prominent American members of the movement, including Richard Perle, Douglas Feith and David Wurmser, wrote a paper entitled *A Clean Break: A New Strategy for Securing the Realm* for the incoming Israeli prime minister Binyamin Netanyahu. The paper argued that Israel had the opportunity to make a 'clean break' with the slogan of 'comprehensive peace' in favour of a traditional concept of strategy based on the balance of power. The document insisted that Saddam should be overthrown, and advocated a programme of neutralizing Syria and of hot pursuit of the Palestinians. It described the removal of Saddam Hussein as 'an important Israeli objective in its own right' and a means of foiling Iraq's regional ambitions. The authors of this report promulgated elements of this agenda through their placing in influential US government positions.

The neo-conservative group that was perhaps the most influential in pushing the US towards war with Iraq was the Project for the New American Century (PNAC), established in 1997. Its members were harshly critical of the Clinton administration's efforts to contain Saddam, namely his embrace of UN efforts and his use of limited, carefully calibrated, military force. In a period of unusually high tension over Iraq's refusal to permit UN weapons inspectors to operate in the country, PNAC published an open letter to President Clinton on 16 January 1998, stating: 'We are writing to you because we are convinced that current American policy toward Iraq is not succeeding, and that we may soon face a threat in the Middle East more serious than any we have known since the end of the Cold War.' The letter called for a forceful new strategy aimed at removing Saddam from power by military means. Among the PNAC members who signed the letter were some who would join the George W. Bush administration and press for an invasion of Iraq from powerful positions in the White House, Defense Department and State Department. These included Elliott Abrams, Richard Perle, Donald

Rumsfeld and Paul Wolfowitz. Another prominent neo-conservative who was key in this effort but did not sign the letter was future vice president Dick Cheney.

As I have already noted, the signing of the Iraq Liberation Act into law on 31 October 1998 was both a concrete example of PNAC's influence in Congress and a major step towards its goal of a full-scale military confrontation. Unfortunately, it opened the door to Iraqi exiles of questionable standing, who were embraced by PNAC and their political allies. This led, in due course, to a series of disastrous policies once the invasion of Iraq had begun.

Despite neo-conservative characterizations of the Clinton policy as 'swatting flies', the president was not averse to using effective force against Saddam. In response to the crisis brought on by the dictator's refusal to allow the UN inspectors to do their work, the president ordered an intensive bombing campaign from 16 to 19 December 1998 (Operation Desert Fox), aimed at Iraq's WMD and missile-related facilities. And as Saddam's defiance persisted even in the face of these bombardments, Clinton kept up the military pressure through the end of his term. As subsequent investigations revealed, these allegedly ineffective attacks in fact were crucial in weakening Saddam and destroying significant portions of his offensive capability.

The neo-conservatives who were bent on invading Iraq used a victory and a tragedy to their advantage in the new millennium. In the wake of George W. Bush's rise to the presidency, they succeeded in occupying some of the most important foreign policy positions in the new administration. From this high ground, they continued to pave the way for a military invasion of Iraq, this time with the means in hand to carry out their plans. Their tragic opportunity was the horrific attacks of

11 September 2001. They were able to press their agenda forward in large part because, in a cool and calculating way, they exploited the American public's sense of momentary panic, uncertainty and outrage, of being pitted against a powerful but elusive enemy. The neo-conservative propaganda machine quickly went into high gear, attempting to link Saddam to the attacks, making frightening claims about his WMD arsenal, and presenting as a certainty the unsubstantiated possibility of his giving these weapons to terrorists eager to attack the US.

Indeed, they argued, Iraq with its WMD capability could pose an even greater danger than Afghanistan, either directly or through its links with terrorist organizations. Removing the regime in Baghdad and replacing it with a US-sponsored group was the best way to eliminate that potential danger. These claims, which would later prove baseless, found fertile ground in the post-9/11 US.

On 20 September 2001, PNAC wrote to President George W. Bush alleging that the Iraqi government might have provided some form of assistance for the recent attack on the US, 'but even if evidence does not link Iraq directly to the attack, any strategy aiming at the eradication of terrorism and its sponsors must include a determined attempt to remove Saddam Hussein from power in Iraq. Failure to undertake such an effort will constitute an early and perhaps decisive surrender in the war on international terrorism.' The letter argued that the US must therefore provide 'full military and financial support to the Iraqi opposition' and that American forces 'must be prepared to back up our commitment to the Iraqi opposition by all necessary means'. It was signed by more than 40 heavyweight figures in the neo-conservative camp.[1]

Some of the flawed methods and outlooks of the neo-conservatives were revealed in the so-called 'Downing Street Memo'. This was a detailed record of a meeting attended by top British officials on 23 July 2002,[2] during which the head of Britain's Joint Intelligence Committee reported on his recent meetings with US officials, including CIA director George Tenet. The memo shows that secret plans were being made to invade Iraq; that the main argument for war was the potentially dangerous but unproven link between Saddam's supposed WMD and terrorist groups; that 'the intelligence and facts were being fixed around the policy'; that the plan relied on circumventing the UN; and that it also sought to create a pretext for invasion if none arose naturally. Most ominous for the people of Iraq was the memo author's conclusion regarding the mindset of officials in the US: 'There was little discussion in Washington of the aftermath' of an invasion.

In a speech on 26 August 2002, Vice President Dick Cheney once again beat the drums of war with the conviction of a true believer: 'Simply stated, there is no doubt that Saddam Hussein now has weapons of mass destruction. There is no doubt he is amassing them to use against our friends, against our allies, and against us.'[3]

The vice president and other neo-conservatives in the administration were able to push the US to invade Saddam for the wrong reasons, and with hardly a thought given to the predictably catastrophic consequences of their other policies.

A new politics of sectarianism

The US-led coalition of armed forces that had been assembled over the years to topple the regime of Saddam Hussein began the major thrusts of its military campaign on 20 March 2003. Less than one month later, Baghdad had been occupied, the Baath regime had been toppled from power with its leaders slinking out of sight, and the people of Iraq thought that they were on the threshold of freedom. But while many Iraqis at first expressed genuine joy and felt hope for the future of their country, subsequent events were cause for great dismay. The poorly planned and executed US-dominated occupation proved to be a profound disaster, and Iraqis feel that the consequences will be horrific.

It is vital to understand why this initial positive attitude towards the invasion was relatively short-lived. Why did the occupation authorities lose the hearts and minds of the population? What went wrong?

It is abundantly clear now that a number of factors contributed to the catastrophic situation that is the lot of Iraqis under the occupation. Chief among these were the occupation's misguided policies, which flowed from a rigid ideological world view promoted by influential figures who raised geopolitics above people and US interests above all others, and who utterly miscalculated the cost, the effort and the complexity of ensuring that Iraq after Saddam would recover quickly and fully. Other factors were the actions of groups and individuals, from inside and outside Iraq, whose incompetence, greed and megalomania brought in untold hardship and loss to the Iraqi people for whom 'Operation Iraqi Freedom' was supposedly carried out.

One of the most destructive steps was the promulgation of policies by the occupation authorities that have fuelled the ethnic and sectarian differences that have become the driving force in the new Iraqi politics. The approach adopted under the occupation of installing political power centres based on religion and ethnicity has made the task of rebuilding a shattered country all the more difficult. The occupation leaders chose to use Iraq's diversity as an opportunity to divide and conquer. Its leaders also changed sides from time to time, confusing their allies and eventually enraging everyone. This use of sectarianism represents a tragic departure for Iraq. A diverse and het-erogeneous society had existed there for as long as history has been recorded, but this diversity was never formally encouraged or recognized as the basis for the new governing edifice.

When, on 13 July 2003, US administrator L. Paul Bremer announced the ill-chosen members of the infamous Iraq Gov-erning Council (IGC), it was the first time in Iraq that the composition of the governing apparatus attempted to mirror the ethnic or sectarian make-up of the population. In advanced societies, diversity can be a source of strength, energy and creativity. However, if diversity begins to dictate the political agenda, it can fuel prejudices and bring negative consequences.

As the London-based International Crisis Group said in its August 2003 report, *Governing Iraq*, the principle behind the composition of the IGC set a 'troubling precedent'. The report said:

> For the first time in the country's history, the guiding assumption is that political representation must be apportioned according to [ethnic and religions] quotas. This decision reflects how the Council's creators, not the Iraqi people, view Iraqi society and politics, but it will not be without consequence. Ethnic and religious conflict, for the most part absent from Iraq's modern history, is likely to be exacerbated as its people increasingly organize along these divisive lines.

The report described the IGC as 'a gathering of political leaders with weak popular followings, very little in common between them, no bureaucratic apparatus and a clumsy nine-person rotating presidency at its helm'. It was 'doubtful that it can become an effective decision-making body'.[4] In my opinion, the occupation forces had the firepower to defeat Saddam's forces, but had no moral authority to engage in social engineering in Iraq.

Propping up dubious outsiders

The occupation authorities put serious obstacles in the way of Iraq's political future by insisting on quickly imposing thugs, warlords and Iraqis of tarnished backgrounds into made-to-order leadership positions in the new government. Some of these men were Iraqis who had been living abroad, but who, after the invasion, were flown in to assume privileged positions in the newly emerging order. They were given preferential access to the occupation officials, enormous financial support, and powerful and influential government posts. These 'political entrepreneurs', a number of whom had challenging track records while in exile, quickly gained an undeservedly influential position in Iraq. They won this initially through the support of the occupation authorities, but they endeavoured to maintain it by obtaining a regular stream of funding (some of it unspecified), as well as by building up private militias to protect their newly won interests.

Ordinary Iraqis resented these political upstarts, insisting that qualified and honest local leaders were more deserving of such high offices. In addition, Iraqis felt no real links to interlopers whose actions were driven more by personal aggrandisement than by public service. Other Iraqis appointed by the US authorities included local warlords. Their power bases were ethnic, tribal and religious, and they too rose to sudden prominence because their large organizations were supported by illegitimate financial resources.

The American decision to promote such a band of intruders generated strong resentment not only among average Iraqis, but also among the vast majority of secular Iraqi professionals. These doctors, scientists, teachers, engineers, lawyers and others who formed the core of Iraq's human infrastructure, its institutions and its civil service now felt excluded from the post-invasion effort to rebuild the country. In any modern society, it is from these capable and ambitious people that political leaders of real worth should arise. Moreover, the injection of funds and weapons into the militias controlled by these ersatz politicians, competing along sectarian lines, fuelled public distrust and outrage.

The spread of corruption and nepotism during the occupation has given rise to intense public disgust, as have large-scale financial scandals and illegitimate entitlements. The old ways of cronyism and corruption so rampant during the era of Saddam seem to have been magnified, with the apparent public approval and encouragement of occupation authorities. Some of the exiled politicians arrived with networks of relatives and supporters who were placed in key positions without any merit or justification. The political disorder was coupled with financial corruption. More and more dimensions of the web of financial corruption have been exposed – corruption that involved the occupation authorities, foreign contractors and the newly emerging local political and business interests.

A plague of corruption and waste

The corruption of the exile Iraqis and the warlords paled in comparison to the fraud, waste and negligence overseen by the occupation authorities themselves, as recounted in the media and official reports. These revelations have been particularly damaging to the US and UK effort because, with the failure to find weapons of mass destruction, the moral and humanitarian reasons for intervention have become ever more prominent. When the occupation authorities fell lamentably short of basic standards of probity, this weakened the justification for sacrificing human lives and a trillion of taxpayers' dollars to 'liberate' Iraq. In awarding billions of dollars' worth of contracts, supposedly for reconstruction and development, the way was left wide open for shameful cases of bribery, embezzlement and theft through weak controls, greed and incompetence.

Of course this has generated cynicism and disillusionment, with many Iraqis fully aware of what was allowed to go on. Corruption has been a major reason for the long delays and poor implementation that have characterized the badly needed reconstruction. This has enraged the Iraqi population further. At the same time, corruption over the purchases of military equipment has badly hampered the rebuilding of the Iraqi army. In a BBC Radio 4 interview, Dr Reinoud Leenders, author of a report on Iraqi reconstruction for the International Crisis Group, said: 'We can only guess how much disappears in private pockets. I really fear that Iraq reconstruction will turn into one of the biggest corruption scandals in history.'[5]

By early 2008 the US had spent or committed $45 billion of its own money on Iraq relief and reconstruction. Also budgeted for this effort has been more than $20 billion of Iraqi money which was controlled by the Coalition Provisional Authority (CPA) in the year following the invasion and which came from the Development Fund for Iraq set up by the UN out of Iraqi oil revenues and certain bank accounts. Some $8.8 billion of this was handed over by the Coalition Provisional Authority to Iraqi ministries and has never been accounted for.

It is reckoned that in real terms, the US has invested twice as much in rebuilding Iraq as it did in reviving Germany through the Marshall Plan after the Second World War, but there is little to show for it. Iraqis still suffer serious electricity shortages, water and sewage systems are inadequate and basic services remain broken. In addition to the vast sums swallowed up by corruption and poor management, the scale of the insurgency meant that large amounts of money had to be diverted into providing security for those involved in recon-struction. In turn, this has led to another Iraqi grievance: the large number of foreign private security firms operating in the country almost as private armies, unaccountable for the often irresponsible way they carry out their duties. The scandal involving the deaths of 17 innocent Iraqis on 16 September 2007 at the hands of the Blackwater security company is one example of many.

The breadth and depth of corruption and economic mis-management in post-Saddam Iraq has begun to be examined not only by the media but by teams from the US Congress and international bodies. But it was particularly shocking to hear the outright admission by a sitting senior Iraqi official of the vast sums that have been squandered. On 23 September 2005 the respected pan-Arab newspaper *Al-Hayat* published an interview with the then Iraqi deputy prime minister, Dr Ahmad

Chalabi, who confirmed that $36 billion spent in the occupation period, starting with the Bremer administration and continuing through the interim Iraqi governments that followed, remained unaccounted for. A month later, the same official told another prominent Arabic newspaper, *Asharq Alawsat*, that 'financial corruption is prevalent and there are thefts of possibly unbelievable amounts of money'.[6]

It has been disgusting to witness Iraqi politicians hurling allegations and counter-allegations at each other over the issue of corruption. The citizens of Iraq outside the Green Zone have been duly incensed.

In late 2006 the US Special Inspector General for Iraqi Reconstruction, Stuart Bowen, estimated that Iraqi government corruption was costing Iraq $4 billion a year, more than 10 per cent of national income. He dubbed government corruption 'the second insurgency' and said that the money thus stolen often funded criminal militias or insurgents. Iraqi businessmen complain that in order even to bid for contracts, they have to pay bribes to Iraqi officials at every level.

In addition, a classified US government report calculated that oil smuggling assisted by corrupt Iraqi officials was bringing the insurgents $100 million a year. One factor hindering the monitoring of oil theft is that the US for some reason failed to install meters when its technicians renovated oil pipes and wells after the invasion.

A US government report, leaked to the *New York Times* in November 2006, estimated that the insurgency was financially self-sustaining, raising between $70 million and $200 million a year from illegal activities, including oil smuggling, ransom from kidnappings, counterfeiting and the connivance of corrupt religious charities. The total included up to $100 million in oil smuggling and other criminal activity involving the oil industry, helped by 'corrupt and complicit' Iraqi officials.[7]

Other estimates of the income of insurgents were even higher. The oil ministry estimated that 10 to 30 per cent of the $4 billion to $5 billion in fuel imported for public consumption in 2005 was smuggled back out of the country for resale. The finance minister estimated that nearly half of all the smuggling profit – $200 million or more – was going to insurgents.

The Corruption Perceptions Index published in November 2006 by the Berlin-based watchdog Transparency International ranked post-invasion Iraq as one of the most corrupt countries in the world. Iraq was at the bottom of the list of 163 countries, together with Haiti, Myanmar and Guinea. The chief executive of Transparency International, David Nussbaum, told Reuters that when there are high levels of violence, 'not only does security break down, but so do checks and balances, law enforcement and the functioning of institutions like the judiciary and legislature. If all that is under strain, the very system that works to prevent corruption is undermined.' The problem persists. The latest Corruption Perceptions Index, released in September 2008, lists Iraq as the third-worst country, after Myanmar and Somalia – with Afghanistan, the Democratic Republic of Congo and Zimbabwe all ranking higher.

A front-page article in the *New York Times* on 12 May 2007 had the headline: 'Billions in oil missing in Iraq, US study finds'. The article stated that between 100,000 and 300,000 barrels a day of Iraq's declared oil production over the previous four years were unaccounted for and could have been siphoned off through corruption or smuggling, according to a draft American government report. The article added that the findings were sure to reinforce long-standing suspicions that smugglers, insurgents and corrupt officials controlled significant parts of the country's oil industry.

During the first years of the occupation, there was virtually no Congressional oversight of this massive ongoing theft of US and Iraqi funds because the US administration found it politically expedient to turn a blind eye to bad news from Iraq. Under Democratic leadership, Congressional committees have begun to reverse this trend. For example, a Senate committee held a hearing in March 2008 to examine waste, fraud and abuse in Iraq. The most dramatic and incisive testimony came from Judge Radhi Hamza al-Radhi, who had been commissioner of Iraq's Commission on Public Integrity (CPI), an organization established with funding and guidance from the US to fight corruption by performing investigations and referring cases to trial.

But from its inception in 2004, the fate of the CPI mirrored the downward spiral of the country as a whole. It became a victim of a dysfunctional government presiding over a sectarian-based spoils system in which government funds were seen as the rightful plunder of those in power, to be scooped up by any means. For example, al-Radhi testified at a hearing of the Congressional Committee on Oversight and Government Reform on 4 October 2007 that the $11 million in cash that he had personally received from US authorities to fund his commission had disappeared from its Rafidain Bank account, transferred into the Iraqi government account, never to be seen again. The same sort of legal theft was carried out with the deposits of other US-funded organizations. Still the commission staff worked tirelessly to carry out their work. One government minister was arrested on corruption charges. The CPI investigated some 3,000 cases of corruption and uncovered at least $18 billion in government funds that 'disappeared' into various ministries. But as the commission's work progressed, the targets of these investigations – up to and including the highest government officials – began to retaliate. More than 31 commission employees were assassinated and 12 family members were killed. Others were kidnapped, held hostage and tortured. Al-Radhi and his family have been attacked on a number of occasions and his house was nearly destroyed by missiles.

In the end, al-Radhi had to flee Iraq because of the violence and because the commission was unable to operate effectively. The central government, in fact, had written a letter stating that no cases referred by the CPI would be prosecuted without its approval, in effect immunizing the Iraqi government from its own watchdog organization. US officials, too, have been doing their part to empower the culture of corruption and intimidation in Iraq. For example, a former State Department official who worked in the now-defunct Office of Accountability and Transparency testified to Senate Democrats in May 2008 that the policy of US officials 'not only contradicted the anti-corruption mission but indirectly contributed to and has allowed corruption to fester at the highest levels of the Iraqi government'. The official added that even when al-Radhi was being attacked by the Iraqi government, the US embassy failed to stand behind him. Once again, political expediency would trump integrity, justice and principles.

Judge al-Radhi is a courageous Iraqi who exemplified the best prospects for the Iraq of tomorrow. He attempted to build a better future for his countrymen, based on the rule of law and equal treatment of all Iraqis. But he and his staff and their relatives have been threatened, tortured and killed by the sectarian, corrupt and thuggish government he was attempting to reform, the sad reality suffered by all those living in the Iraq of today. And the cruel logic of the occupation led US officials to stand by during this travesty for fear of offending the dysfunctional government leaders they themselves had put in power.

A reign of violence and lawlessness

In the immediate aftermath of the invasion and the collapse of the regime on 9 April 2003 there was a total breakdown in law and order which might perhaps have been avoided if martial law had been declared and a curfew imposed. Unconstrained mobs stormed out of the poorer areas of Baghdad, stripping anything and everything of value in complete anarchy. Among many other public buildings, the National Museum in the heart of Baghdad was stormed and looted of objects dating back to the dawn of civilization. Too little was done by the occupying forces to prevent this orgy of theft and vandalism. The outcome was that looting, criminality and violence dominated the Iraqi scene, inspiring fear among the general population and causing untold destruction to infrastructure, government buildings and businesses.

The pillaging and burning continued unchecked for weeks. This caused the civil service to fall apart and the very mechanisms of the state to grind to a halt. The absence of security and stability, together with shortages in basic services such as water, electricity and fuel, made Iraq a dangerous place. People who were not protected by their own militias or private security – although even these could not completely guarantee personal safety – have faced unprecedented risks. Kidnappings and incidents of violence against women have soared. Suicide bombings and torture have become the daily norm for Iraqis.

The figures for Iraqi deaths as a result of the invasion, occupation and continuing terror attacks and lawlessness are much disputed, but are undeniably high. The levels of violence have fluctuated during the years of the occupation, with little hope for any serious abatement in the near future. The UN stated that violent civilian deaths in October 2006 reached a high of 3,709, or 120 a day. The *Lancet* estimated in October 2004 that the invasion and occupation of Iraq had led to nearly 100,000 excess deaths (civilian and non-civilian). A year later, its estimate had risen to 655,000 deaths – that is, 2.5 per cent of the population. The US and Iraqi governments and other supporters of the war criticized the methodology used, but many epidemiologists and statisticians defended the survey. Iraq's health ministry in late 2006 estimated deaths related to the war and violence at between 100,000 and 150,000. At the same time Iraq Body Count, which bases its figures only on reported deaths, estimated that between 49,642 and 55,048 civilians had been killed.

Reports of torture have also been increasing. In a statement reported by the BBC on 21 September 2006, the UN Special Rapporteur on Torture, Manfred Nowak, said that torture, much of which was carried out by security forces, militias and insurgents, might be more of a problem than under Saddam Hussein.

Social volatility and instability have been exacerbated by an alarming polarization of society between those reduced to poverty and those who have at once grown super-rich. Iraqis had of course suffered under economic sanctions and the policies of the Saddam regime, but rather than alleviating conditions for Iraqis, the invasion ushered in a period of even greater poverty. In October 2006 the UN humanitarian news agency IRIN quoted a senior official in the ministry of labour and social affairs as saying that nearly 5.6 million Iraqis were living below the poverty line. Of these, at least 40 per cent were living in 'absolute and desperate deteriorated conditions'. This degree of poverty was a 35 per cent increase over the pre-2003 level. There has been a boom in consumer goods for those who can afford them. Others have spent all their savings trying to survive, and some people have been forced to pay large sums of money to gangsters and kidnappers.

Another reason for the increasing poverty is that women are no longer as economically active as they were, for security and religious reasons. Unemployment has also soared, partly as a result of the misguided policy of sweeping de-Baathification. In late 2006 it was reported that in some parts of the country, unemployment was as high as 70 per cent. Inflation in the year beginning June 2005 was put at 70 per cent. The ongoing violence and lack of security have made it difficult for businesses to operate and many businessmen who could afford to do so have relocated outside Iraq. At the same time, those with the right connections have been able to benefit lavishly from the post-invasion situation.

Iraq has seen high levels of external and internal migration since the invasion. The UN High Commissioner for Refugees (UNHCR) estimated in the spring of 2008 that more than 2 million Iraqis – nearly 10 per cent of the population – had left Iraq since 2003. The report added that more than 100,000

Iraqis per month were fleeing to Syria and Jordan. These included well trained and highly qualified professionals. The brain drain that started with the rise of dictatorships has now reached a scale that has severely crippled the economy, destroying the educational system, the provision of healthcare and other important areas.

The UNHCR also estimated that following the invasion there were 700,000 Iraqis living in Jordan and another 1.2 million in Syria while 2.2 million citizens have been displaced within Iraq. While some Iraqis might have returned to their homes in late 2007 and early 2008, the problem of emigration and internal migration persists. Some returnees from abroad might have been encouraged by a relative decline in the level of violence, mainly in Baghdad. The majority simply ran out of money and could no longer afford to live abroad. Until there is a political solution that ensures widespread peace and security, many Iraqis will live at home or abroad in fear and uncertainty.

The George W. Bush administration's agenda for Iraq resulted in a botched occupation of the country, with looting and chaos followed by factionalism, corruption and criminality worse in scope than during the Saddam era. It is not surprising that many Iraqis suspect that the entire enterprise was engineered to ensure that their country would end up destroyed, divided, insecure and forcibly subject to an uncomfortable US military occupation for the foreseeable future. And while occupation authorities have been struggling to undo the damage of their early mistakes, they have yet to grasp the basic changes needed to rescue Iraq.

Before I discuss how I think the future of Iraq could be

improved, I will describe in greater detail in the following chapter how the occupation period has been counterproductive to the cause of democracy, economic development, national unity and regional security.

5

Giant steps backward

Although the military campaign in 2003 was swift and successful, it was clear from the moment US forces entered Baghdad that enormous miscalculations had been made as to what to do next. The history of the occupation of Iraq provides a handbook of how not to build a new state. One major failure was to place the fate of the entire country in the hands of people who, for the most part, knew very little about Iraq. Other mistakes included the provision of US support to expatriate Iraqis who were unqualified for leadership positions; raising the status of warlords and other scavengers at the expense of more qualified Iraqis; and instituting policies that all but ensured that if Iraq survived as a country at all, it would be economically weak and politically fragmented.

As a result of the damage done by these policies and actions, the people of Iraq have suffered, some losing their lives and others losing faith in the possibility of a new Iraq. Many have expressed this despair by leaving their homes and their country; others wait passively on the sidelines, or join the sectarian and ethnic forces bent on tearing Iraq apart.

A government dismantled

General Jay Garner was appointed in January 2003 to head the Pentagon's Office of Reconstruction and Humanitarian Assistance (ORHA). He was chosen to lead the postwar rebuilding effort in part because of his involvement as the head of Operation Provide Comfort, the US military's provision of safety and sustenance to Kurds fleeing attacks on their villages by Saddam's forces after the 1991 Gulf War.

Garner's tenure began horribly. He was supposed to ensure the security of Iraq's people and the smooth provision of necessary services after the occupation of Baghdad on 9 April 2003. Instead, a massive spasm of looting and sabotage broke out in much of the country, especially the capital. As I have noted already, government buildings, schools, hospitals, museums, military installations and businesses were stripped of anything of value. Countless government records were destroyed and offices ceased to function. Basic necessities such as food, water and electricity became scarce or ran out.

Because US officials failed to heed warnings that such a breakdown of law and order was likely to occur, they made no provision for keeping the people and property of Iraq safe. Some order was restored in May, but by then untold damage had been done. Iraq had suffered one of the greatest mass thefts of modern times, and the Iraqi people lost all confidence in the professed intentions and competence of the occupation authorities.

Garner did not stay long in his position. In May he was replaced as head of the CPA by Ambassador L. Paul Bremer. Bremer had no previous knowledge of Iraq and no experience in managing such a complex country at such a difficult time.

He was also in too much of a hurry to impose his own brand of authority. As Thomas E. Ricks writes in his account of these events, 'Bremer headed for Iraq in early May, determined to show that there was a new sheriff in town.'¹ As a result, he made reckless decisions with disastrous consequences.

Bremer arrived in Baghdad on 12 May 2003. Within three days he announced his 'De-Baathification of Iraq Society'. This policy called for all members of the Baath Party to be dismissed with immediate effect from their government jobs and barred from being rehired by the new government. Since party membership during Saddam's rule was mandatory for all mid- to high-ranking government officials, this move resulted in the firing of more than 50,000 qualified civil servants, which in effect eradicated Iraq's administrative machinery and abolished authority.

Whether Bremer was instructed to take this action by the Department of Defense or was talked into adopting such a policy by the gang of Iraqi opportunists who were flown from exile by the US Air Force to take a leadership role in the future Iraq, the decision proved catastrophic. Firing the entire core of Iraq's government structure, including doctors, engineers, teachers and law enforcement officers, was an unmitigated disaster.

To make matters worse, on 23 May Bremer issued his second order: the abolition of Iraq's armed forces. How wise was it to take away the jobs of over 400,000 individuals, all of them with military training and many with access to weapons and explosives? Not only did these men now have a serious grudge against the new government, they had the means, the training and the leadership to pose a serious threat to the country's order.

On 13 July 2003, as I have mentioned, Bremer announced the appointment of the Iraq Governing Council (IGC), whose members he chose not for their competence, qualifications or integrity but because they were part of the former opposition groups who were recognized by the US as having complementary ethnic, tribal and religious affiliations. Most of the 25 council members had been living in exile. The office of the president was also based on an ethnic and sectarian formula, unprecedented in Iraqi history, whereby a person from a different group served a monthly term in rotation.

Obviously, the IGC proved to be not only highly ineffective, but also counterproductive. It became evident that IGC members were busy pushing their private agendas rather than engaging in joint decision-making on key issues. Bremer himself complained that at any given time more than half the IGC members were outside the country.

Initially, the Iraqi public was impressed by the quick collapse of Saddam's dictatorship, but its joy turned to dismay when the occupation proved incapable of maintaining law and order. Moreover, Iraqis were outraged by the CPA's decision to dismantle the functioning governing infrastructure and impose discredited individuals in leadership roles.

Many atrocities were committed in Iraq by Saddam; new ones came from those who rushed to inherit his power thereafter. As an example, I would like to refer to the removal of the Baath Party archives from the country upon its occupation. Millions of pages that documented the depredations of the Saddam Hussein regime were seized shortly after the fall of Baghdad by Kanan Makiya, who heads a private group called the Iraq Memory Foundation. The importance of these documents can hardly be overemphasized. They are part of Iraq's cultural assets, a vital tool for holding the Baath regime accountable. Despite protests from the director of Iraq's National Library and Archives, the documents were shipped to the US in 2006 by Makiya's foundation.

The Society of American Archivists announced that seizing and removing the documents was 'an act of pillage' prohibited under the laws of war. Iraqi officials expressed the Iraqi government's 'absolute rejection' of Makiya's deal. The documents 'are part of the national heritage of Iraq' the statement declared, 'and must be returned to Iraq promptly'.

Makiya had received permission from the Coalition Provisional Authority, which ruled Iraq following the fall of Saddam, to move the documents to his parents' home in Baghdad. In 2005, his foundation reached an agreement with the US military to move the documents to the US.

Makiya may claim that his intention was to protect and restore the documents and that he considered their presence in Baghdad, as things stood, to be unsafe. And it may be true that chaotic and violent conditions in Iraq following the invasion could endanger the survival of such critically important records. But what should have taken place is for the occupying powers to assume the responsibility to protect and preserve the documents along with other objects and institutions, such as museums, that were part of the cultural heritage. Protecting valuable material should be the task of the Iraqi government or its occupiers, not of a private entrepreneur, still less one who proceeds to ship them out of the country. Those records belong to the Iraqi people.

An insurgency inflamed

By the summer of 2003, the arrogance, incompetence and misguided policies of the occupation authority and its superiors in Washington had fuelled such widespread anger and discontent among broad segments of the populace that the political situation in Iraq was near to exploding. Just as in the pre-invasion period, decision-makers in Washington were more intent on pushing forward with their preconceived agenda than actually improving the situation. One of the many serious flaws of US policy was that the welfare of the Iraqi people was the last thing on the minds of those in charge.

Because policy was based not on the realities on the ground, but on the ideological dictates of the occupiers' agenda and the so-called global 'war on terror', the occupying forces failed to identify the true source of the insurgency. As their political programme called for a foreign menace, US officials blamed many insurgent attacks on foreign members of al-Qaeda and other radicals, notably the Jordanian Abu Musab al-Zarqawi (whose death in a US air strike in June 2006 did virtually nothing to dampen the insurgency). True, the insurgency included barbaric foreign terrorists who took advantage of open borders post-occupation to move into Iraq in order to fight the US. In addition, many of the insurgent attacks at this time were being carried out by remnants of Saddam's regime who had lost power and privileges but had enormous amounts of cash and weapons at their disposal. However, the largest part of the insurgency came from former members of the armed forces as well as ordinary Iraqis who initially may have welcomed the invading troops on 9 April 2003, but were outraged by the mismanagement, destruction, corruption and injustice that they faced thereafter.

Finally, the rise of sectarianism after the invasion caused many men to join militias motivated by religious identification, while others joined together to defend and protect their own neighbourhoods in the presence of a serious security vacuum.

Although undoubtedly hostile to the US occupation and its newly appointed government, in December 2006 foreign terrorists were estimated by the Iraq Study Group, the bipartisan group chaired by James Baker III and Lee Hamilton, as numbering only around 1,300 – an insignificant figure compared, for example, with the tens of thousands of Iraqi nationals participating in the insurgency at one time or another.[2]

Nor could these foreigners have operated effectively had Iraqi public opinion not already been angered by the outcome of the invasion. This political atmosphere of discontent with the occupation had created an environment that was fertile ground, unfortunately, for insurgents as well as criminals.

The conditions created by the occupation have also boosted the substantial rise of Iranian influence among Shias opposed to the government as well as within the government itself. In this way, the different currents of ideology in Iran, as well as different parts of the Iranian regime, have been given free rein in the Iraqi political arena, to the detriment of Iraq's security, unity and long-term prospects. Shia insurgents have received arms, funds and training from Iran, complicating the efforts of the US and the Iraqi government. The greatest irony is that the US-led occupation has been midwife to an Iraqi government dominated by religiously motivated Shia politicians whose values are diametrically opposed to the secular-minded, pro-Western Iraqi nationalists. These men and women have been forced to leave the country or compelled to abandon any hope of meaningful political participation in shaping the future of their nation.

For too many years, the ideologically-driven approach to battling the insurgency added fuel to the flames rather than quelling the unrest. It was telling that a world public opinion poll conducted by the Program on World Policy Attitudes found, in September 2006, that the percentage of Iraqis supporting attacks on US troops had risen sharply to 61 per cent. Seventy-nine per cent of those canvassed thought that the US was having a negative effect in Iraq; only 14 per cent rated the US impact as positive.[3]

The hope for liberation had turned out to be a hated occupation.

The myths of the 'surge'

The escalating violence and disorder of the insurgency was like a stewpot boiling over. Unfortunately, US officials didn't turn down the heat. Instead they chose a short-term solution, the so-called 'surge' policy, which had the effect of slamming a tight lid on the pot, creating a pressure cooker: a potent mix of unresolved tensions just waiting to explode. In short, the influx of more US troops and the institution of new policies that included giving arms and funds to former insurgents had temporarily reduced the level of violence, but it utterly failed to deal with the root causes of the insurgency, or with the broader conflicts pulling Iraqi society apart. In fact, some of these policies made the prospects for peace even more remote. Once again, policies by occupation authorities were aimed more at placating the American public than benefiting the people of Iraq in the long term.

This message needs to be spelled out because most Americans only know the rosy myth rather than the reality. Hungry for good news from Iraq, many Americans have eagerly accepted upbeat and unrealistic statements by Bush administration officials and pundits touting 'the success of the surge'. But these eager proponents of a temporary fix for their failed Iraq policy have intentionally ignored or downplayed the caveats attached to progress reports from Iraq. Over and over again, for example, US military and civilian analysts have conceded that the security and political gains made under the surge remained 'fragile and reversible'. But this message has rarely got through to the American public. And why are these gains called in question? I return to the analogy of the pressure cooker. Even after the troop increase and the reduction in violence, the fire was burning, the steam pressure building. Unless the core questions revolving around the establishment of a stable, just and unified Iraq are addressed, the situation stays potentially explosive.

Misperceptions about the surge have made it more difficult to analyse the situation in Iraq and to map out a plan to solve the country's many problems. So I would like to address these myths systematically.

First, the surge was not the only or even the most important factor in the reduction in violence that occurred in 2007 and 2008. Even before President Bush unveiled his surge policy (30,000 additional troops were sent to Iraq with a strategy of 'holding' areas and remaining in them after 'clearing' out insurgent activity in a policy announced under the Iraq Strategy Review on 10 January 2007), years of brutal ethnic cleansing by sectarian militias and gangs had nearly run their course, forcibly separating ethnic and religious groups from formerly mixed areas. In this phase of Iraq's tragic civil war, regions, cities, towns and neighbourhoods that had enjoyed peaceful diversity now endured a forced homogeneity. Another cause for the temporary decline in violence was the decision by

Moqtada al-Sadr in August 2007 to impose a tactical ceasefire, calling his Mahdi Army militiamen to stand down until further notice. This effectively ended the inter-Shia attacks that had plagued large portions of Baghdad and southern Iraq, but only so long as it suited the needs of the militias. Nonetheless, these groups have already shown that they can trigger serious violence outbreaks at the drop of a hat. Finally, the foreign-dominated al-Qaeda in Iraq employed violence so extreme and sought changes so distasteful to Iraqis that they lost most of their local support and began to face opposition from Iraqi armed groups.

Another myth of the surge was that it would contribute to Iraq's political reconstruction. But the opposite was true. One of the controversial and counterproductive cornerstones of the surge policy has been to fund and arm former insurgents and others to provide 'security' in once unsettled areas. Recall that it was the US failures in the early months of the occupation that gave rise to the utter breakdown in security. Thousands of unemployed and disgruntled men from the armed forces rose in opposition. Tribal leaders felt the new order had deprived them of past influence and sources of income. And because Iraq's borders were no longer adequately controlled, al-Qaeda was able to infiltrate from outside the country in order to inflict further damage on US forces and the civilian population. These and other groups contributed to the horrific violence and disorder during the worst years of the occupation, and the US authorities sought a way out of the morass.

One way was to exploit the divisions that had emerged between Iraq insurgent groups and the foreign-dominated al-Qaeda. This was clearly a short-sighted and politically cynical decision. For the former insurgents, the relationship was based purely on money and power. With the blessing of the US occupation authorities, they could build little sectarian fiefdoms and criminal operations, so long as they kept 'order' in their areas, fought against al-Qaeda, and refrained from attacking US targets. A US Army intelligence officer quoted by Mir Rosen in an article titled 'The myth of the Surge' in *Rolling Stone* magazine (6 March 2008) had no illusions about the motives of these new 'allies': 'The only reason anything works or anybody deals with us is because we give them money.' The US architects of the policy were willing to sacrifice the future of a unified Iraq for the temporary calm brought by their surge policies.

Former US ambassador Chas Freeman is quoted as saying that the surge policy is 'supporting a quasi-feudal devolution of authority to armed enclaves, which exist at the expense of central government authority'. The same article paints an almost apocalyptic picture of the once prosperous and attractive Dora neighbourhood of Baghdad: 'lakes of mud and sewage' in the streets, 'mountains of trash', broken windows in countless deserted and looted houses, and 12-foot-high walls surrounding it all, built by the US to separate warring factions.

There are many other independent critiques of the surge. For example Steven Simon, writing in *Foreign Affairs*, makes the important point that the surge 'is not linked to any sustainable plan for building a viable Iraqi state'. In fact, he adds, this policy has made peace and unity in Iraq less likely. 'Financing and arming Iraqis outside of the formal state establishment, I believe, can be counter-productive. It will further Iraq's disintegration, put more weapons in the hands of the wrong people, and create serious dangers for the future.'[4]

American officials packaged their controversial new military escalation with a seemingly conciliatory and optimistic political programme. And these promises have not been fulfilled. For example, when the surge was announced in January 2007, US officials promised that Iraq would take over security in every province by November 2007. That did not happen. They also promised that Iraq would pass legislation to share oil revenues among all Iraqis. Again, that did not happen. They said Iraqis would hold provincial elections in 2007. That did not happen. In short, reconciliation in Iraq to share power and resources has never taken place in spite of five years of occupation.

With all these failures on the political front, officials still had the temerity to hail the 'success' of the surge. All the while, the Iraqi government remains non-existent in many areas outside its 'Green Zone' fortress. The country is divided. The hatred and vendettas between Shiites, Sunnis, Kurds, Arabs, Christians and Turkomans that started in 2003 have not been reduced. A reduction in US casualties and a decline in al-Qaeda effectiveness are positive results of the Petraeus plan. But in order to achieve that, Iraqis have been armed and bribed to fight against each other, thereby increasing the hatred and expanding the potential danger. Therefore, the reference to achieving more peace in Iraq under the 'surge' is misleading.

The situation is reminiscent of Afghanistan in the 1980s, when the US supplied arms to the Mujahiddeen and other fundamentalist groups to use against the Soviets. While the immediate objective – the expulsion of the Soviets – was achieved, the consequences of this short-term strategy continue to plague the US administration to this day.

It is an undisputable fact that before the occupation, al-Qaeda had no presence in Iraq. Nor were there any US casualties. In claiming to be winning against al-Qaeda, the US administration is doing no more than fix a problem of its own making. The prospect of a strong, prosperous and unified Iraq is further away now than at any time before.

Kurds press for autonomy

The Kurds of Iraq have had a troubled history, suffering cruelly at the hands of Saddam. After his forces were expelled from Kuwait in 1991, there were uprisings among Shia populations in the south of Iraq and among the Kurds in the north, hoping to finish off a Baathist regime deemed to be on its last legs after its bloody losses in the Kuwait debacle. When Saddam brutally crushed these uprisings, the US imposed no-fly zones over the north and south of Iraq in order to severely reduce Saddam's ability to attack these areas. As a result, the three predominantly Kurdish provinces of northern Iraq effectively became disconnected from the rest of the country, which remained under Saddam's rule.

In this way, the Kurdish region gained de facto independence. It opened its borders with Turkey and Iran and engaged in active commercial trading with both countries. The Kurdish tribal leadership identified their new entity as Kurdistan, with its own flag, government and parliament. Kurdish became the official language in schools and government offices. These events were seen as a long-overdue victory in their struggle for autonomy, but they clearly bode ill for the prospects of returning to a unified Iraq.

When Iraq was occupied in April 2003, the challenge of how to reintegrate this Kurdish entity into the rest of Iraq became a serious issue for those who continued to dream of a reunified

Iraq. The Kurdish leadership realized that it would not be in their self-interest at that point to declare formal independence. For one thing, they were surrounded by neighbours who strongly opposed the creation of an independent Kurdistan. At the same time, the Kurdish authorities had no wish to share any part of their newly gained command and control with any government in Baghdad.

The president of the Kurdistan Regional Government, Masoud Barzani, and other Kurdish leaders have often said they don't want independence for the time being but insist on having the right to call for a separate Kurdish state. Barzani has said: 'what we have received in the current atmosphere is better for us than to announce an independence that is not supported and will lead to losing what we have now. As for the issue of establishing a Kurdish state, this is a natural and a legitimate right. Yet when will it happen? This we leave to coming generations and perhaps to our generation. God knows.'[5]

In Iraq's national elections of 30 January 2005 there was a high Kurdish turnout and Kurdish candidates gained an impressive block of seats: 75 out of the total 275. On the same day, Kurds elected members to their own Kurdistan parliament. In an exit poll on voting day, the vast majority of Kurds, influenced by their tribal leaders, expressed a preference for total independence and secession from Iraq.

In the drafting of Iraq's new constitution during the summer of 2005, the Kurds pushed hard to keep the privileges and autonomy they had enjoyed since 1991, while remaining part of a loose federation under an Iraqi umbrella. The constitution approved in the 15 October referendum endorsed Kurdistan's self-rule. It also stated that Kurdish laws and decisions in force since 1992 would remain valid, provided they did not contradict the constitution. The 2005 constitution described Iraq as a single, federal, decentralized state and designated Kurdistan as its first semi-autonomous region. It allowed for further new regions to be designated, in accordance with its provisions.

The Kurds succeeded in removing from the draft constitution language that referred to Iraq as an Arab nation. Instead, the constitution identified Iraq as 'a country of many nationalities, religions and sects', and as 'part of the Islamic world'. But as a concession to Sunni Arabs and others furious at a draft that had said only that Iraq's Arab people were part of the Arab nation, the constitution stated that Iraq is 'a founding and active member of the Arab League and is committed to its covenant'.

The constitution recognized Kurdish and Arabic as the two official national languages. The Kurds were permitted to keep their own army, the Peshmerga. And Article 117 stated: 'The regional government shall be responsible for all the administrative requirements of the region, particularly the establishment and organization of the internal security forces for the region such as police, security forces and guards of the region.'

The Kurds have long aspired to have oil-rich Kirkuk, a fourth province in the north of Iraq, added to Kurdistan. The 2003 constitution stipulated that a referendum should be held no later than 31 December 2007 in Kirkuk and other 'disputed territories' on 'normalization'. The proposal to conduct a 'normalization' process based on ethnic population swaps has faced much opposition, and its advocates have had trouble implementing it on a large scale. The plan has been delayed several times as the UN and Iraqi politicians try to find a way to make an impractical policy work.

Since the approval of the constitution by the referendum of October 2005, the Kurds have moved decisively to consolidate their position. In September 2006 the Kurdish regional government banned the flying of the Iraqi national flag and announced that only the Kurdish flag would be flown on offices and government buildings throughout the Kurdish region. Furthermore, 'Kurdistan's' efforts to forge an independent oil policy, including the drafting of its own oil law, and offering concessions to foreign oil companies independently of Baghdad, caused disagreements with the central government which was drafting an oil law for the whole of Iraq.

The Kurds cannot continue indefinitely along this political course in which the leaders shelter under the umbrella of Iraqi sovereignty when faced by threats from the outside, but assert a bold, de facto Kurdish independence in their domestic affairs. A moment of reckoning must come. In my view, they must once and for all make the hard choice: either declare full independence and create a real, separate 'nation', or abandon their reference to 'Kurdistan' and their policies of strongly independent and isolated identity and become a full and committed partner in building the new Iraq.

The course of world history has shown that unity has tremendous political and economic benefits. From Asia to Latin America to Europe, people have been turning their backs on the old politics of ethnicity and division that had been the root of chronic conflict, isolation and economic ruin since the dawn of history. The unification that the European countries have chosen provides a compelling example. Former imperial nations such as France, Germany, Austria and others came to realize that in the twenty-first century none of them individually could provide the highest standards of living for their citizens. But united, they would increase their chances of success in a competitive world market.

In this global economic context, then, how can anyone believe that an underdeveloped country like Iraq can be better off divided? If Iraq, for example, is split into two or more separate units, how much would each one have to spend on defence and armaments to safeguard its new borders? It seems to me that only some warlords driven by greed would choose that path. The vast majority of Iraqis would end up less secure and less prosperous. Still, those who back fragmentation may yet be able to promote their separatist causes by employing appeals that arouse an emotional ethnic or religious response. But I can only hope that the majority of Iraqis have learned from the catastrophic failures of the past 50 years, when leaders used high-sounding slogans to manipulate the hearts of the people. Time and again, politicians with only their own power and wealth in mind would advance their self-serving agendas by using such words such as 'nationalism', 'patriotism' and 'identity' in a calculated and cynical way. And the people of Iraq have repeatedly succumbed to such ruses, their economy plundered and in ruins, their society in tatters.

The argument for unity is compelling, and Iraqis should look at their own country's pre-1958 history as well as worldwide trends demonstrating the benefits of joining together rather than splitting apart. By doing so, they can reject the counterproductive and self-serving propaganda of the warlords and others hoping to benefit from what would be left in a divided Iraq. The future Iraq needs all its regions to contribute to the nation's recovery. Unless they work in synergy and exploit their interdependence along the lines I propose in the following chapters, all Iraqis will continue to suffer poverty, paralysis and chaos.

The question of Kirkuk

I was born in Kirkuk, and so were my parents, grandfathers and many generations of their ancestors. And although the city's political and cultural life has historically had a strong Turkoman character, there were also Kurds, Arabs, Christians and Jews all living in an integrated society. My grandfather represented Kirkuk in the first Ottoman parliament in 1908 in Istanbul. Following the formation of modern Iraq, and throughout the Hashemite monarchy from 1921 to 1958, my grandfather, then my father and finally my oldest brother were elected members for Kirkuk in the parliament in Baghdad. I find it painful, therefore, when some claim that Kirkuk belongs to a specific ethnic group. Like other parts of Iraq, the Kirkuk of today is a battleground in which warlords and political operators with narrow, selfish agendas are tearing apart the city's sense of community and the country's sense of unity.

It is true that some of today's problems date to the era of Saddam, who ordered the deportation of Turkomans and Kurds, replacing them with Arabs in order to change the demographics of Kirkuk. But the Kurdish leaders of today are not motivated solely by the desire to reverse this population transfer to achieve justice. Their aim is also to claim the oil wealth around Kirkuk and to tear the region away from a unified Iraq. In my opinion, such a step would create just as much injustice as Saddam did. I believe that those Arabs who were moved to Kirkuk some 20 years ago should not be forced to relocate again. They are Iraqi nationals and should therefore be allowed to live wherever they choose in Iraq. Equally, those Kurds or Turkomans who were unjustly forced to leave should be entitled to move back to Kirkuk, or stay or move to anywhere else they choose within Iraq. For how can Iraq aspire to be democratic if it denies its citizens the freedom to reside wherever they choose within one nation?

Policies encourage disintegration

The overthrow of Saddam offered the people of Iraq the prospect that their country would eventually become democratic, cohesive and resilient, united yet enjoying the benefits of a substantial degree of administrative decentralization. This would be an Iraq based not on sectarian and ethnic differences and divisions, but on consensus and a commonality of purpose; a tolerant nation where plurality and diversity would be sources of social enrichment rather than strife. To undertake such a transformation in a society shattered politically and economically by decades of dictatorship and war represented an enormous challenge, but I believe it was achievable over time. It needed a leadership that possessed integrity, wisdom, vision, dedication, patriotism and a long-term strategy.

It is deplorable that the type of politicians that the occupation chose to impose have not been conducive to the development of a united, secular, stable and democratic Iraq. Far from it: Iraq was steered towards becoming a failed and dismembered state. The disintegration of Iraq along sectarian and ethnic fault lines would be a disaster for the Iraqis themselves and for regional stability. The creation of a number of mini-states could potentially cause explosive upheavals in the region, and the resulting political instability would empower terrorists.

The occupation took four catastrophic steps.

The first was to dismantle the existing administrative structure. The second was to create the Iraq Governing Council, with members selected not for their integrity, merit or qualifications, but instead for their sectarian, ethnic or tribal affiliations. The third step, taken in January 2005, was the rush to premature elections for the Transitional National Assembly. The fourth step was to choose untested and inappropriate individuals to assume power and engineer a defective constitution that served their own religious, ethnic and tribal agendas more effectively than the wider interests of a civil, secular, united and modern Iraqi nation.

These four interrelated steps stemmed from the underlying fatal error of the occupation: the segmentation of the Iraqi body politic along ethnic and religious divides.

Under the constitutional monarchy, people organized themselves politically along ideological and economical lines, not dissimilar to those in modern Western countries. After the Baath Party took over by force in 1968, political differences became confrontational: one was either pro-Baath or anti-Baath. But when Saddam turned against some of his leading comrades within the Baath Party, the choices became more provocative and indeed violent: one was either with Saddam or against him, and it was he and his inner circle who were the judges.

After the overthrow of Saddam, the occupation should have established a new environment in which religion and politics were kept separate. Instead it took the divisive path I have described, driven by short-term interests and personal agendas rather than by any long-term vision for the future of the nation as a whole.

While it may be true that up to 60 per cent of Iraqis are

Shia, this group had never before been conceived of or treated as a simple political bloc purely on the basis of religion. Other considerations tended to shape the political identities of Iraq's Shia; they were Baathists, Communists, conservatives, monarchists and so on. The occupation authorities did not realize, and still may not admit, that before the invasion there were more Shias than Sunnis enlisted as Baath Party members.

In its first two and a half years, the occupation fabricated a shaky political edifice whose shape and timetable corresponded less to the real needs of Iraqis than to the interests of the occupiers and the mainly undeserving clique of Iraqis to whom they handed the reins of power. As a result, the occupation has been successful only at alienating most educated and secular Iraqis. This vital segment of the population was sidelined while warlords and carpet-baggers propped up by militias, financial capital and foreign support were put in the political driving seat. At the same time, a well-organized insurgency using ever more sophisticated weapons inflicted death and destruction on a horrific scale, and the violence took on an increasingly sectarian character.

While fighting the insurgents, the occupation forces, in effect, have been protecting the imposed Iraqi government, isolated within the heavily fortified Green Zone. The zone itself symbolizes the divorce between the current ruling class and the masses of Iraqis from whom they are insulated.

The Iraqi public has been incensed by the daily toll of violence, the absence of security, the corruption, the lack of electricity, water and other services, and the evidence that the Iraqi government was indulging in, or turning a blind eye to, torture and other human rights abuses that were probably worse than the horrors of the Saddam era.

A policy based on 'spin', not reality

In the US, the Iraq War is often described as the most 'spun' conflict in history. The invasion was originally marketed to the US public as a vital measure taken to pre-empt any potential link-up between Iraq's arsenal of WMD and al-Qaeda's terrorists. The war was justified in terms of Saddam's repeated failure to comply with UN Security Council resolutions. The claims of links between the Iraqi regime and al-Qaeda were hyped up by the Bush administration and repeated long after the invasion, even though they had by then been entirely discredited.

After the failure of the invading forces to find WMD in Iraq, it was clear to the US administration that to counter a threat that turned out to be non-existent could no longer be presented as a valid justification for the loss of thousands of lives and the spending of hundreds of billions of US taxpayers' dollars. A new 'spin' must be put on the war, and the new rationalization was that the occupation was leading to democracy in Iraq, which would in turn act as a beacon for democratization throughout the Middle East.

The introduction of genuine, rather than cosmetic, democracy in a country that has lain under brutal repression for more than four decades is not possible without a diligent and far-reaching transition to establish the underlying institutions and other prerequisites of a free civil society. Attaining democracy requires far more than citizens casting their votes: after all, many illiberal societies hold elections, as indeed Saddam did from time to time.

But the occupation authorities chose not to make the deep-seated long-term transformation that was required. They kept trumpeting the rhetoric of democracy and handed the trappings of power to those they picked to serve on the Iraq Governing Council. They then formed the interim government, expedited elections and allowed the same basic group of Iraqi politicians to write a constitution that would fulfil their personal agendas. The aim, unfortunately, was to provide the occupation with a face-saving formula for domestic consumption rather than to lead Iraq to the best possible future.

There are those who hoped that the US would be as successful in Iraq as it was in transforming Germany and Japan following the Second World War. But the US experience of building democracy in postwar Germany and Japan shows that achieving such a transformation required a long transition period. In postwar Japan it took seven years of authoritarian rule under General Douglas MacArthur to lay the foundation of democracy and introduce a new constitution. In Germany, postwar nation-building took five years.

Planning for postwar political reconstruction in Germany and Japan started some three years before the war ended. But for Iraq there were no such effective strategies. The US State Department did initiate the Future of Iraq Project in 2002, but General Jay Garner was told to shelve the project.

The rebuilding of the Japanese and German political systems was difficult and lengthy, but in some ways Iraq poses an even greater challenge. Japan and Germany were devastated countries that had been through years of war and destruction, and this made their populations more receptive to a new order. In addition, Japan and Germany were far less heterogeneous societies than Iraq with its complex structure of religious and ethnic groups. Both had been formidable modern and industrial societies and could look back to periods of liberal democratic rule. Iraq did have some experience of a parliamentary system and pluralism under the monarchy, but this had ended 45 years before the invasion. The bulk of its overwhelmingly youthful population had known nothing but dictatorship. Saddam had done a thorough job of destroying the fabric of a civil society.

A study published by Rand in July 2003 entitled *America's Role in Nation-building: From Germany to Iraq*[6] found that the most important factor for success was the level of effort the US put in, measured in time, people and money. The study concluded that there is no quick route to nation-building.

The premature elections of 2005

The interim government that took over in the 'handover' of power on 28 June 2004, when the IGC and CPA were dissolved, was mandated to manage Iraq up to the elections for a Transitional National Assembly to be held on 30 January 2005. It had to cope with an unenviable number of challenges on all fronts as it worked against the seven-month artificial deadline. It faced increasing insurgency and multiple uprisings in different parts of the country. Prime Minister Ayad Allawi had an impossible mission.

It was undeniably moving to see the Iraqi people turning out to vote on 30 January in greater numbers than had been anticipated. They expressed excitement and enthusiasm and showed remarkable courage and determination at the prospect of regaining electoral power denied them for more than 40 years. But these premature and theatrical elections were portrayed almost as if they were an end in themselves, as if they proved that democracy had finally arrived in Iraq.

In my view, the elections were seriously flawed. First, a premature electoral process based on ethnic, tribal and religious differences and sectarian affiliations could only damage the fabric of national unity and strengthen the chance of Iraq's disintegration. Second, treating the whole country as a single electoral district did not serve the interests of voters. Geographically bounded voting districts should have been used instead. This would have allowed citizens to elect people they knew and trusted in their own districts. As it was, voters had to vote for a long list covering all of Iraq without even knowing the names or qualifications of those on the list. Third, the installation of democracy is a long-term process. It requires the development of a mature cultural mindset as well as economic independence, and must be based on institutional foundations. As Andrew Rathmell, the director of Rand Europe's Defence and Security Program, states, 'there was a simple view that holding elections equates with nation-building success, providing the international community with an easy exit strategy.'[7]

The 'democratization process' in Iraq was clearly cobbled together and carried out in a manner that put a priority on appearances rather than establishing a genuinely representative government. The result was the elaborate orchestration of a sham democracy, clad in all the customary trappings of candidates and slogans and elections, but serving only to further entrench some of the most unqualified and anti-democratic political operators in the country. Rushing to elections in an environment lacking such foundations may do more harm than good and can make society vulnerable to destructive passions deliberately fomented. Only when individuals feel free to choose, uninfluenced by intimidation or religious, ethnic or tribal directives, can they fully exercise their rights based on what they consider best for the country in terms of security, economic needs and public services.

In the January 2005 elections, the Shia religious leaders used their power and prestige to steer followers to vote for a favoured list of candidates. The Kurds were directed by their own leaders to vote for autonomy – in effect, semi-separation. The Sunni Arab leaders felt excluded from the whole process leading to elections, and told their constituencies to boycott them. Such blatant manipulation of the electorate by religious, ethnic and tribal leaders is anti-democratic because it deprives the individual of the right to exercise discretion. This is a form of enslavement and recalls the days when Saddam would prescribe the way to vote.

In summary, the 30 January elections were not based on political or economic programmes or platforms that addressed the needs of the citizens as one nation. Instead they conformed to sectarian interests directed from the top. Warlords, religious parties and tribal heads exploited the fears, prejudices and suspicions of the voters and, with the help of their armed militias, influenced people to vote for their lists as directed. Thus, what had been inculcated by the CPA in terms of politically partitioning the country along divisive ethnic and religious lines was reproduced, reinforced and legitimized by these elections.

Further, it can be said that as long as Iraq lacks a proper taxation system, it can have no true democracy. In a full democracy the individual pays taxes and different contenders in elections present different programmes on how the resultant income is to be spent. A government is judged on its performance, and voters can remove it through the electoral system. Without a proper system of taxation and government accountability for spending, there cannot be real democracy. The individual is more likely to vote on the basis of top-down instructions and tribal and sectarian influence than according to his choice of specific government programmes. And if oil wealth directly funds state spending, there will be less pressure to establish a reasonable taxation system.

For the December 2005 elections, certain cosmetic improvements were made to the voting system. Instead of considering the whole country as a single electoral district, the elections were organized on the basis of provinces, with 230 of the seats divided among the provinces so as to match their share of the total number of registered voters in the January elections. The 45 remaining seats, known as the 'compensatory seats', were allocated at the national level. However, the proportional representation structure that had been introduced in the January 2005 elections remained unchanged. Voters were thus required to vote for entire lists of candidates, under one banner or another, rather than for individuals. Moreover, they did not vote for policy but for religious or ethnic solidarity and protection. Citizens voted as Shias, Sunnis, Kurds and so on, and not as independent Iraqi nationals.

Contrary to their portrayal by some optimists, the elections were not a turning point for Iraq. Powerful centrifugal forces led to further deterioration and fragmentation. Under the government of Nuri al-Maliki, a member of the religious al-Dawa Party, Iraq slipped further into violence, sectarian killings and ethnic cleansing. Attacks by insurgents and the operations of death squads and kidnappers became ever more audacious and horrifying, and the power of the private militias continued unchallenged. The incompetent government, confined as it was to the relative safety and isolation of the Green Zone in

Baghdad, was both incapable and unwilling to take meaningful steps to deal with Iraq's problems or to engage in meaningful nation-building. Rather, it was paralysed by a failure to compromise and was rent by growing factionalism.

There was also a failure to reconstruct the army and police into reliable forces loyal to the nation rather than to sectarian, criminal or insurgent interests. The new army and police were riddled with sectarianism and prone to desertion. Public distrust in these new forces grew, especially after attacks were carried out by men wearing army or police uniforms. On top of the new government's failure to bring about security and stability, rampant corruption continued to flourish.

Towards the end of 2006 the occupation's impatience with the Iraqi government became more evident. The bipartisan US 'Iraq Study Group' suggested that in order to encourage the Iraqi government to be more active in resolving the situation, it should be made to abide by 'milestones' towards national reconciliation, security and governance. The US should make its continuing military, training, political and economic support contingent on the government meeting these milestones, the Study Group recommended. There were grave doubts as to whether the Iraqi government would be able or willing to live up to what was expected of it.

A destructive constitution

The constitution, announced on 15 August 2005 and approved by the referendum of 15 October 2005 in order to fit the occupation-imposed timetable, was written by those same politicians who were appointed to the IGC and then reinstalled in parliament by the January 2005 elections. For this reason, it is a fatally flawed document, more a recipe for disaster than a path to peace. It reinforces ethnic and religious disunity and stipulates the counterproductive utilization of oil and gas resources. It defines Iraq as a federation, but the strong powers bestowed on the regions in relation to the central government suggest a model closer to a weak and dismembered nation.

For example, the constitution allows the Kurds to maintain their autonomy, with their own government, army and flag, and envisages the creation of other such autonomous regions. It has also given the Kurds effective commanding control over their oil and other natural resources. The Shia in the south will seek to obtain similar authority and privileges if, as seems probable, they set up an autonomous region. Each region, in turn, will adopt its own governing constitution dictated and led by self-imposed warlords. In fact, the Supreme Islamic Council of Iraq has already 'begun to demand an autonomous Shia zone in the south under a loose pan-Iraqi federation'.[8]

The formation of an oil-rich southern Shia region, in addition to Kurdistan in the north, would mean that an irrelevant central government based in Baghdad and the disenfranchised and resource-starved provinces in mid-Iraq would be left behind. The result would be outrage, devastation and more than enough genuine grievances to drive many Iraqis into the arms of those advocating further terror and instability.

As for Iraq's vital hydrocarbon resources, the constitution has been widely interpreted as meaning that the future exploration and development of oil wealth will be under the control of the regional authorities in the areas where such resources are concentrated.

On 11 October 2006 the Iraqi parliament approved the law

setting out the mechanism for creating federal regions, although the session was boycotted by the largest Sunni political bloc and by two factions within the large Shia alliance. Sunnis predicted that the law would lead to the formal disintegration of Iraq.

The constitution has also disappointed those who want to see a secular state with a clear separation between state and religion. It stipulates that no legislation can be passed that contradicts Sharia law. One area in which those Iraqis who dream of a modern and progressive nation see the document as a fundamental setback concerns the rights of women, whose status has been jeopardized in post-Saddam Iraq.

In December 2003, the US-appointed Iraq Governing Council voted for Resolution 137, which cancelled Iraq's existing family and personal status laws. Issues formerly covered by that law were placed under Sharia law. Iraq's family and personal status laws had for the previous decades protected women's rights. For example, the previous law set the minimum age of marriage at eighteen, while arbitrary divorce was prohibited and men and women were required to be treated equally for purposes of inheritance. Although Resolution 137 was repealed in March 2004, it was a strong indication of what was to come. Women have seen their rights severely eroded, with the strengthening of conservative trends enshrined in the constitution.

At one time, the position of Iraqi women was among the most secure in the Arab world. They participated in the workforce, occupied many jobs in the professions and had equal rights. It is important to remember that the first female judge in an Arab country, Zakia Haqqi, was Iraqi, as was the first Arab government minister, Naziha al-Dulaimi. In the

1950s, my mother was an active member of the executive committee of the Association of Iraqi Women. This was chaired by Mrs Asiya Tawfiq Wahbi, the wife of Tawfiq Wahbi, of Kurdish origin, who served at various times as minister of economics, education and social affairs.

In stark contrast, since the occupation women have faced intense social and religious pressures. They have often found themselves edged out of their former jobs, and many former female workers are now confined to their homes. They have to be covered up when they leave the house and may be threatened and beaten by men in the street. Men are nervous about the women and girls in their families venturing outdoors in case they are attacked, kidnapped or murdered. And yet the occupation, which stressed the need for democracy and human rights, including women's rights, has been oddly quiet about the loss of Iraqi women's rights and the violence against women. Although there are some women members of the Iraqi parliament, they tend to be of a conservative bent, fully agreeing that all laws should be in accordance with the Sharia and even arguing in favour of polygamy. Is it not an outrageous irony that the status and security of the women of Iraq have declined precipitously under the occupation compared with the era of Saddam's dictatorship?

Before the invasion, mixed marriages between people of different ethnic or religious groups were quite common. Now, couples in mixed marriages are increasingly feeling compelled to divorce, out of fear or under pressure from insurgents, militias or religious authorities.

I repeat: the constitution in its current form is a recipe for a dismembered Iraq. A fractured Iraq, whether it ends up as separate states, a confederation or a loose federation, would find it impossible to realize its full economic potential. It would also be less secure than a united country against external aggression or internal disorder. There could be further sectarian strife and ethnic cleansing as the parties jockeyed for position in a state with weak central government. Some of the neighbouring states would be deeply concerned at the dismemberment of Iraq, to the point where they might try to intervene. A fragmenting Iraq might export terror and instability to its neighbours, and could be a threat to security at a regional and even global level.

The US–Iraqi agreements of 2008: preserving a defective status quo

The length and nature of the US occupation are among the most contentious and complex political issues facing the people of Iraq. It is clear that the occupation gave rise to violence, division and a deterioration of the quality of life. Therefore, most Iraqis have been eager for it to end. But American officials were reluctant to let go of their powerful military position, saying that anarchy would follow any hasty departure. Still, the people of Iraq grew ever more impatient with the many indignities, insults to national honour, economic decline, public health crisis and other failures of the occupation. They wanted an end to the abuses, some stringent checks on US military actions, and a firm commitment that the occupation would not be permanent.

Eventually, the position of the US authorities began to change. As the level of violence began to decline in 2007 and 2008, and as American public opinion turned increasingly against the US presence in Iraq, occupation officials began to seriously discuss a way out of the current situation. Thus, after many months of hard bargaining, during which Iraqi officials were able to win a number of concessions from the Americans, two agreements were signed by American and Iraqi officials, and ratified by the Iraqi parliament in November 2008.

As I examined the terms of these agreements, I found cause for vindication, for hope and for apprehension. To begin with, my view that the occupation had trampled Iraqi interests is implicitly acknowledged in the terms of the so-called 'status-of-forces' agreement. For example, over and over, the US is called on to 'respect Iraqi laws, customs, traditions, and conventions'. This is a clear reference to one of the main grievances of the people of Iraq: that the occupation authorities had ridden roughshod over their interests, rights, welfare and dignity, and that this must end. This agreement, it appears to me, for the first time acknowledges that the US and Iraqi governments must treat each other as equals, with mutual respect. That is a good start, in theory at least.

The sense that the military forces, and especially some civilian contractors, had in the past acted improperly is also implicitly recognized in Article 12 of the agreement, which deals with legal matters. This section recognizes 'Iraq's right to determine and enforce the rules of criminal and civil law in its territory', and specifically gives Iraqi authorities jurisdiction over US contractors and their employees. The people of Iraq wish to see no more 'Blackwater massacre' incidents.

Iraqi and American leaders also agreed that the past practice of random, unjustified and unauthorized detentions and abductions by occupation authorities was no longer acceptable. Article 22 stipulates, for example, that US forces may not arrest or detain anyone 'except through an Iraqi decision issued in accordance with Iraqi law . . .' And even when US forces arrest or detain someone, he or she must be handed over to Iraqi authorities within twenty-four hours. From the well-publicized abuses at the Abu Ghraib prison to the routine detention of thousands of Iraqis without charge or trial, the outrage felt by the people of Iraq over the issue of improper US military detention practices clearly has reached the attention of the highest levels of both governments. Hopefully, this sad chapter of the occupation can now be closed.

There is a small glimmer of hope and cause for some optimism in the agreement's most notable provisions: those for the withdrawal of US forces from Iraq. It is laudable that the main thrust of the agreement seems to be to ensure that the occupation shall end by the last day of 2011. In addition, a major step in this direction is the promised withdrawal of US forces 'from Iraqi cities, villages and localities' no later than 30 June 2009, providing conditions allow.

However, unmentioned in the many terms of this optimistic agreement are the many uncertainties and questions and problems that lie ahead. One of the main problems of the agreements is that they seek to maintain a highly questionable and problematic status quo. For example, they pledge support for Iraqi 'democracy' when the reality is rule by sectarian leaders and warlords. The agreements call for a 'unified and federal Iraq' when the forces of disunity and secession are ascendant. And both sides have enshrined a constitution which is deeply flawed, a document which cannot provide the basis for a truly unified, democratic and prosperous Iraq in the long term.

Finally, there is the biggest question: Will Iraq plunge once again into violent anarchy? The prospects for peace and unity are not good. Militias, criminals, terrorists and other armed groups have been increasing their stocks of weapons, not handing them over to the government. Many are eager for a chance to assert themselves. Despite some small gains, the Iraqi government has not become a bastion of national unity and reconciliation. It is deeply divided, and many of its leaders encourage the politics of greed, sectarianism and disunity. And we should not forget the harmful role of outside factors, whether meddlesome nations or terrorist groups. We have the example of Lebanon to show how competing external forces can exploit internal discord to create a breakdown of order, benefiting no one inside the country.

Is Iraq irreparably damaged and now at the point of no return, or is there still a chance that this disastrous course can be reversed? My hope is that the educated, secular and modern-minded Iraqi men and women living outside the Green Zone will unite and refuse to accept the political process that has been imposed by the occupation and promoted by the country's current leaders; that they will organize a political force to counter the current anti-Iraqi trend. With an enlightened mindset and energetic organization, they, hopefully, will be able to gain widespread support for an effective reversal of the political direction pursued since the foreign invasion and begin to move towards a secular, undivided, liberal and progressive Iraq.

It is my hope that such groups would become deeply concerned about the way matters have been moving and would make themselves increasingly heard. Such a grouping might lack the militias of the sectarian and ethnic groups, but might have the commitment, energy, vision, dedication, ideas and talents so desperately required by the new Iraq.

The long litany of failures of the occupation authorities to provide security, stability and good government in the wake of the invasion is well known. The policies of de-Baathification, supporting infamous Iraqis in exile along with local warlords, and ignoring the need for maintaining security until it was too late, all added to the alienation of large segments of the Iraqi population and contributed to destructive and divisive insurgency. Rather than building a new Iraq based on equality, the occupation's policies instead encouraged division, sectarianism and the politics of corruption and cronyism. The so-called 'surge' begun in 2007 was simply misguided. It could not be anything more than a short-term way to deal with symptoms rather than treat the real root of the problems in Iraq.

Everyone who cares about the Iraq of tomorrow wants to be optimistic, and I would not have written this book if I did not think the current situation could be turned around. And so, in the following chapters I will lay out a blueprint for a new Iraq, starting with the terms for political stability. It is time to start thinking about saving Iraq's future.

PART THREE

Iraq future:
A blueprint for prosperity and peace

6

Making a new political start

During the first years of the post-Saddam era, the only thing worse than the occupation's bad policies has been the speed of their execution. One example I have discussed was the occupation authority's rush to create 'democracy'. This plan had many fatal flaws, not least that its chief purpose was not to strengthen the Iraqi state and broaden political participation, but to impress Western and international public opinion, justifying the invasion on the grounds that the people of Iraq could now vote and be led by elected officials. This sham democracy, hastily cobbled together, based on sectarian differences, a flawed constitution and premature elections, has made the goal of a just and stable political order in Iraq impossible to attain. In short, the current dysfunctional system, built on dubious principles and a shaky foundation, is sure to result in the end in no democracy at all.

The original mission of converting a post-totalitarian state into a free nation has now become the unprecedented task of turning a failed state riven by civil war into a true democracy in the face of extreme hostility from armed groups and the centrifugal tendencies of irredentist groups and thugs working to unravel the nation-state. By rushing to build their sham

democracy, the occupation authorities have allowed the electoral laws and constitution to be manipulated by sectarian
extremists who have emerged as the new, incompetent leaders
of the Green Zone government. This political charade has
legitimized their claims and led to a regime crippled by
corruption and unable to project authority beyond the fortress
walls of its compound.

All this can only be regretted, and the past cannot be
changed. So I would now like to discuss my hope for ways in
which this horrific damage can be undone and how it might
be possible to build a strong, unified and genuinely democratic
Iraq of tomorrow. The political order in this new Iraq should
be based on time-tested principles, many of which influenced
the political life of the country during the constitutional
monarchy. These guidelines can provide a solid foundation
upon which real democracy in Iraq can be built by its future
leaders – a goal which I believe is still possible. It is time to
employ some lessons from the past.

Separating religion and the state

In my opinion, one of the prerequisites for true democracy and
prosperity in Iraq is to establish a secular state with a clear
separation of state and religion. Theocracy and democracy are
incompatible. The current relationship between religion and
politics in Iraq does no good. The new constitution is one
reason for this, specifying, as it does, that Sharia should count
as one of the sources of legislation. In this system, religious
leaders have elevated themselves to become powerful political
actors, some of them heading insurgent groups as well as

political parties. I believe this arrangement is mistaken: the constitution should not empower a specific religion, and leaders of religious groups should be barred from political activity.

Religion is based on faith, and its message is sacred, supreme and absolute. It is based on God's word and therefore it cannot be subject to compromise. Religious scholars and leaders are individuals deserving of the highest esteem, respect and reverence. Their mission is to guide and motivate their followers to adhere to the teachings of their faith and to live up to the highest moral standards. They are there to help their fellow believers fulfil their spiritual needs and religious obligations. In order to be able to perform these duties, religious leaders need to devote themselves to constant study, worship and the furtherance of theology. Religious leaders are, by definition, strict and autocratic. They have to temper their judgement to comply with what they interpret to be God's will. They cannot allow flexibility and independence.

Government, on the other hand, is a body for providing public services. In a democracy, it is expected to be subject to critique, disagreement, debate and change. Governments serve at the mercy of the electorate, which may express its dissatisfaction through the ballot. Governments must mediate the demands of different groups in society and be open to debate and compromise.

A secular state in the new Iraq would maintain two sets of rights for each individual – the right to worship freely, and the entirely separate right to choose his government according to his judgement of the needs of the country and the qualifications of the candidate. In short, the individual must be entitled both to exercise his citizenship rights and, in parallel, to freely satisfy his spiritual needs. Religious leaders should not participate in politics, and the state should not support one particular religion or sect over others.

Another reason for keeping religion and politics apart is economic performance. Strong economic growth will be essential to Iraq's future. I believe that proper economic management requires competent and qualified leadership. Obviously, religious scholars are well trained in their field of specialization, but this does not give them the qualifications or experience to direct a modern economy or to formulate social programmes.

Some of the ugliest scenarios occur when religion sets out to dictate government policy, thus causing religious leaders to compete among themselves for power and authority. Clerical meddlers in politics neglect their supreme spiritual mission and engage in rivalry and jockey for political position. When they do so they exacerbate the conflicts between their followers and among different religious factions. Political establishments subject to religious control become dysfunctional, unresponsive and inflexible.

Historically, examples are many from around the world in which the mixing of religion and government has produced unrest, disunity and oppression. Religion becomes debased in its contact with power, and power can become distorted when influenced by religious leaders. Furthermore, under such circumstances, there is always a risk that failings by those leaders in government may be attributed to religion itself. Any religion or religious clerics should be kept high above and totally immune from the possibility of attracting blame to their noble mission.

It is interesting to note that Ebrahim Yazdi, a devout Muslim, a follower of Ayatollah Khomeini, who followed him into exile in Paris, and who served as the first foreign minister in the post-revolution provisional government under Khomeini following the fall of the Shah of Iran in 1979, has stated thirty years later: 'The clerical establishment made a historic mistake when it was dragged into politics, leading people today to blame clerics for government failings.'*

The separation of state and religion should not imply any hostility between the two. Rather, it is a means of protecting and safeguarding the independence and integrity of each. There are millions of faithful Muslims around the world who accept, rather than reject, this separation and enjoy its benefits. For example, many millions of Muslims live in the US and western Europe. They provide tangible evidence of the ability to achieve higher standards of living in societies where religion and state coexist in separate spheres. Also, in certain Muslim states such as Indonesia, which has the largest Muslim population of any country, the separation between state and religion has been in effect for decades. In India, 170 million Muslims live under a democracy with the freedom to practise their religion and separately cast their votes in ballots for political choices. Turkey, with a population of over 70 million Muslims, is perhaps the most inspiring example of a secular state that clearly distinguishes between the fulfilment of spiritual needs and the exercise of citizenship.

The future constitution of Iraq should make no reference to Sharia as a source of legislation. It should also prohibit religious leaders from influencing or holding political office.

* *Financial Times*, London, 9 February, 2009.

The state as guarantor of individual rights

One of the most formidable challenges facing Iraq is to convince its citizens that the state both grants and protects their full rights. Under the Baath regime of tyranny and terror, it is not surprising that Iraqis were fearful of government and so looked to their religious, ethnic or tribal leaders to protect them and to meet their social and economic needs. Establishing a new civil society that ensures and safeguards individual rights requires an enormous amount of confidence-building. Without the creation of an environment in which individual rights are guaranteed, Iraqis are unlikely to give up their sectarian identities.

In a new and unified Iraq, people must feel they are entitled to equal rights, regardless of gender, sect, opinion, belief, ethnicity, religion or origin. They must be equal before the law, and every individual must have the right to life, liberty, security and equal opportunity. The freedoms of thought, conscience and religious belief must be unassailable. Individual rights to security, education, healthcare and social welfare must be basic and permanent.

If individual rights are granted across the board, separate group protection, whether based on ethnicity, tribe or religion, will not only be unnecessary but actually harmful. Such group protection promotes disunity and is certainly undemocratic. Equal rights and equal opportunities must belong to all of a country's citizens, without exception. An Iraq based on freedom, liberty and equality can unify a population of diverse ethnic and religious backgrounds.

It will take a long time to weave the fabric of the new Iraq into the design many of us wish to see. The stress in the constitution of 15 October 2005 on ethnic, national and religious differences is not a good omen, and has set the country on a path towards division and strife rather than unity and peace.

A responsive and limited government

After 45 years of brutal dictatorship and five years of disastrous and divisive foreign occupation, Iraq needs a long transition period in order to achieve security and stability, and to re-establish its national unity and identity. The transitional government needs to be headed by an authoritative leader, able to combine command and control with integrity, vision, dedication and competence. To assert that it would be difficult to find such people cannot be credible, considering the size, diversity and rich background of Iraq's population. Sought in good faith, a leader with the necessary skills should not be impossible to find.

Given my forty years' absence from Iraq, I am not qualified to offer names. On the other hand, I certainly do not wish to be interpreted as implying that the Americans should find that leader. My aim is to draw attention to the crying need, right now, for a new leadership to emerge. It may come from the current group of political leaders, or from an underground movement or from among military veterans. Or perhaps the solution will come from a future generation of young Iraqis who do not accept what they have been subjected to and who aspire to rebuild their nation on the basis of unity, modernization and prosperity.

The transitional government should focus on rebuilding Iraqi nationalism and setting in motion a massive economic development programme capable of transforming the lives of

Iraq's citizens in every corner of the country – from its borders with Turkey in the north to those with Kuwait in the south. The new government should abolish federalism, tribalism and ethnic and religious divides, offering instead a better lifestyle, personal freedom and the rule of law to every Iraqi, irrespective of gender, religion or ethnicity.

Once economic prosperity starts to be felt at grass-roots level, the transitional authority should then move towards political transformation. Such a change would require the authority to lay the foundations for an effective democracy. This in turn would depend on building the necessary institutions and nurturing public education and awareness to encourage a constructive political process.

Governing Iraq should no longer mean the lust for power, unlimited authority and unfair privileges. Nor should it be reliant on force, fear and corruption. Since 2003, the occupation has allowed the rise of an ugly form of government based on ethnic and religious divides. As a result, power has been wielded by unqualified leaders who have used either force or demagoguery to rule. By exploiting religion, ethnicity or nationalism, they have justified their hold on power for the sake of personal gain. Warlords chosen by the occupation authorities have used such differences to form their own militias and create political parties centred on personalities. Different factions have sided with their respective leaders and have not hesitated to attack others when instructed to do so.

In a break from this destructive spiral, the new government should be held accountable for delivering security, the rule of law, economic prosperity and a higher standard of living. It should see its role as providing that whole range of public services (health, education, housing and so forth) that individuals

need but cannot achieve on their own. To meet this responsibility, citizens should employ competent and qualified individuals in the same way that an airline employs trained pilots
and a bus company uses licensed drivers to provide the service
its passengers expect.

Once it has set the economic engine in motion, the transitional authority should start the next drive for political reform.
The first step would be to educate the public on the role of
good government. This would be essential in order for the
electoral system to function properly. The educational programme should cover the responsibilities of voters, what to
expect from elected officials and the principle that having more
government services requires higher taxes while less government
means lower taxes.

The step after that, I hope, would be to establish a two-party
system. The parties themselves should not be based on any individual, but should be distinguished by their underlying philosophy. One party would stand for more government services,
achieved through higher taxation. The other would advocate less
government and therefore lower taxes. People would be free to
belong to either party or to remain independent.

In Iraq, traditionally, the practice has been for the leader of
a political party to build the party around himself and act as
the central power. Party members would then be expected to
follow him blindly. It is the party leader, for example, who has
tended to decide almost single-handedly whom he appoints to
his party's list of parliamentary candidates. I hope that in the
new Iraq these roles would be reversed. It should be up to any
individual to decide which party best meets his and his country's
expectation of a better standard of living. Once he has made
up his mind to join a political party, it should be his prerogative

and responsbility to select the most competent political leaders to represent the party platform and implement its programmes. Elections are for voters to decide which party would form the most effective and productive government.

I have already mentioned the need to separate religion from politics, and this point must be reiterated. During the occupation, religious leaders have been allowed to use their spiritual influence to dictate political positions. Religious leaders should be free to promote the practice of faith and worship, but should not be entitled to influence the political process.

Before the 2003 invasion, Iraqis clung to two assumptions – first, that their country had all the ingredients necessary to make it one of the most prosperous in the world (an assumption I believe is still valid); and second, that Saddam was the only obstacle preventing Iraq from unlocking its potential and that a bright future was certain to follow once he was ousted. Tragically, the second assumption has proved to be false.

Five years of ugly and disastrous occupation may have convinced Iraqis that governing is not an entitlement, one to be seized and exploited by any religious majority or minority, or any ethnic or tribal head. Indeed, the concept of entitlement should no longer be accepted. If Iraqis have learnt this bitter and costly lesson, they may now understand that governing is a responsibility to be assumed by competent individuals with the necessary talent, skill, experience and integrity.

The structure of government

For Iraq to advance, it needs capable leadership. The fault of the occupation was to promote the wrong leadership. Individuals seeking to govern should be chosen for their qualifications, not their affiliations. Only those who are not qualified will use and abuse religion, ethnicity or tribal stature to justify their claim or entitlement to wield power.

The leaders of the future Iraq should put in place the foundations of government that have proven effective over the long run in other parts of the world. One quality of a successful government is the ability to ensure fairness and the rule of law by balancing centres of power and ensuring accountability and representation through the election of people's representatives to local, regional and national legislative bodies.

In the new Iraq, I would like to propose that there should be three independent branches of government – executive, legislative and judicial. Iraq must have a robust central government to conduct foreign affairs, defend itself from invaders, reconstruct the economy and pursue a unified monetary policy. But this central government needs muscular checks on its power. The most important of these is an independent judicial system that protects the constitution and ensures that the law is being justly implemented by the executive branch. Cementing the rule of law into the foundations of the country is the single most important requirement for establishing a new and prosperous Iraq.

Organizationally, Iraq should have three geographic levels of executive branches, each headed by an elected chief executive who appoints a qualified cabinet to assume responsibility in various departments of public administration. The central government would be headed by a prime minister, the regional government by a governor and the local government by a mayor, all of them elected.

At central, regional and local levels, there should also be

elected legislators who would appropriate government funding and act as checks and balances to the executive branch. At the central level, this would be a parliament; at regional level, a chamber of deputies; and at local level, a municipal council. While the central government has important functions, the governing system in the new Iraq must also place as much authority as practicable in the hands of regions and municipalities. Decentralized government is a key means to preserve freedom by spreading power. Citizens can express their discontent through the ballot if the government is inefficient, repressive or corrupt. The Iraqi constitution should specifically reserve for the regional and municipal governments all power not directly given to the national government.

Decentralized governments are much closer to the people they represent and are therefore less likely to treat their constituents like subjects in a distant land. Iraqis should know their local representatives by name, in contrast with the occupation-orchestrated January 2005 elections in which they voted for long slates of faceless names and had little knowledge of the backgrounds and policies of the candidates. In addition, decentralized governments are more responsive to local needs and priorities and have stronger and more familiar institutions. A decentralized system is also the best way to empower all segments of Iraq's diverse population. This kind of empowerment will provide valuable cohesion for a young nation.

The creation of a strong decentralized system should take as its basis Iraq's current 18 provinces. These geographically divided provinces should be identified as 'regions' in the new Iraq. The concept of federalism imposed to make the splitting up of Iraq sound more palatable should be abolished. Federalism has worked in countries like the USA and Germany because it was a means to unite divided entities, not a system imposed on a united country to divide it.

Moreover, the new political order should include term limits for serving in government positions. At executive level, political party heads should either win the next general election and assume government, or resign and be replaced. At central government level, the prime minister should serve only one term of seven years. This is a long enough period to implement his or her strategic vision while not allowing too prolonged a period for rule under the same leader. It will also eliminate the distraction of re-campaigning for the same position. At regional and local levels, governors and mayors respectively should serve a four-year term with a maximum of two terms if re-elected. Term limits at legislative level should be four years, with a maximum of three terms if re-elected. That will ensure constant renewals of leadership.

A fair tax system

Citizens of the new Iraq should expect to pay separate taxes to the central government, the regional government and local municipalities for services rendered by each. Iraq cannot establish a democracy without an effective, transparent and fair fiscal system. Such a system not only provides revenue for necessary government operations, it also forms a set of relationships between the citizen and the state. With legislative bodies at all levels of government deciding how tax revenues will be spent, and with government agencies putting these funds to work, there develop bonds of participation on the part of the taxpayers (who become stakeholders in all levels of government) and of accountability on the part of elected officials and government employees (who will be held accountable for the responsible discharge of their duties).

The centralized and oil-dependent character of today's government system is a primary cause of misuse and corruption. Distributing wealth directly to the citizens and then asking them to pay taxes to their elected governments will eradicate corruption and make government more accountable and efficient.

I therefore propose that the net income generated from natural resources should be used to satisfy the required annual national investment needs of a National Economic Development Board and an Education and Technology Board (both discussed in detail in the next chapter). The remaining balance should be paid directly to the citizens as annual cash dividends.

Obviously, there should be a law to define an equitable entitlement standard. My preference would be for the distribution to be to all citizens who are expected to pay taxes. However, should minors also be considered eligible, I would hope there would be a differentiation between those children who attend schools and those who do not. Also, setting a maximum limit for each family's entitlement to those dividends will have the collateral advantage of discouraging a potential undesirable population growth.

Iraq is in desperate need of a new political settlement. The four principles outlined above would, I believe, give the country a chance to develop into a real democracy in the long term. Critics may point to these four principles and say they are a blueprint for a 'Western' liberal democracy, a system that may not work in Iraq. To these, I answer: Iraq had successfully embarked on a similar political course during the Hashemite constitutional monarchy; therefore such a system did work in the past and can again in the future Other critics may claim that Iraqis themselves want something else − for example, a theocracy. Here, I would counter by saying that only those Iraqis who want a divided, unstable country would want a theocracy. I believe most Iraqis recognize that peace and unity are possible only when religion is not mixed with politics.

Hand in hand with drastic reform of the political system must come changes in Iraq's economy. In the following chapter I discuss how oil revenues can be maximized and then used to fuel economic growth and social development.

7

Fuelling progress with oil

Iraq's economic revival must begin with the oil industry. The country's vast oil wealth has the potential to fund a large portion of its needed transformation. Iraq's oil reserves have yet to be fully explored. However, estimated reserves of about 115 billion barrels place the amount of Iraq's oil second in the world, outranked only by Saudi Arabia.*

Harnessing this lucrative resource will be central to Iraq's development, but it cannot be done under the current system. Unfortunately, mismanagement, neglect, corruption and adventurist wars during the Saddam years have severely diminished the capacity of this vital industry. The destruction of facilities and the drain of critical personnel in the subsequent occupation period have crippled the industry. Still, even with today's relatively inadequate production, oil revenues comprise around three-quarters of Iraq's GDP and 95 per cent of government revenue. The sooner Iraq reaches full production capacity, the more financial resources it will have to develop and diversify its economy.

---

* The American Energy Information Administration (EIA), Official Energy Statistics from the US government, puts it at 112 billion barrels. The EIA estimates that 90 per cent of the country remains unexplored and these regions could yield an additional 100 billion barrels.

But attempting to build a new Iraq using the current system of oil exploration and production would be fruitless. Instead, I recommend a wholesale reconstruction of the oil sector. This would include creating new organizations and structures to improve efficiency and ensure that revenues are spent in a wise and equitable manner. This plan also calls for foreign participation in order to inject fresh management expertise, state-of-the-art technology and new sources of investment.

A legacy of inefficiency

As well as bringing about political decline in Iraq, the era of junta leaders and dictators that followed the 1958 coup was marked by an absence of efficiency and rationality in developing the oil industry. In 1961, for example, Abd al-Karim Qasim issued Law Number 80, which was detrimental to the oil industry in a number of ways. First, it stipulated that the government would take control of more than 98 per cent of the IPC concession. The government also took over areas that had been explored but not yet developed by international oil companies, and confiscated a number of productive oil wells in the southern Iraqi fields. Second, the foreign oil companies reacted to this arbitrary government action by reducing their oil exports. This badly affected government revenue. Finally, the companies immediately suspended all exploration and drilling operations in the confiscated areas. This loss of revenue and the pullback in exploration were doubly harmful because they came at a time when Iraq lacked the financial and technical expertise to develop the areas it had confiscated.

Despite these drawbacks, oil output reached its highest level in 1979, with total production of 3.5 million barrels per day (b/d), of which over 3 million b/d were exported. However, the Iran–Iraq War (1980–88) caused immeasurable damage to oil installations and export facilities, reducing production to 900,000 b/d and exports to 600,000 b/d. Following the long and costly war, production rose to 3.2 million b/d by early 1990, but with the Iraqi invasion of Kuwait in 1990, production dropped drastically to 300,000 b/d. The subsequent sanctions degraded Iraqi oil facilities further. In 1997, with the initiation of the UN-supervised Oil for Food Programme, production increased to 1.2 million b/d.

Between 1990 and 2003 the Iraqi oil industry suffered terrible devastation. During this period, Saddam Hussein used oil revenues to expand his political authority and prevent the regime from collapsing under the weight of discontent and economic dislocation brought on by the international sanctions regime. As a result, the oil industry witnessed rapid degradation and production capacity fell due to lack of investment and loss of hundreds of qualified engineers and experts who decided to emigrate to escape the regime's brutality. The lack of access to technology due to sanctions meant that the only way to maintain production was to use obsolete technology such as water flooding and over-pumping, which damaged oil wells. It was also during this period that Saddam awarded contracts to Russia, China and Asian companies, hoping to win their political support but knowing in advance that these projects could not be implemented due to sanctions.

In 2003, Iraqi and non-Iraqi oil experts expected that once Saddam had been overthrown, production would return in a couple of years to its pre-Kuwait invasion level of 3.2 million b/d. More optimistic projections by some experts forecast that,

by the end of this decade, Iraq would be increasing its production capacity towards 8–10 million b/d. These optimistic
estimates were based primarily on Iraq's potential proven oil
reserves, without adequate assessment of the challenges faced
by the industry.

The reality, however, is quite different. As of early 2008,
Iraq's oil production does not exceed 2.4 million b/d, with
exports not exceeding 1.6 million b/d. Most analysts agree that
there will be no major increases in the next three years. In the
short term, the best scenario is one in which Iraq maintains its
current production. It is clear that things have not gone
according to plan. A number of factors such as attacks on
oil installations and pipelines, ageing and poorly maintained
infrastructure and criminal activity are hindering development.
According to the Office of the Special Inspector General for
Iraq Reconstruction (SIGIR), by 2006 Iraq had lost a potential
$16 billion in revenue from oil exports. On top of that, Iraq is
paying billions of dollars to import petroleum products.[1]

Challenges facing the oil industry

An immense infusion of investment is needed to develop the
oil industry. According to some estimates, several billions would
be needed to restore oil production to its previous levels, and
more than $20 billion if Iraq decides to increase capacity to 5
million b/d. Given these large requirements, Iraq would have
to rely primarily on foreign investment and foreign capital. On
top of the issue of finance, Iraq would have to rely on foreign
companies to enhance the skills of its oil workers and transfer
technology and management skills to the national oil company.

Throughout the 1990s, Iraq lacked access to state-of-the-art technology such as 3D seismic data, gas injection and directional drilling. Furthermore, skills to manage large oil projects have also been degraded. I would like to re-emphasize that Iraq needs foreign capital more for the expertise that comes with it than just for the money.

The biggest obstacle to developing the oil industry and increasing production has been the lack of security. In 2003, the occupying forces disbanded the army and the police without providing a substitute to restore law and enforce order. The impact of the lack of security on the oil industry has been devastating. It has been manifested in a number of areas: the regular sabotage of pipelines and oil installations, which is limiting the ability of Iraq to increase its exports of crude oil and undertake necessary maintenance work; the kidnapping and killing of oil engineers, technicians and employees, which is badly affecting the human capital needed to run the industry; the smuggling of crude oil and products by militias and gangs, which is forcing the Iraqi government to increase its dependence on imported products; and corruption at all levels, which is causing large loss of revenues to the Iraqi people. Consequently, the first and most crucial precondition for attracting highly needed investment to develop the oil industry is to restore security.

Another precondition is to resolve the uncertainty that affects the political future of Iraq. Oil companies are reluctant to make irreversible investments unless the issue of sovereignty is clearly settled. Unfortunately, the future of Iraq as one entity is highly in doubt under certain scenarios. Aspirations for Kurdish independence remain very high and the borders of the Kurdish region are not defined. For example, the incorporation of

Kirkuk in the Kurdistan region remains one of the central platforms of the Kurdish political parties.

The future of the south of Iraq is equally uncertain. In 2005, the head of the Supreme Council for the Islamic Revolution in Iraq, one of the main ruling parties, called for the creation of a federal southern state. The locally powerful al-Fadhila Party, which controls key oil industry jobs in Basra where most of Iraq's oil is found, oppose the creation of a Shia 'super-region'. Disagreement among the different groups could threaten national reconciliation efforts.

It is hard to attract foreign investment amid this ambiguity and uncertainty. Any development of Iraq's oil industry would have to await the settlement of these issues, as it is not clear what authority and which law would prevail in the producing regions. Thus, the most important step is for the future leadership of Iraq to hold on unequivocally to the unity and stability of their nation.

A new petroleum law

Another key reform will be a new petroleum law that would state clearly the objectives of the government and address the major principles of exploration, development and production. The law should establish some general aims and guidelines to govern the relationship between international oil companies and the government. It should also provide a framework for stable and transparent taxation, enhance credibility by emphasizing respect for the sanctity of contracts and provide assurances and guarantees against outright and/or creeping expropriation.

Unfortunately, there has been an absence of clear strategy towards the restructuring of the oil industry in post-invasion Iraq. For instance, in April 2003 the US Department of State's Oil and Energy Working Group completed recommendations that favoured an oil policy reliant on production-sharing agreements. Later in the same year, former Iraqi prime minister Ayad Allawi provided the Council for Oil Policy with a set of guidelines recommending that existing fields remain under the control of the Iraq National Oil Company (INOC), but that the development of new fields be undertaken exclusively by private companies. Allawi also recommended that INOC be partially privatized.

In May 2006, Iraq's oil minister, Hussein al-Sharristani, announced the need to pass a new hydrocarbon law that would guarantee the conditions needed for oil companies to operate in Iraq. The draft of the Iraqi Oil Law was approved by the Iraqi government in February 2006 and was sent to the parliament. One stumbling block was apparently removed in April 2008 when it was announced that Iraq's central government and the Kurdish provincial government had come to an understanding. Iraq's parliament has yet to pass the law.

However, rather than strengthening cohesion, the new oil law seems to have had the opposite effect of deepening the divisions within Iraq. It has brought to the fore a number of sore points involving federal versus regional control of oil, the types of contracts that should be awarded, the sharing of oil revenues and the role of the new INOC. The absence of a clear vision for the future of the industry is creating tensions, undermining cohesion and inhibiting investment.

The new petroleum law need not be exhaustive and should cover only general principles that can then be augmented by decrees and regulations as development goes on. Here the experience of Norway is instructive. Norway enacted a comprehensive petroleum law only in 1985, almost twenty years after the start of production! If that country managed to administer a successful, growing petroleum industry without comprehensive legislation over such a period, Iraq, too, can afford to take a measured, if somewhat different, approach. The first law in Norway focused only on general issues related to sovereignty, the stability of the fiscal regime and the general framework for issuing licences. Detailed legislation followed later on when needs arose and when the authorities became sufficiently familiar with the existing challenges and had gained experience in negotiating with international oil companies.

This approach of gradual legislation might not necessarily be applicable to Iraq, as allocating licences without proper legislation could open the way for corruption and abuse and could discourage foreign companies from investment. But the gradual approach would work if accompanied by the appropriate institutions (discussed below) to ensure fairness, openness and transparency.

While the petroleum law and subsequent legislation will create the legal basis for the relationship between the government and oil companies, there is also a need to fashion a model agreement that covers the specific details and the fiscal terms. This would help facilitate negotiations and could prove a useful tool for attracting investment. Models may include production-sharing agreements (PSAs), concessionary agreements, joint ventures, buyback contracts or service contracts. In principle, Iraq could rely on any of these agreements as long as it achieved the objective of maximizing the return to the country and provided enough incentives to the international oil companies to invest.

The yield to the country should not be limited to financial returns, but should cover overall benefits in terms of technology transfer, upgrading local skills and protecting the environment. Furthermore, the fiscal regime should be flexible, varying according to the nature of the project. For instance, if exploration risk is high and rewards are modest, then the fiscal terms could be lenient. On the other hand, fiscal terms should be stricter for areas with relatively well-proven potential and low risk. Furthermore, the fiscal regime should contain a sliding scale so that the Iraqi government would benefit from higher production and higher oil prices. For instance, in Libya or Indonesia, government profit from oil (i.e. revenues remaining after royalty payments and cost recovery) is split according to the rate of production and/or an R factor that measures the ratio of contractor's accumulated receipts to accumulated costs. The higher the R ratio or production rate, the lower the profit share of the contractor.

In devising the contracting and fiscal terms, it is always important that the country offer attractive returns, adjusted for risk. The fact that a country has great geological potential does not mean that it is able to attract oil companies regardless of the fiscal terms. In fact, the existence of large reserves may have the opposite effect of hindering investment. Because of the existence of large reserves in resource-rich countries, exploration and development risks are relatively low or at least perceived to be so. As a result, national governments are unlikely to grant international oil companies a high return on their investment. These low returns are likely to continue throughout the life of the investment. This is in contrast to more difficult locations: although the quality of reserves is lower and risks are higher (with margins therefore low at the start), margins can increase over time as operations proceed. Iraq should avoid falling into this trap and ensure that it offers attractive fiscal terms to oil companies.

A new institutional framework

Given the great challenges that the oil industry faces, it is imperative that Iraq devises new institutions that would regulate and administer oil operations. It should also construct a petroleum policy to develop the national resource in an efficient way that maximizes the return to the Iraqi people. Degree and ease of access to reserves are highly dependent on the institutional framework of the host country, which governs the relationship between the national oil company, the foreign company and other bodies involved in the industry. Vagueness about the roles of the various players and possible overlap in their functions can lead to uncertainties and delays in carrying out investment projects.

Right from the start, there should be complete separation between the legislative, regulatory and commercial functions of the state. In many countries it is customary to combine these separate functions and entrust them to the national oil company. The national oil company is also subject to the control of the ministry of oil. This structure has usually produced very poor performance and resulted in low investment, preventing the development of productive capacity. It is important to move away from such an arrangement towards a more open and transparent system. This would require the creation of new institutional structures.

In 1952, Iraq successfully negotiated with IPC a deal that would generate more revenue for the government, raise production capacity and permit Iraqi nationals to assume managerial positions in the company. It was agreed that the government of Iraq should receive 50 per cent of the oil profits from foreign companies operating within its borders. For the first time in its young history, Iraq had a fair claim on its natural wealth, and it promptly made use of this newly earned fortune. The key step was the allocation of 70 per cent of oil revenues to a new Development Board. By another stroke of wisdom, the board was distanced as much as possible from politics. At the top of the organization were a chairman and five technically competent board members, including two experts, one British and one American.

The Development Board was a source of great hope, expressed particularly in the annual celebrations of its achievements. Had the country not been thrown into turmoil in 1958, I am confident that students of economic development would today be referring to Iraq's transformation as a shining example of success and prosperity.

A new oil company with foreign participation

One way to avoid the shortcomings of the national oil companies of other countries would be to create a new company to replace INOC. It would have a new name, but for the sake of convenience let us call it the International Iraqi Oil Company (IIOC). The important thing is that this new company would be designed to encourage participation by the best companies in the world so that Iraq could benefit.

The IIOC would be organized so that the government would retain majority ownership and control of the petroleum industry, but foreign companies would be invited to participate in the country's petroleum production. This would improve exploration, production and management in Iraq by providing a constant influx of highly trained experts and state-of-the art technology. In addition, these companies would offer an important source of investment in the industry. Foreign companies would be permitted to retain all revenues from their share of exports until their investment costs had been recouped. After this, revenues would be shared, with the government receiving 85 per cent of IIOC profits while the company would retain 15 per cent.

The IIOC management would operate to the highest international standards, incorporating a high degree of transparency. Through guarding against the creation of an inefficient oil bureaucracy, Iraq's petroleum resources would be rationally and professionally utilized. A large portion of the income from Iraq's 75 per cent share of the IIOC would go towards funding the country's economic and social development, providing operating funds for the National Economic Development Board (see below) as well as cash payments to every Iraqi along the lines of what is done in Alaska to distribute a portion of the state's oil-generated wealth.

The National Economic Development Board

What worked in the past could work today if a few simple but crucial principles are followed in re-creating the National Economic Development Board. In my suggested blueprint, the

NEDB would be empowered to reconstruct Iraq and to direct the investment of oil revenues so as to develop other sectors of the economy and establish alternative sources of income.

First, a new board must be kept independent and at arm's length from political manoeuvring, just as was done during the constitutional monarchy. Second, its members must be of the highest technical and intellectual calibre and include world-class foreign experts. Finally, in order to attract the best talent, pay must be commensurate with responsibilities and achievements. Here, the example of Singapore may be followed, where top officials have always been paid on a scale in line with the private sector. Such high levels of compensation not only attract the best talent, but reduce corruption and the need for excessive perks.

Needless to say, the challenges facing the new development board will be profound. Its mission will be to transform Iraq into a truly first-rate, world-class nation. In order to do this, the board must seize the initiative in many areas including agriculture, housing, tourism and healthcare. But more importantly, the NEDB would play vital roles in the investment of Iraq's oil income, which is bound to play a central role in the development and transformation of the new Iraq.

At the first stage of the board's work, priority should be given to the restoration of facilities relating to crude oil production and export operations that were damaged during successive wars and by economic sanctions. This could enable oil production to reach the level of 3.5 million b/d achieved before the war with Iran interrupted production in 1980.

At the second stage, the board should devise a policy aimed at rehabilitating existing oil refineries which have been heavily damaged in the last two decades. Due to the deterioration in security and lack of maintenance, Iraq's refining capacity is under-utilized. At present, oil products and gas are mostly imported from abroad, costing the Iraqi people billions of dollars a year. Securing oil products to the people has become more difficult because of smuggling. The large discrepancy in oil prices between Iraq and neighbouring countries has made smuggling oil from inside Iraq to neighbouring countries a very lucrative business. The weaknesses in the measurement of the flow of oil, the poor control over the borders and over land and sea outlets, the lack of planning of distributional and organizational policies and lax legal and judiciary measures against offenders have all encouraged smuggling. A top priority for the NEDB is therefore to phase out subsidies and take immediate action to enforce a strict system of measurement of oil flows.

After the rehabilitation of existing oil installations and refineries, the NEDB would embark on plans for oil prospecting and drilling to increase Iraqi capacity towards the 5 million b/d mark. The NEDB would determine which areas of Iraq should be offered first for exploration and production, when to offer them, under what terms, and how fast to develop them. The main objective of such a policy is to optimize the potential life and use of the resource. In order to achieve this, the NEDB should establish a data centre containing detailed information about all oilfields in Iraq. The oil companies operating in Iraq would transfer data regularly to this centre, and it would be made publicly available to help oil companies establish the potential of certain sites.

The NEDB would also be responsible for matters involving licensing. Licences would be market-oriented and based not only on the largest monetary offer, but also on the work programme. The procedure, evaluation, discussion and decision on all bids should be transparent and made publicly available to all bidders. At early stages of oil sector development, licences should include clauses that would commit the international oil companies to share state-of-the-art management and technology to the IIOC. The NEDB could also enforce a national content element requiring a certain percentage of work in the oil sector to be performed by local personnel.

Health, safety and environmental protection should also be a top priority for the NEDB. The performance of international oil companies should be closely monitored, and incentive and penalty schemes devised to make sure that certain health and environmental benchmarks are met.

The National Oil Regulatory Board

In addition to the NEDB, there is a need to establish a National Oil Regulatory Board which would act as the regulatory arm for the state. The NORB will monitor oil companies, including the IIOC, in areas related to exploration, development, health, safety and environment, technology transfer and national expertise development. In the areas of exploration and development, the regulatory arm would establish whether oil companies have carried out the work programme specified in the agreement. In the areas of health, safety and development, the regulatory arm would set certain benchmarks and monitor the companies' performance on that basis. In the areas of technology transfer and national expertise development, the board should monitor the training programme and whether the operator is transferring the best available technology.

An important part of the board's work would be to monitor the production-sharing agreements. PSAs are complex and a typical agreement usually contains an array of elements including royalty, cost recovery, profit oil, signature bonuses, production bonuses and taxes. Since PSAs allow the contractor to recover costs out of revenues, one of the main responsibilities of the NORB would be to ensure that contractors were recovering only those costs listed in the contract. Another responsibility is to make sure that profit oil is split according to the agreed formulas.

Distribution of oil revenues

It will be vitally important, as well, to establish a way to effectively distribute the oil revenues. First, it is essential that part of those revenues should be invested in new productive capacity. Iraq should avoid the situation that exists in many other oil-exporting countries, where revenues are lavished upon social projects such as education and health while the national oil company starves for funds. In the long term, this would have devastating effects on investment in the oil sector and the competitiveness of the national oil company.

Obviously, a large portion of oil revenues should be transferred to the NEDB. Centralizing oil revenues in a competent institution of that kind is essential for the unity of Iraq and for deciding rationally and fairly how to spend oil profits. It is also important to implement a strategic plan to place the country on a new development path. The NEDB would have the purpose of investing oil revenues to promote economic and human development in the areas of education and health. A top priority would be to restructure, rehabilitate and upgrade the country's infrastructure and provide for the basic utilities required by the people. Oil revenues should also be invested in diversifying the Iraqi economy, thus preparing it for the post-oil era.

To enhance transparency and accountability, all oil revenues and expenditures should enter the federal budgetary process. There is a need for an audit board that would monitor accounts, give annual reports to the parliament and have the authority to investigate any discrepancies.

Another portion of the revenues should be transferred into an oil stabilization fund designed to deal with external shocks. Since Iraq will rely heavily on oil for its development, an oil stabilization fund is important for three main reasons: to lower the risks associated with stop-go public expenditures when oil prices go up or down; to maintain fiscal discipline and try where feasible to decouple public spending from oil-price volatility; and to avoid excessive real appreciation or depreciation of the national currency. The management of the oil stabilization fund should be entrusted to fiscal authorities and the central bank rather than an independent body, since these authorities will have a better grasp of the macroeconomic situation. With this knowledge, these authorities could best judge when it would be necessary to engage in counter-cyclical fiscal policy.

Many have suggested that Iraq should establish a special fund that would receive a constant share of oil revenue, to be used to benefit future generations. There are two models that are worth mentioning and which could become relevant in the Iraqi context, but only in the very long term. Alaska established the Alaska Permanent Fund (APF) in 1976 to provide for future generations once its oil reserves ran out. At least 25 per cent of certain oil receipts are placed directly into the fund. The principal must remain in the fund, but 42 per cent of the annual investment earnings are paid out in dividends. Every eligible Alaskan resident receives an annual dividend. In 2006, this amounted to $1,107 per person, up from $846 in 2005. Norway provides another example of a successful oil fund. It instituted the State Petroleum Fund (SPF) in 1990 as a way to save for the retirement of its baby-boom population. The SPF had grown to $205 billion at the end of December 2005, enough to provide more than $44,000 per Norwegian.

At the early stages of Iraqi reconstruction, it may not be sensible to focus too closely on these particular models. They both exist in mature, capital-rich economies, and the funds are constituted on the premise that the return on the underlying portfolio of financial assets under the fund's management exceeds the need for fixed capital investment. Given the large reconstruction efforts that it faces, Iraq is likely to be capital-scarce, so that the return on portfolio of financial assets is likely to be dominated by investment in fixed capital, especially in infrastructure investments in Iraq itself. Thus, there are few lessons that one can draw about the investment strategies of APF and SPF at the early stages of reconstruction. Once Iraq has attained a degree of economic prominence – with a modern infrastructure and an educated and prospering population – establishing such funds could provide an effective way to manage Iraq's future oil revenues.

Renewing and managing Iraq's oil industry will be a monumental task, and the foregoing plan offers just a few suggestions for how this might be done to maximize the benefit to the people of Iraq. Any future leaders of Iraq would do well to take special care in reviving the country's oil industry, because revenues from this source will be central to the country's future.

The challenges facing the oil industry are immense. However, it is not too late to turn things around. The ideas presented here can serve as a guide to future leaders of Iraq, who will require a clear vision about the future of the Iraqi oil industry so that they can develop the appropriate institutions to carry this vision forward. But the Iraqi economy has many other facets. In the following chapter I explore ways to rebuild and improve some of the important non-oil sectors.

8

Building a vibrant economy

Iraq's economy has been ravaged by war, corruption, mismanagement and the well-documented shortcomings of the US-led occupation. Even though billions of dollars have been channelled into the country since 2003, the economy remains a shambles, with little improvement in socio-economic conditions and living standards.

Turning this situation around will be a monumental challenge, even once the political system is overhauled and a new leadership takes over. However, such a drastic change of course is not impossible. Recent history has shown that under the right conditions, countries can overcome major obstacles and achieve remarkable growth rates and a high level of economic development within a reasonable amount of time. Ireland, South Korea, Singapore and Taiwan have all achieved impressive economic development in the past few decades. Each of them followed its particular development trajectory, and it would be difficult to replicate in Iraq the historical experience of any of these countries. But behind these success stories we can identify common factors such as a stable macroeconomic situation, a favourable business environment that sets predictable rules and provides support and incentives for the private sector, and appropriate governance mechanisms. If such measures are implemented in Iraq, then it too can become an economic success story.

To build that future, the first step must be a clean break in terms of Iraq's current leadership. It will require the emergence of a competent and authoritative government under a UN mandate and UN protection to take charge of the nation's destiny for an extended interim period that might run for several years. During this period, the UN must also guarantee Iraq's territorial unity and integrity. The new transitional government must be dedicated to following a new and different path in order to build a stable and prosperous country, free of ethnic and sectarian tendencies. It must create an effective road map for restoring law and order and for turning Iraq into a vibrant economic success. And before it can achieve political democracy, it must establish the institutional foundations for an economic democracy. In other words, political democracy can flourish only once Iraq's shattered economic infrastructure, its civil institutions and social services such as healthcare and education have been given the time and resources to recover.

Some requirements for recovery

In places such as Singapore, Taiwan, Ireland and South Korea, the clarity of vision and the dedication and skill of national leaders played a large part in achieving spectacular successes. These leaders employed some common strategies including the use of long planning horizons and resisting pressures from powerful groups with narrow interests so that they could implement a broad strategic plan benefiting wide sectors of the economy.

Streamlining government is also a priority for creating a dynamic economy. This will involve drastically trimming the bureaucracy and privatizing most government-owned economic enterprises. Under the dictatorship, Iraq's government was chronically bloated, and this pattern has not improved under the occupation. Government at all levels should be lean and efficient, just large enough to perform its functions and not used as a patronage system to reward those in power. Similarly, as soon as the appropriate financial infrastructure is in place, government-owned economic assets should be privatized. This shift of financial power from the public to the private sector would reduce the risk of corruption and reinforce democratic processes.

I would like to add five more key principles that must prevail in any vision for a new Iraqi economy: 1) the openness and transparency of national institutions, including measures aimed at fighting corruption; 2) the creation of strong incentives for private-sector development; 3) close economic and financial integration with the international community, and a governmental ethos of fiscal responsibility; 4) the implementation of world-class standards and best practices, with a view to reducing red tape and promoting efficiency; and 5) a social safety net that addresses the needs of all Iraqis, with special emphasis on opening up all possible avenues of social and economic participation to women.

Future Iraqi leaders should employ these and other strategies, but long-term prosperity will rely on how well they achieve economic diversification. While Iraq will be dependent on oil revenue to maintain its consumption-driven economy in the near term, measures should also be employed to diversify the economic base away from oil. This can be done by using profits from the petroleum industry to build infrastructure that supports a broader real economy, and in particular encourages investors to develop a financial services community.

To ensure long-term prosperity, oil revenues must be used to invest as well in Iraq's agricultural, tourism and industrial sectors. This broad-based diversification strategy will be one of the most important tasks of the new Iraqi National Economic Development Board. The following is a more detailed discussion of the development of the non-oil sectors of Iraq's economy.

From the first farms to the farms of tomorrow: agriculture

Lying at the eastern end of the Fertile Crescent, Iraq has for millennia been endowed with some of the most productive agricultural lands in the Middle East. Indeed, the region was the site of some of the world's first settled agriculture. The well-watered plains between Iraq's two mighty rivers, the Tigris and the Euphrates, along with the foothills in the north and the date palms of the Shatt al-Arab, represent an endowment of rare productive potential. But this potential has not been well managed since 1958. Before that, Iraq was an exporter of food – mainly grain and dates. For example, Iraq exported 1 million tons of wheat in 1957. After 1958, the country became a net importer of wheat, the agricultural system became a political pawn, and production plummeted. With investment and the right policies from Baghdad, Iraq can fulfil its potential as an agricultural producer. This would serve to diversify the economy and bring work and purpose back to depressed parts of the country.

Under the constitutional monarchy, Iraq realized a significant expansion in agriculture, the area under cultivation nearly quadrupling. By the 1950s it boasted an exportable surplus of grain. Investments from the Iraq Development Board accorded agriculture a high priority, and the future was bright for Iraqi farmers.

The coup of 1958, however, led to a series of ill-considered policies that precipitated a collapse in production and the end of large-scale public investment in the sector. In October 1958, large estates were broken up and land was confiscated for redistribution, an effort at land reform meant in part to improve output. The programme was a disaster, however, and agricultural production collapsed as large parts of the land were not redistributed. And those who received a plot of land lacked financing, equipment and know-how.

Through the next 45 years, agriculture remained in turmoil, with periods of collectivization and episodic investment followed by longer periods of neglect. During this period the state remained deeply involved in the agricultural sector. Even during the 'privatization' reforms of the 1970s, the profitability of farming was driven by the availability of subsidized inputs. Livestock levels continued to decline. Agricultural production failed to keep pace with a rapidly growing population, and Iraq became more and more dependent on food imports. By 2000 almost 95 per cent of cereals were imported. The onset of UN sanctions in 1991, after Saddam's disastrous war in Kuwait, devastated Iraq's agricultural sector, and only rationing and then the Oil for Food Programme after 1997 helped Iraq's poor to avoid starvation. Overall, Iraq's governments since 1958 have failed to achieve the considerable potential of the land.

In the wake of the US occupation in spring 2003, there has been a modest level of investment in agriculture through various reconstruction schemes. However, there has been no sign of the kind of large-scale projects and fundamental reform that could dramatically expand and improve production. A small part of the IRRF scheme was dedicated to agriculture, through the USAID-administered US Agriculture Reconstruction and Development Program for Iraq (ARDI) between 2003 and 2006. Money was spent on veterinary clinics, the introduction of improved cereal grain varieties, repairing agricultural equipment and training farmers and ministry staff. Some of this work is being carried on in the 'Inma' (Arabic for growth) project from 2006 to 2009, which is scheduled to spend around $100 million every year on training farmers, with some investments in irrigation management. While welcome, these investments are not on a scale to match the opportunity, and they ignore some of the more fundamental challenges.

Irrigation is central to Iraqi agriculture. Iraq's two most important agricultural products are cereals and dates. Cereals account for around 85–90 per cent of cropped areas, while dates were Iraq's most valuable export before oil (in 1970, Iraq was producing half of the world's supply). Most of the dates and two-thirds of the cereals are grown in irrigated areas in the centre and south of the country, which creates two major challenges for Iraqi agriculture: managing the land and irrigation systems, and ensuring that sufficient water enters the country by river.

To address these twin challenges requires a comprehensive recovery programme. The first step is to establish clear property rights for Iraqi farmers. State intervention in agriculture was pervasive during the post-1958 era and took many different forms. In particular, the programmes of land requisition and redistribution have left a complex legal legacy including a frustrating and paralysing lack of clear land ownership records in many places. Farmers will not invest in land if it is not clear whether they are working for themselves, for others or for the government. In all cases where there is a dispute between an Iraqi farmer and the government, the default option should be to grant the land to the farmer so that it can be quickly put to use. Resolving disputes between individual Iraqis should also be a priority for the judicial system.

Iraqis must also learn to farm smarter. The government must phase out heavy subsidies that distort production. Subsidizing inputs like fertilizer has led to their excessive use, which is both wasteful and damaging. The government should also establish extension schools to ensure that advanced techniques are taught to farmers. State control of the agricultural sector in Iraq has been a disaster and should be reversed.

A second step is to reform Iraq's food-rationing programme, shifting from a market-distorting rationing scheme to one targeted at just the poorest Iraqis. Domestic farmers cannot compete with subsidized imports and deserve a fair chance to sell their produce. As long as Iraqis are able to buy imported packs of food for just a few cents, domestic production will never revive. By using cash grants, the government could ensure that those who cannot pay do not go hungry.

A third step is to upgrade the quality of Iraq's irrigated land. Difficult flat conditions, combined with mismanagement, have led to considerable degradation of existing farmland. Three-quarters of Iraq's arable land is affected by salinization, nutrient depletion or high water tables. Agricultural yields have fallen gradually since the 1960s.

Techniques are available to restore fertility to these lands, but they require considerable investment in both infrastructure and education for farmers. The development board should invest heavily in upgrading existing irrigation and drainage schemes. There is also considerable potential for new irrigation schemes. The UN's Food and Agriculture Organization (FAO) concluded in 1990 that Iraq had potential for cultivating 5.5 million hectares of irrigated land. In 1993, only one-third of that was actually irrigated.

The fourth and most fundamental step is to ensure an adequate flow of fresh water. The key input for Iraq's irrigated agricultural sector is river water. Around 50 per cent of the flow from the Tigris and 90 per cent from the Euphrates comes from outside the borders of Iraq. The flows of these rivers are down 50 per cent from their historical rates, primarily due to the construction of mammoth dams in Turkey and Syria. This decreased flow, combined with pollution, has caused widespread damage. It used to be possible to fish the Tigris year-round for a number of edible fish (such as *shabbut*, *gittan* and *bunni*), but this is now possible only in the spring and early summer. And the problem is only getting worse. Iraq needs quick action on a lasting agreement with Syria and Turkey on the allocation of water rights.

Finally, rebuilding Iraq also means rebuilding national pride. A quick step towards this goal would be to have the development board replant Iraq's historic date palms. These stately plants – the *nakhlas* – have played a significant role in the country's history. Some even credit the date palms with being the primary reason Iraqis have never starved. Just as Russian soldiers used to carry sunflower seeds in their pockets during winter, Iraqis, especially Bedouin, knew that the date palm could always provide their next meal. There were once 30 million date palms in Iraq, but decades of war have severely reduced the numbers. As a first step in date palm revival, these trees should be planted proudly along the routes from international airports to all centres of business. Singapore's founding father, Lee Kuan Yew, once noted that his strategy of planting beautiful trees along the routes travelled by foreign investors was his most cost-effective development strategy of all.

Agriculture in Iraq has never met its long-term potential. Iraq's rich natural resources make farming a strong candidate for investment to diversify the economy, and would have the additional benefits of delivering employment to rural areas and improving food security and nutrition. Large-scale public investment must be backed by fundamental reforms to land ownership rules to unlock private entrepreneurship which has been suppressed for too long by state domination.

Building on an ancient legacy: tourism

Iraq is a land full of religion, romance and legend. It is the land of Imam Ali, Abraham, the hanging gardens of Babylon and the Arabian Nights. Iraq has religious, historical and archaeological sites worthy of a flourishing tourism industry. In the near term, the security situation makes the development of these assets virtually impossible, but in the longer term tourism should become an outstanding part of the Iraqi economy.

There are several reasons for optimism. Iraq's neighbours are attracting an enormous number of visitors. The Middle East has been the world's fastest-growing regional destination in recent years, with the World Tourism Organization estimating annual growth of 16 per cent per year (compared with a global increase of just 4 per cent).

In 2007, the Middle East earned tourist receipts of $34.2 billion, almost trebling over just 10 years. Turkey generated 18.5 billion and Egypt $9.3 billion, but the most ambitious plans are for Dubai. By 2012 the dazzling city on the Gulf is expecting to host 15 million foreign visitors, more than double the 2005 figure of 6.2 million. The money spent by these tourists is essentially foreign investment without any need for repayment, and each satisfied visitor is a potential friend and ambassador for the country.

Iraq's violent recent history need not discourage investors from developing the country's tourism sector. Vibrant tourism sectors have been rapidly developed in several war-torn countries such as Vietnam and Cambodia. The recent history of war has created considerable curiosity among tourists. Vietnam has devoted considerable resources to promoting and developing tourism and saw growth of 20 per cent in 2006, earning $2.5 billion from foreign visitors.

In the shorter term, religious tourism is the most likely market segment for Iraq to exploit. This is a strategy followed by Saudi Arabia, which has seen tourist receipts soar in the last few years from $4.4 billion in 2003 to $7.9 billion in 2006. In Najaf, Karbala and Samarra, Iraq has some of the holiest sites in Islam. Mosul and Baghdad also have many sites important to other religious denominations.

In the longer term, Iraq's tourist industry should focus on great historical sites including Uruk (the city of King Gilgamesh), Ur (home of Abraham), Hatra (an archaeological Roman treasure) and Najaf, the resting place of Imam Ali and the fourth holy city of Islam. These sites are potentially as lucrative as Egypt's pyramids or Jordan's Petra. Turning these places into major tourism centres will take time. The development board must refurbish the sites with creative architecture and develop the supporting infrastructure including roads, airports, hotels and recreational and shopping facilities. The board will develop the hotels initially, but it should sell them to the private sector soon thereafter.

The future leaders of Iraq should not shy away from grand, inspirational undertakings. One such example would be the construction of a national opera house using the design created by Frank Lloyd Wright nearly 50 years ago under commission of the Iraqi government. Such a magnificent building would be a striking symbol of Iraq's progress and an architectural gem in Baghdad.

The story of the lost opera house is little-known, but fascinating. In 1957, the great American architect was summoned to Iraq to design an opera house that would be built by Iraq's Development Board. While in Baghdad, Wright spotted an underdeveloped island in the Tigris near the outskirts of the city. When Wright asked King Faisal II if he could build on the island, the king replied: 'The island, Mr Wright, is yours.' Wright renamed the building site 'The Isle of Edena' in reference to the Garden of Eden. He was so captivated by Baghdad that he went beyond his mandate and designed art museums, shopping kiosks, a university and even a planetarium. His designs were respectful of Middle Eastern tradition, incorporating domes, spires and ziggurats. But the assassination of Faisal II in 1958 and the resulting decline in Iraq's fortunes meant the large project was stillborn.

Fortunately, Wright's designs remain intact. In addition, the designs could be brought up to date by Iraqi architects such as the world-renowned, Iraqi-born Zaha Hadid. Ms Hadid should also be able to design other monumental architecture for the future Iraq.

Channelling funds towards growth: financial services

If the Iraq of tomorrow is to have a vibrant and dynamic economy, it will need an efficient and robust financial services industry that is able to transparently and effectively channel resources to where they are needed. Given the large investment outlays needed both for reconstruction and in order to develop new industries and sectors in Iraq, the new financial system must play a central role in the funding of investment opportunities. The ability to attract foreign capital to help diversify the sources for this capital, and to help underwrite the economic transformation, is vital to the future story of the state. Among the services that will be required are consumer finance, project finance, insurance, private banking, asset management, private equity and particularly venture capital.

Surveying the region, one sees that leading global financial services firms have an increased interest in establishing and expanding their institutional presence in the Middle East. Dubai, Bahrain, Saudi Arabia and Qatar are all eager to attract such institutions. The surge in oil revenues has triggered a business boom in the Gulf Cooperation Council (GCC) countries, creating a variety of business needs and therefore opportunities for financial organizations across the major sectors. It is absolutely essential for an effective economic transformation in Iraq that a sophisticated and comprehensive financial services sector be established.

Indeed, the story of this section is that Iraq can attract its share of such lucrative opportunities by building a world-class platform commensurate with its industrial, agricultural and tourism potential on top of its hydrocarbon wealth. And not only is Iraq *able* to engineer such capital inflow, it must. The existing financial system is totally inadequate. The necessary financial machinery must be attracted and encouraged to play a vital role in the new Iraq. It will include a sophisticated stock exchange, debt and equity markets, commercial banks, investment banks, venture capital and other specialized financial institutions and resources. Underpinning the entire sector, however, must be a framework of sound regulation and market oversight for ensuring fair competition, total transparency and the rule of law.

Currency reform provides a model

If financial services are to be revitalized in an Iraqi context, then financial capital – that is, currency – must play a foundational role in the reconstruction project. Towards this end, the successful introduction of a new currency provides reason for hope. The replacement of old national currencies with a new and unified national currency in 2004 was the first step in a broader process of national integration. It bridges the economic and political streams of integration and paves the way to finance more forward-looking development.

This ambitious plan for currency reform was successfully implemented as scheduled between 15 October 2003 and 15 January 2004. According to John B. Taylor, US Undersecretary of the Treasury for International Affairs, the scale of this reform is not easily overstated. In testimony before the Senate Banking, Housing and Urban Affairs Committee, Taylor noted: 'The equivalent of twenty-seven 747 plane loads of currency were delivered to Iraq and distributed to the public through approximately 240 exchange sites, mostly bank branches, under a significant security threat.'

In addition to its introduction, the sustainability and performance of the new Iraqi currency are also noteworthy. In terms of sustainability, the new notes are more difficult to counterfeit, and they circulate more effectively through the real economy. In contrast to the old currency regime of two denominations, the new Iraqi dinar has six denominations available.

Reforming the conduits of reconstruction: banking

As the conduits of financial reconstruction, Iraq's state-owned and private banks are the potential lifeblood of the country's reform efforts. It is therefore important that the current banking system undergo wholesale reform in order to make it more efficient and up-to-date.

For example, according to a study of Iraq's banking sector, the Rasheed and Rafidain banks – the two largest and wholly state-owned banks which control over 85 per cent of total banking assets – are undercapitalized and heavily constrained by a high concentration of non-performing loans in their overall loan portfolios. These difficulties are further compounded by a lack of comprehensive, modern accounting standards and systems. While these two banks have an extensive and well-established countrywide network of more than 360 branches, individual branches operate as independent units, inhibiting the potential economies of scale in any forward-looking reformist programme. Another finding of this study was that Iraq's state-owned banks unfortunately lacked centralized management and an integrated system for making and clearing payments.

Rafidain was established in 1941 as the primary commercial and central bank (the central bank function was transferred to the National Bank of Iraq in 1947). A press report from May 2003 stated that '60 out of 70 Baghdad branches are believed to be destroyed or looted' and the Iraq Policy Unit within the UK Foreign Office estimated three months later that 'one-third of the branches are open, performing minimal servicing of accounts. The majority of them are in Baghdad.'

Rasheed Bank was established in 1988–9 to compete with Rafidain and is focused exclusively on domestic banking. Its current status is, much like Rafidain's, unclear. The *Middle East Economic Digest* Special Report published in June 2003 estimated that it 'seems to have disappeared'.

It is clear that Rafidain and Rasheed, which hold 34 and 54 per cent of the total assets ($US791 million) respectively, are potentially in disastrous shape. Nevertheless, corporate relations, branch locations and brand awareness might still represent useful assets. In this sense, reinvigorating and privatizing the existing banks within Iraq should play a large part in the broader reform of the financial services sector.

Going forward, changing the orientation and objectives of state-owned banks in Iraq will be critical for any sustained reformist programme. Iraq's banks will be able to offer better service and compete regionally and globally only in the aftermath of privatization and a fundamental and sustained restructuring of management, organization, personnel and systems. As well as laying the groundwork for a more diverse financial services infrastructure, policymakers need to ensure in the near term that these institutions are able to provide basic services such as taking deposits, clearing cheques and making loans to support small and large business activities. What is needed is to establish the foundation of a responsive and competitive credit market.

An analysis by McKinsey & Company outlined a comprehensive growth outlook for Iraq based on a number of assumptions. One of these is the stable and secure development of Iraq towards a free market economy with a pro-business legal environment, implying rapid GDP growth over a ten-year period. Another assumption is the absence of numerous security issues which currently retard reform. The purpose of the exercise was to demonstrate the *potential* of a new Iraqi economy and to state persuasively that, should the war effort come to a conclusion and should the necessary reconstruction resources be provided, the Iraqi economy – both financial and real – has great potential.

The analysis projects a scenario for the future Iraqi economy. GDP is forecast to reach $US44 billion in Year Three, $57 billion in Year Five, and $88 billion in Year Ten ($47 billion in oil, $41 billion in non-oil). The supporting rationale for this scenario is that oil production will grow rapidly to reach 3.5 million b/d by Year Three, 4.5 million b/d in Year Five, and 6.5 million b/d in Year Ten, and furthermore that the non-oil sector will grow rapidly at 20 per cent per annum for four years, then at 15 per cent, finally slowing down to 8 per cent per annum.

The development of banking assets in Iraq begins from a baseline estimate that a total of $1 billion is held in the

Iraqi banking system. Based on the significant Iraqi holdings identified in other Middle Eastern banks, many of which could be quickly transferred to Iraq's banking system, three potential futures are outlined for the development of banking assets in Iraq. It is estimated that the total banking assets held there will reach $13 billion in Year Three, $29 billion in Year Five, and $88 billion in Year Ten.

The conclusion emerging from the study of banking asset development in Iraq is that while this market is still very small by international standards, and despite its high margins, the low-income market would represent a marginal business opportunity. A relatively strong presence in the corporate and small business segments is a required move for any player aspiring to have a leading position in the banking industry in Iraq.

It is forecast that Iraqi banking revenue pools will evolve from substantially all-corporate (including government) relative to retail and non-client (specifically, 2003 statistics imply that 85 to 95 per cent of revenue derives from corporate, 5 to 10 per cent from retail, and 0 to 5 per cent from non-client, including income from securities held, treasury activity, etc.). In Year Ten, the percentages of total revenue deriving from corporate, retail and non-client are 55 to 70 per cent, 20 per cent and 10 to 15 per cent respectively. (This is comparable to the 1997 split in Saudi Arabia.)

Not all paths of financial development are equal, and the Iraqi financial system should avoid becoming strictly an outward centre shifting funds away from the country towards international financial markets, or an exercise in exclusively recycling petrodollars. Iraqi bankers have a comparative advantage in assuming this funding role, given their local knowledge of the market and the business culture. To realize this potential, however, bankers must develop skills in screening, monitoring and assessing risk profiles of projects, and financial institutions themselves must develop high skills in project and structured finance. Central to both will be engagement with international firms and industry leaders, regionally and globally.

Towards a mature capital market: stocks, venture capital and regulation

At the heart of the new financial system, the stock market should have a leading role. The stock market is not only helpful for raising much needed capital, but has other useful functions to perform. If Iraq embarks on privatization, many of the public assets can be sold through the stock market. The stock market can also help family businesses to reorganize their corporate structure and obtain access to funds that would allow them to grow and compete internationally.

Many economists have argued that the stock market is also best positioned to provide effective governance mechanisms that improve the efficiency of firms and lead to an efficient allocation of resources. The very large number of publicly listed firms and the very tight disclosure rules imply that a great deal of information is disclosed. Stock markets can also help investors with risk-sharing and risk-diversification. This will lower the cost of capital for firms, ultimately enabling more competitive growth prospects as the country emerges from decades of regressive leadership.

But the mere existence of a sound conventional banking system and stock market is not enough to guarantee the due availability of seed capital for new business enterprises such as technology start-ups. It is the presence of venture capitalists and business 'angels' that generally enables entrepreneurs to develop their products sufficiently to bring them to market. Middle East and North Africa (MENA) countries do not generally have a well-developed venture capital sector, but the industry has been growing in some neighbouring countries. Iraq should aim at developing an environment that helps venture capital to nurture and finance future Iraqi entrepreneurs.

An important precondition for attracting venture capital will be to establish a legal system that can effectively protect intellectual property rights. Once the venture capitalists arrive, they can provide, among other things, an important source of funding, for micro- and small enterprises (MSEs) by providing microcredit and unlocking the potential of those Iraqis who are entrepreneurial but who lack the collateral for conventional borrowing. Microfinance – which became more widely known when the Bangladeshi economist Muhammed Yunus and his Grameen Bank shared the Nobel Peace Prize in 2006 – provides very small loans (microloans) to the unemployed, poor entrepreneurs and to others living in poverty who are not considered bankable. Because these individuals lack collateral, steady employment and a credit history, they are unable to meet the minimum requirements for traditional bank credit. Many of the microcredit borrowers are women, and the default rate has been negligible. The objective of microcredit has been to encourage the start-up or expansion of microenterprise. For example, ambitious individuals could use a small loan to buy a sewing machine, fishing rods, or any other item to help them begin to earn a steady income. Borrowers could also engage in selling craft products or agricultural produce.

A primary prerequisite of a sophisticated financial system is to establish a world-class regulatory and legal infrastructure that includes standards, processes, legal certainty and enforceability. Good governance, fairness, protection and transparency are the foundations for a robust and reliable financial sector. The independence of the central bank is another prerequisite. By preventing the central bank from engaging in inflationary financing of the government, the central bank law ensures the process of rolling out a sound and confidence-inspiring monetary policy regime.

Creating a sound supervisory and regulatory regime is a further critical step on the way to establishing a credible financial system. One way to realize this goal is to employ technical assistance from advanced countries, but best practices are observable in financial services sectors worldwide.

Looking towards future growth: technology

For Iraq to truly become a first-world nation, it must embrace the information age. Technology and innovation are the primary drivers of productivity growth in advanced economies. These gains come from the application of new engineering and scientific knowledge, the use of better management processes such as just-in-time inventory, and the process of creative destruction whereby innovative firms take market share from stagnant firms. The stories of Silicon Valley, Bangalore and Hsinchu provide clear examples of how great economies have risen from a technological spring. The creation of an Education and Technology Board would help Iraq in this regard. The board could oversee the development of investment parks in Iraq that become magnets for profitable ideas.

Silicon Valley grew from such a seed, evolving from the Stanford Research Park, which was established by the visionary electrical engineering professor Fred Terman. Early in his career, Terman had sought ways to encourage his best students to stay in California, especially ones who would work in the new field of radio engineering. One of his first steps was to bring together two of his former students, William Hewlett and David Packard, who founded Hewlett-Packard in 1939.

Not satisfied with his earlier success, Terman in the early 1950s devised a way to accelerate the development of technology companies in the area. He helped set up a small industrial building on Stanford land that was rented to technology companies at a low cost. Terman also arranged ways for the top employees of the new companies to study at Stanford. Eastman Kodak, General Electric, Lockheed and Hewlett-Packard were early tenants of his project. Also during this time, Terman encouraged William Shockley, co-inventor of the transistor, to return to his home town of Palo Alto, and by 1956 Shockley was producing four-layer diodes. Only a year later, in a move that would signal how fast technology companies would evolve, eight of Shockley's talented young engineers left to establish Fairchild Semiconductor, the foundation of the semiconductor industry. Employees from Fairchild eventually founded 38 other new companies, including Intel.

Terman himself summed up the amazing success of the Stanford Research Park: 'When we set out to create a community of technical scholars in Silicon Valley, there wasn't much here and the rest of the world looked awfully big. Now a lot of the rest of the world is here.'

A decade later, another visionary, Kwoh-ting Li, was just as determined to make Taiwan a leader in technology. Li, who over his career served as chairman of the Industrial Development Commission, minister of economic affairs and minister of finance, pushed for decades for Taiwan to look outward in its quest to develop. His efforts led in 1973 to the creation of the Industrial Technology Research Institute, an R&D centre for industry focused on hardware and semiconductor technologies. They also led in 1980 to the creation of the Hsinchu Science-based Industrial Park, Taiwan's version of the Stanford Research Park. Since Hsinchu was established, the Taiwanese government has invested $1.7 billion in park infrastructure and facilities and has earned a high rate of return for this investment. At the end of 2004, 384 high-tech companies were located in the park and were generating $15.7 billion a year in exports – 8.5 per cent of Taiwan's total.

Minister Li made sure that the investment park received the capital and talent it needed to succeed. He invited overseas Chinese investors to set up local venture capital operations to invest in Taiwanese companies. As a result, Taiwan now boasts one of the more sophisticated venture capital industries. Li also set up government offices in Silicon Valley, where tens of thousands of Taiwanese worked. The elite National Taiwan University had created a pool of talent that was ready to come home. In essence, Taiwan had all the ingredients for success, and businesses, anticipating knowledge spillover benefits, clustered in Hsinchu Science-based Park.

A decade after Taiwan's growth explosion, India emerged as a technology leader. In the late 1980s and early 1990s, India took substantial steps to end its long, painful experience with autarky. One of its better policies was the establishment in

Bangalore of Software Technology Parks of India (STPI), which gave tax exemptions to export-oriented firms in designated zones for five years and guaranteed these firms access to high-speed satellite links and reliable electricity. This policy, combined with other liberalization measures, led to the creation of STPI Bangalore, an envy of the developing world. Bangalore has always been one of the most beautiful Indian cities, with hundreds of acres of green parks and imposing granite buildings. Today it is one of the software capitals of the world as well.

Like Taiwan, Bangalore had a large pool of expatriates to draw on. Nearly every student from the elite Indian Institutes of Technology emigrated during the 1970s and 1980s. By 1998, there were 30,000 Indian professionals working in Silicon Valley, with Indian engineers running more than 775 technology companies that accounted for turnover of $3.6 billion. With the right policies, India – and particularly Bangalore – was able to lure many of these expats home. As these professionals returned, they transferred technological know-how and other business skills. They brought capital, advanced managerial techniques and global business networks – all key ingredients in innovation. Bangalore also offered an advantage that surpassed even Taiwan – an abundance of English-speaking, low-wage workers.

Looking at these three examples, the elements of a successful science and technology park emerge. First, high-quality universities are needed to train students in science and engineering. Second, these students must be encouraged to hone their skills in the leading technological centres of the world. Third, science and technology industrial parks should be formed near these universities. Fourth, firms that locate in such parks must be offered incentives such as lower taxes, a stable power supply and access to the most advanced communications infrastructure. Fifth, the location of the science and technology park should be as beautiful as possible, so that the brightest expat workers will be attracted to return home.

Iraq has a long road ahead of it before it becomes the next Bangalore. But if it finds a leader with the determination and skill of a Kwoh-ting Li, anything is possible. At the start of the twentieth century, no one would have guessed that Taiwan, India and California would become technological centres of the world. And no one knows what countries or regions will be at the forefront in another 50 years.

In terms of manpower, Iraq already has a vital ingredient for success. Like India, it has numerous nationals scattered abroad, working in various fields of science and technology, who could in the future use their skills for the benefit of Iraq itself. They must have the right environment and facilities to encourage them to return permanently or as visitors. There could be a network of Iraqi professional scientists and technology experts spread across the world, linked through the internet and other modern communications. This could help Iraq in the vital process of technology transfer.

To expedite its integration into the modern technology- and knowledge-driven global economy, the new Iraq must overcome any inhibitions about utilizing foreign expertise. During the 1960s, Singapore made a deliberate decision to reject the conventional wisdom that foreign multinational corporations were exploitative. In fact, Singapore benefited from their technology transfer, and it used American multinationals to lay the foundations of its large high-tech electronic industry. Sectors where significant foreign know-how is going to be critical in Iraq include oil, economy, education and technology. Leading international figures could serve on the boards of establishments in these sectors. Foreign experts are equally essential to run training centres and provide administrative skills. Other areas where foreign know-how will be vital are tourism, healthcare, agriculture and financial services. In these sectors, in particular, foreign companies should be attracted to invest and engage in long-term development.

The approach being adopted in Singapore is one example of top leadership preparing for this new world. Prime Minister Lee Hsien Loong embraces the fact that globalization has moved beyond industry and is penetrating the knowledge economy. He has said: 'New technologies allow us to embed knowledge processing in every object, and link people and organizations in networks that are always on, always connected.' Countries are positioning themselves for the growing competition in the knowledge economy, and Lee thinks Singapore is likely to do well. This is partly because 'our ethos is open, cosmopolitan and pragmatic. Our society is meritocratic and egalitarian.' Singapore has long made a living from knowledge, but 'we still face a sharp change of phase, and we must move fast to adapt'.

Lee is keen for every person in Singapore to have the opportunity to access and exploit information: 'There will be no barrier to knowledge, information and lifelong learning.' He says that globalization will 'force nations to reallocate resources, restructure their economies and reorient their societies for the future. Singaporeans accept this as a given. We are remaking ourselves into a key node in the global knowledge network, securing our place under the sun.'

Building a new capital city: a bold stride into the future

The new Iraq, I recommend, should have a new capital. I strongly believe that this would be one of the most exciting, dramatic and beneficial projects that could be undertaken by the country's future leaders. A shining new city would be a symbolic as well as a concrete break with the past, presenting limitless horizons for new generations.

For the past 50 years, the Iraqi people have been impoverished by a closed economy, isolated by closed borders, stifled by a closed intellectual climate and traumatized by a tyrannical and violent political system. The regimes that ruled the pre-1958 Iraq shredded the fabric of society. They drove away some of the country's most talented and ambitious citizens and cruelly oppressed those who stayed behind with stifling laws, a rigid bureaucracy and an economy choked by corruption and cronyism. What better way to erase this malign legacy than with a new and inspiring capital city?

A new capital could go a long way towards freeing people from the psychological shackles of the past and helping them to raise their aspirations. Its well-planned and generously funded facilities and institutions would nourish the new Iraq's principles of cultural vibrancy, academic excellence, technological innovation, economic dynamism and political freedom. The new capital would become a shining example for Iraq's other cities, as well as for those of the region and indeed the world. Rather than fleeing, as they did from the old Iraq, the country's brightest and best will flock to the new capital, glad to live and work in a place where they can make their dreams come true.

To see why a new capital is so necessary, one need only

look at Baghdad. Centuries ago, Iraq's present capital was a prosperous and beautiful world centre of science, philosophy, medicine and the arts. Unforgivably, the oppressive military takeovers allowed large parts of the city to become crowded, disorganized and unhealthy. And those few residential quarters that used to be pleasant, prosperous and safe have, under the chaos of the occupation, deteriorated as well. In short, the city has more stacked against it than it has going for it. Most significantly, the fighting since the 2003 occupation has taken a terrible toll, not only in physical destruction, but also in massive population shifts and the division of the city into walled, ethnically based, heavily armed sectors.

As well as overcoming the problems of an overpopulated Baghdad, a new city could avoid the inefficiencies of contemporary suburban sprawl by planning in harmony with the natural environment, by facilitating a broad spectrum of economic activity and by encouraging social integration. Masterminded by the Iraqi National Development Board, the new capital would offer a fresh start and embody the hopes of a rising nation.

While the idea of a new capital may seem shocking to some Iraqis, there are many precedents around the world for such a dramatic undertaking. In the past, leaders have created new capitals for a variety of reasons. Brasilia, for example, was established in 1960 to help develop Brazil's underpopulated interior. Ankara was created in 1923 to help integrate Turkey from a central location and to escape the entrenched interests of Istanbul. Canberra was created in 1911 after a long dispute over whether Sydney or Melbourne should be the capital of the new Commonwealth of Australia. And Washington, DC was created in 1790 as part of a complicated compromise.

Alexander Hamilton wanted the new government of the United States to assume the war debts of the individual states, and it was the northern states that had the largest debts. The southern states agreed to the debt plan, but only after the north conceded that the capital would be located in the south. George Washington subsequently chose the site of the capital a few miles up the Potomac river from his home.

In a similar way to Washington, new capitals in other countries have symbolised a new political direction and created a unifying focus for different groups. Ottawa, for example, forged a link between French Canada and English Canada while Chandigarh unites two states of India. In the same way, Iraq's new capital could potentially bring together the country's ethnic and religious groups.

Within the Gulf region itself, there are several examples of new cities rising high above sparkling waters, offering a vision of modernity, prosperity and cultural vibrancy. Visiting Dubai, for example, is always an inspirational experience. This modern and cosmopolitan city is described as the jewel of the Gulf because of the sparkle of its daring and beautiful skyline. The best architects in the world have fashioned uniquely bold skyscrapers and world-class communities where once there was little but sand and water. Abu Dhabi, for its part, is building an entire new cultural city and encouraging museums such as the Louvre and the Guggenheim to establish a presence. Both have developed in the past 25 years and both are currently attracting millions of international tourists every year.

Iraq – a vast museum in itself, with considerable archaeological treasures – deserves a central, modern capital. Baghdad, of course, will maintain its historical, industrial and commercial importance. But a new Iraqi capital would offer a host of advantages. The construction of such a project would be likely to take between four years (the time it took to build Brasilia) and ten years (as was the case with Washington). Such a massive undertaking would help absorb Iraq's unemployed workers and would develop a whole new class of skilled builders. And though it would be an expensive undertaking, it would cost far less than attempting to upgrade Baghdad to a similar level. Indeed, once the government had taken the lead in setting the parameters of the capital's development, it would quickly become a magnet for private real estate investment and a boost to Iraq's economy.

The location of this new city will be very important, and I would like to suggest the shores of Lake Tharthar. Situated in the middle of Iraq north of Baghdad, this lake is the largest body of water in the country and its shoreline is now mostly unpopulated. Residents of the new capital would be able to look out on a vista as broad and bright as the future of their country.

As always, real estate developers create value by transforming less expensive land into high-priced property by creating demand. The land surrounding Lake Tharthar is a vast tract of empty desert, currently owned by the government. Today it is worthless due to lack of demand. Designing a world-class future capital for one of the wealthiest countries in the region should be an attractive value-creation project. Conceptually, this should be a self-financing venture. It would undoubtedly be one of the most valuable real estate value-creation projects in the Middle East.

Other examples in the region speak for themselves. In the case of Dubai, Abu Dhabi, Doha, Riyadh and Jeddah, one has only to compare real estate prices before and after development to realize the appreciation in value. The proof is also evident elsewhere in places such as Singapore, Sardinia in Italy, Palm Beach in Florida, Las Vegas in Nevada and Bangalore in India.

From its very beginnings, the new capital would need to be organized and managed by a National Capital Commission, similar to those in many other countries. Reporting directly to the Prime Minister, this body would comprise a few select members chosen from the national and international community. It could have a national figure as its president and would also include prominent architects, landscape designers and city administrators.

The commission's first task would be to organize an international design competition to come up with a master plan for the new capital. Once the design was chosen, the commission would then marshal resources for delivering the project. While the new capital would obviously evolve over time, its development ought to adhere to the pre-agreed plan in both its visionary and its practical elements. Following the initial competition, the design of all major public institutions could be put out to competition in the same way. The city's various neighbourhoods should then be constructed and integrated into the overall framework established by the original plan. The commission would supervise the necessary design competitions and coordinate the work of all the architects involved. It would also appoint administrators to manage the city's various functions and services on a day-to-day basis.

It is important that the new capital avoids industry pollution: products, after all, can be manufactured elsewhere. Instead, it should provide a base for high-tech, Silicon Valley-type industries. As well as adding a highly productive sector to the capital's economy, these industries would create an outlet for research carried out at the city's new university. At the same time, the development of first-rate financial, educational, tourist, recreational and official government infrastructure and institutions will attract further wealth-creating traffic to the city.

Turning this vision into reality will require top world-class urban planning. It must take into consideration the need to build on a human scale, provide attractive parks and other public spaces, and take advantage of the views, atmosphere and activities that a waterside location offers.

The new capital should have at its heart a system of parks linking conservation areas and the lake-front promenade with small neighbourhood gardens and play areas for children. This series of public spaces should incorporate ceremonial routes, plazas and squares and tree-lined avenues and boulevards. It should be a showcase for landscape development in the region and could help to develop a local landscape know-how. This in turn could become known all over the world in the same way that Brazil and Mexico fostered their own landscape traditions with designers such as Roberto Burle-Marx and Luis Barragan.

In my mind's eye, I see the crowded, narrow and deteriorating streets and structures of Baghdad giving way to clean, beautiful avenues and boulevards, flanked by the most attractive and functional buildings imaginable. Iraq's new capital should of course adhere to the highest environmental standards and base its development on an eco-friendly local economy. From its overall design to the detail of its buildings, the city should embody energy-efficient concepts and be a model of sustainable development. The emphasis should be on buildings of architectural excellence housing government ministries and other non-polluting facilities. Such a beautiful, clean and well-planned metropolis would then become a tourist destination in itself, like other great world capitals, adding another sustainable pillar to its economy. And critically, the new city should be designed for security, making it a safe place to locate a new government.

Through good design, I see the capital fostering genuine communities. Architecture and landscaping should reflect the traditions, history and expectations of local people. Streets and squares should be safe, convenient and interesting, encouraging people to get out and enjoy their environment. Each neighbourhood should be compact, pedestrian-friendly and mixed-use. Within each locality, housing of different types and price levels can bring people of different ages and incomes into daily interaction, strengthening the personal and civic bonds essential to an authentic community.[2]

The new capital should also have a comprehensive, energy-efficient public transport system, both within its boundaries and with links to the rest of Iraq and to international destinations. Rail connections would be particularly important to reduce dependence on the automobile (a rapid transit system to Baghdad would be a prime requirement), but the system should also include superb air and road links.

Iraq's new political capital, in my view, should also become the country's main centre for culture, education, medicine, sports and technology. I envisage museums of all kinds, some displaying the artefacts of Iraq's rich and ancient civilization; others devoted to the vibrant creations of today's and tomorrow's artists. Centres for the performing arts would showcase dramatic and musical performances of international calibre. And young people eager to become actors, singers, musicians, painters or sculptors would flock to this new capital's many academies for training in the arts.

For higher education in other fields, there would be universities and colleges rivalling the best in the world for the youth of Iraq. Sports, too, will be an important part of the new capital, not just for professional athletes, but for everyone. In addition to modern stadiums there would be training facilities, sports centres and fields where people of all skills could enjoy the benefits of exercise, friendly competition, and camaraderie. And perhaps some day these facilities could be the site of important regional competitions and even the Olympics.

I envisage the new capital as a world-class centre for high-tech education, innovation and application – the Silicon Valley of the Middle East. One of the most important functions of the new capital will be to help Iraqis escape the country's past isolation and take full advantage of globalization. By embracing the possibilities that technological expertise offers, Iraq can join the leading ranks of the world's most dynamic economies, taking its place alongside Taiwan, Indonesia, China and Singapore.

As part of this endeavour, the new capital should include an international university linked to other centres of research and learning around the world. As well as teaching traditional subjects in the arts and sciences, the new university would research fields that lend themselves to the geography and culture of this part of the world. I have in mind subjects such as water conservation, desert agriculture and solar energy. In these different ways, the university could become a centre of excellence in some of today's leading scientific and academic disciplines.

The technology park in Iraq's new capital should be well planned, totally integrated and an excellent place to work. World-class educational facilities will attract Iraq's top students to study engineering, computing and other sciences. Side by side with these will be research centres aiming to find practical and profitable applications for new technologies.

Finally, I envision a third, connected campus, containing innovative high-tech companies. An attractive and environmentally sound physical setting is crucial, as has been demonstrated by the well-planned high-tech centres in Taiwan, Singapore and India. People work best in an environment that is conducive to the safe, clean and attractive completion of their duties. Along these lines, the physical and mental welfare of those working in the technology park would be served by excellent exercise facilities; lush, peaceful, landscaped parks, and splendid living quarters. I believe this component of the new capital would ignite the spirit of the new Iraq, enabling bright and ambitious young Iraqis to attain their highest aspirations in their own country.

This dream of a high-tech paradise is based on similar successes in the real world. In an age of globalization, Western companies have taken advantage of the time and money savings made possible by outsourcing back-office work such as accounting, human resources and IT. Some international financial institutions outsource their stock research and data maintenance. Highly trained radiologists read and interpret medical scans sent from the other side of the globe. The potential profits and benefits for Iraq would be significant. For example, US firms spend more than twice as much, on average, for IT services and software as for hardware. Once it becomes connected to the high-capacity data routes that make this possible, the technology park in Iraq's new capital could perform these functions, and offer stiff competition to similar centres in India, Singapore and Taiwan.

Businesses in the new capital would benefit from locations

that were attractive to their employees and conducive to their operations. Shops and restaurants would be built alongside residential areas that housed Iraqis from all segments of the population, for cities come to life only when they are filled with people, day and night – working, learning, playing, eating and sleeping. I see children running and laughing in green and pleasant parks; families enjoying a meal at a waterside restaurant; the country's best students studying earnestly at a new, world-class university, eager to reach their potential in their own country, in their own capital, rather than leaving their homes to go abroad. This is all part of my dream for the Iraq of tomorrow.

The economic transformation that Iraq must undergo is both challenging and comprehensive. It is difficult to overstate the extent of the redevelopment and progress that must be achieved to make possible a positive and viable future for the Iraqi people. Iraq must be rebuilt in every corner and in every sector. The country has a long journey to travel before it is transformed into a vibrant, dynamic and prosperous nation integrated with the rest of the world. But with the right institutions and development strategies, and an honourable, skilled and determined leadership, Iraq has the potential to achieve prosperity and development.

Indeed, the story of this chapter is that Iraq can attract its share of such lucrative, global opportunities by building a world-class platform commensurate with its industrial, agricultural and tourism potential on top of its hydrocarbon wealth. And not only is Iraq *able* to engineer such capital inflow, it *must*. The existing bank-based financial system should undergo fundamental structural reform. The necessary financial machinery must be brought in and encouraged to play a vital role in the new Iraq. This will include a sophisticated stock exchange, debt and equity markets, commercial banks, investment banks and specialized financial institutions. Underpinning the entire sector, however, is a necessary framework of sound regulation and market oversight, set in the political arena.

One also hopes that Iraq's future planners will try to ensure that Iraq equips itself to participate fully in the new, global, knowledge economy. As in Singapore, it would be beneficial for Iraq's future leadership to have a forward-looking and creative outlook.

But the most dramatic, symbolic and inspirational project that needs to be undertaken is the construction of a new capital to embody the aspirations of the people of the new Iraq. Such a massive but necessary and exciting undertaking would focus the population on the future, encouraging Iraq's people to work as one nation towards a brighter tomorrow.

In the following chapter, I discuss how this brighter tomorrow must take into consideration not only the political and economic well-being of the country, but the social and physical well-being of its people.

9

Developing the greatest resource

Iraq can become a great country only if its people are healthy, educated and comfortably housed. Oil may be the foundation of the economy, but the chief resource is the people, a fact too often ignored by the country's past leaders.

One of the lessons from the coup of 1958, which curtailed the activities of the previous Iraqi Development Board, is that infrastructural investments alone, whatever their economic justifications, are slow to deliver benefits to ordinary citizens. Worse, they can be seen as biased towards the wealthy, who tend to benefit most directly as the productivity of their assets is enhanced. Thus, while previous chapters have shown how to develop various sectors of the economy, I would now like to focus on the need for Iraq's future leaders to pay special attention as well to the more immediate and tangible needs of the people, providing them with education, housing and healthcare.

Reviving a proud past: education

A first-class educational system is the key to Iraq's future. An educated electorate is one of the building blocks of an advanced society. For example, once Iraqi children are taught about the promising first steps their country took after independence, their psychological horizons will expand, making it natural for them to imagine a unified, prosperous and free Iraq which they can help build. In addition, a system of public and private schools that accepts the children of all Iraqis, and presents a curriculum that promotes tolerance and respect, would provide a crucial first step in the long process of national reconciliation and healing that must take place in the years to come. In addition, the teachers and schools of tomorrow will also be responsible for preparing their students to enter an economy that will demand the best talents in all fields of knowledge, but especially mathematics, sciences and technology.

The rehabilitation, reconstruction and renewal of Iraq's education system, once the best in the Arab world, will require sustained investment, attention and care from all involved: parents, teachers, administrators, government officials and those in the private sector. A substantial down-payment on the country's education will provide untold dividends in the future.

There are three principal reasons to be optimistic about education in Iraq.

First, Iraq possesses a centuries-old intellectual tradition. In fact, at one point, the country had one of the oldest universities in the world – Mustansiriyya University, founded in 1280. The Abbasid rulers, with their capital in Baghdad, presided over a golden age in which the city was the intellectual centre of the world, attracting the best philosophers, mathematicians, poets and medical practitioners. Iraq is fortunate to have a legacy of learning, during its modern history as well. Having made a good start during the constitutional monarchy, the country achieved almost universal school enrolment by the 1970s. Iraq, in fact, used to boast one of the best educational systems in the entire Middle East region.

Second, there is now space for reform without concern. Because conditions are so desperate, Iraqis are begging for change. This circumstance would provide educational reformers with a wide degree of latitude.

Third, Iraq may have domestic access to rich resources and a natural endowment base with which to finance a substantial investment in education.

However, like all sectors, Iraq's population of teachers, professors and other education professionals has been seriously harmed by the unrest of recent years. A precise assessment of the state of education in Iraq is necessarily complicated by years of repression and violence. As a result, reliable data over the past decade is unavailable. Nevertheless, a two-pronged strategy has been proposed by the United Nations Educational Scientific and Cultural Organization (UNESCO), focused on both restoring normalcy in the short term and creating national capacity-building in the long term.

According to research by UNESCO published in 2003, 'Recent events and the backlog of unmet needs after two decades of war, dictatorship, sanctions and isolation have created a unique challenge now confronting both the Iraqi people and the international community.' As their report, *Situation Analysis of Education in Iraq*, states,[1] the key asset of Iraq is the education of its citizenry. Consequently, the renewal and resumption of educational services is a precondition for any broader strategy designed to promote national unity and dem-ocratization processes.

Notwithstanding the historical ambition for education in Iraq, the process of reconstruction is advancing slowly by all accounts. While the US-led occupation in Iraq can cite some limited progress as it tries to restore basic services – such as having funded the repair of nearly 2,400 schools – it has fallen well short of its goals in key areas. And education is no different.

The renewal of Iraq's education sector requires the simultaneous renewal of all levels of education, so that no generation – let alone no child – is left behind. In particular, addressing the state of education in Iraq requires tackling five main concerns.

First, the right to education in Iraq must be ensured. Undermined in the past, as indicated by the stagnation in enrolment rates and the weak internal efficiency of the system, the fundamental right of all Iraqis to receive a quality education must be established.

Second, the National Education and Technology Board must address the issue of the quality of education by specifically rectifying the terms of service, on-going retraining, remuneration and qualifications of teachers. Low salaries encourage teachers to supplement their minimal income by providing private tuition, and many of the best teachers have simply left the profession. Raising teachers' pay to a level that is appropriate and sufficient to support the individual's necessary financial obligations is a critical step in advancing the state of education in Iraq.

Third, central to any education reform or restoration is the rehabilitation of school buildings. Physical infrastructure in Iraq, educational facilities included, has suffered intensely during recent decades. Damage and looting have taken a heavy toll on all school premises. In order to lay the groundwork for phased rehabilitation and reconstruction activities, the first step is to undertake a comprehensive survey, isolating the pockets of greatest need. It will then be necessary to ensure the safety and functionality of all facilities from elementary to professional education. In the longer term, a more systematic programme for modern infrastructure development should be undertaken, maintaining the highest standards.

Fourth, beyond the physical facilities, the curriculum must also be totally renewed. Related to the task of upgrading teacher credentials and teacher training, the task of formulating an effective curriculum that meets the needs of Iraqi children and young professionals today is central to the wider process of educational reform and is bound to entail a phased approach. The paramount principle is that the quality of education matters more than the quantity. The new Education and Technology Board should set clear educational standards and then hold local schools accountable for them: funding must be linked to results. This means regularly testing students to ensure that they are advancing. If a school's performance does not measure up to the expected standards, parents must have the option of sending their children to other schools. Furthermore, integrating modern pedagogy with current information and communications technology and, importantly, the methods of distance learning, can allow Iraqis themselves to knowledgeably participate in developmental processes.

Similarly, at the vocational level there is an urgent need to review the curriculum and replace outdated equipment. Establishing an effective network of technical and vocational schools that train workers for employment would be an important step towards returning talented young individuals to the workforce. Such training could take place in existing schools, new schools or even private training centres. In Singapore, public–private training centres were created to give workers four to six months' experience of operating in a factory-like environment to become familiar with the work systems and culture of foreign employers.

In particular, national educational standards must place a heavy emphasis on maths and science, which have an obvious strong link to economic growth. Eric Hanushek of Stanford calculated that a one standard deviation difference on maths and science tests was related to a one percentage point difference in GDP per capita growth rates. This has a major and cumulative impact over time, and helps explain why the countries known as the Asian Tigers (Hong Kong, Singapore, South Korea and Taiwan) grew so rapidly in the second half of the twentieth century. An economy that grows annually at 2 per cent instead of 1 per cent will, over 50 years, attain incomes that are nearly two-thirds larger. Unfortunately, only 5 per cent of students in Arab universities study for a scientific degree, compared with 20 per cent in South Korea – an example Iraq should emulate.

Fifth and finally, no reform is possible without an improvement in educational management and information services, inspired by the deep experience of the ministry of education. Staff will need to be retrained and reacquainted with modern methods of pedagogy as well as with information and communications technology.

Despite many challenges, I believe the educational system in Iraq has great potential because there has long existed among the population a culture of learning and merit-based advancement. I have already mentioned the rise of Fadhil al-Jamali, largely due to his academic achievements. In addition, the national baccalaureate exam, which for decades has been taken at the end of high school, continues today. The exam has allowed children of humble origins who achieve high scores to get a free college education in Iraq or abroad.

Creating a world-class educational system will mean nothing if it is not accessible, well-governed and firmly rooted in the community. I believe these goals can be attained if schools receive the benefits of participation by both the private and public sectors. Although local government should fund and operate free public schools that serve the majority of the country's communities, private schools should also play a major part. And financial need should not prevent any Iraqi child from attending a school chosen by their parents. One way that parental choice can be guaranteed is through a system of providing vouchers that would pay for private school tuition. Every child in Iraq must have the chance to learn, and if a child possesses the qualifications, he or she should be able to study at any school. Competition among schools to attract the required number of students would ensure the highest standards.

Each level of government would have its role in ensuring quality education for all. Among the ministry of education's duties would be to maintain a department devoted to establishing world-class standards and making certain that schools comply with them. This department would also act as a rating agency for all schools and would issue examination questions for nationwide graduation exams at elementary and secondary levels.

Regional governments, in turn, would fund and operate institutions of higher education that would offer free education to residents of the region. Of course, there would also be private universities and colleges that would charge tuition and offer scholarships. The voucher system would not apply to higher education. In addition to operating colleges and universities, regional governments would also establish and operate vocational colleges and training centres. These would also be free and could, in certain circumstances, offer payments as an incentive to students who are studying a vocation deemed particularly necessary in the community.

The healthy effects of local control and community involvement are best seen at the elementary and secondary school level. Here, local taxes would fund the public school system. This would be overseen by local boards made up of parents and elected or appointed officials who would guarantee the kind of accountability that improves performance. Private schools would obtain funds from other sources, but they would be required to meet nationwide educational standards and be licensed by local government.

The returns on education are among the highest of any government spending. Education is also an essential element of productivity growth – the key to higher living standards. Not only are workers in educated populations more efficient, but new technologies and information are diffused more rapidly.

Educational benefits spill over into all aspects of society. For example, improved nutrition and early diagnosis of illness have both been linked to education. One study has shown that an additional year of maternal schooling in developing nations leads to 5 to 10 per cent decline in child mortality rates. Education even brings agricultural benefits. In India, educated farmers switch to better-yielding seeds and their less-educated neighbours follow their example, reducing poverty all round. Especially important in the case of Iraq is the fact that education is essential to achieving democracy. The Harvard economist Robert Barro has demonstrated that the propensity for democracy is linked to primary schooling and the educational attainment of women. Moreover, an educated population is more likely to hold its government accountable.

The ancient Greek biographer Diogenes Laertius wrote in the third century: 'The foundation of every state is the education of its youth.' This is even truer today because education and knowledge are the heart of any modern society. If Iraq succeeds in building a world-class education system, it will eventually succeed in everything else.

A workforce for the future: labour markets

Many of Iraq's economic problems and labour-market failures stem from the political disputes, security crises and bad economic policies endemic during the dictatorship, followed by the afflictions of the occupation period. However, I believe that once stability and order have been restored, it will be necessary to address the problems that prevent the country's workforce from being fully utilized.

Present labour market dynamics in Iraq's formal economy – slow job creation in the public sector resulting from the de-Baathification programme, and the inability of the formal economy to absorb surplus labour in a time of rapid population expansion – have not only contributed to absolute unemployment but have also forced many Iraqis to work for sub-standard wages in the growing informal economy. Addressing slow job creation in Iraq's formal economy and the growing participation in the country's urban informal economy, together with current demographic trends and rapid population growth, is further complicated by the unavailability of reliable statistics. Iraq's last official census, conducted in 1977, reported a population of 21.7 million people. However, there are serious doubts about the reliability of this figure. And in addition to questions about Iraq's absolute population, the rate of growth is similarly unclear. As of 2004, the International Monetary Fund estimated that the country's population was growing at the alarming rate of 2.7 per cent per annum, in line with the high population growth figures throughout the Arab world.

What is clear from the available data is that Iraq's population reflects trends broadly consistent with the experience in the Middle East, resembling, in particular, patterns found in the region's other oil rentier states. To consider the region at large, nearly 36 per cent of the population is less than 15 years old. And more than 20 per cent are between 15 and 24 years of age. Consequently, a 'youth bulge' has emerged in Iraq, exacerbating the implications of underemployment and informal economies. And among the youth, unemployment in Iraq is particularly problematic. One report estimates that 60 per cent of Iraqi youth are unemployed, double the national average. (Unemployment is variously estimated at between 25 and 60 per cent.)

So long as population flows remain unstable, there is little hope of laying the foundations of a thriving formal labour market. A recent report by the UNHCR contends that the current conflict in Iraq has created the largest population displacement in the Middle East since the displacement of Palestinians in 1948. As many as 2 million Iraqis have fled the country to Jordan and Syria since 2003, and another 1.7 million have been internally displaced. The poor conditions in the country during the near term guarantee that the problem of population displacement and emigration will continue. And while the UNHCR estimates that an additional half a million people will be displaced within the next year, the Iraqi Red Crescent anticipates twice as many. In October 2003, the UNHCR estimated that more than 4.7 million Iraqis had left their homes, many in need of humanitarian care. Of these, more than 2.7 million Iraqis were displaced internally, while more than 2 million had fled to neighbouring states, particularly Syria and Jordan. Many were displaced prior to 2003, but the largest number has fled since. In 2006, Iraqis became the leading nationality seeking asylum in Europe.

The root cause of displacement has been sectarian violence, which has, of course, had negative consequences for the labour pool. Without a secure environment, the labour market cannot bounce back. The principal consequence of displacement for labour markets is the broad-based depletion of the professional class, which is crippling efforts to rebuild Iraqi society.

Having failed to provide for security, the occupation-installed Iraqi government lacks a comprehensive policy towards the informal economy. This defect is complicated by a lack of available data, making it hard to ascertain the extent of structural labour market failure. The Iraqi informal economy is the product of a number of factors – a rapid expansion of the youth population, commensurate with regional demographic trends; a long era of indoctrination, touting the prestige of the public sector over the private sector; a workforce with an unrenewed if not diminishing skill-set; and minimal private-sector growth. As a result, a two-tier labour market dynamic has arisen, where the informal economy is both large and growing despite the wretched status of its workers. These trends, evident in the 1980s and beyond, have become even more acute as a result of the occupation and failed reconstruction.

Because it is structural in nature, Iraq's labour market rigidity is unlikely to cease in the short term. Nevertheless, encouraging private-sector investment in Iraq (related quite closely to the security situation) will go a long way towards rebuilding the underlying fundamentals. In the past, the choice of major studies at university was distorted by government hiring and promotion policies. Consequently, labour skills deviated sharply from the skill mix required by the private sector. According to a recent survey by Zogby International, the highest-priority needs in Iraq's workforce are for more English-language training and computer skills. The education system should respond to the requirements of the private sector by establishing more effective links between universities and companies and by setting up training centres to rehabilitate the labour force.

Rising public-sector wages, and the attractiveness of employment in the public sector more generally, are rendering the private sector largely unable to compete for talented workers. This dynamic is not new to postwar Iraq, having originated with the dictatorships of the 1960s. In 1968, for example, Iraq adopted a full-employment policy, obliging the public sector to provide jobs for all individuals. With similarly destructive implications, the private sector was kept at a distance from technically trained university graduates, stifling the development of the formal economy and leading to employment imbalances, lower national productivity and inflationary pressures. To address this structural problem, the government should set strict limits on hiring in the public sector and cease treating employment in that sector as a means of distributing oil dividends – a policy that in the past has resulted in overstaffing and the under-utilization of human resources in the public sector.

Iraq has numerous nationals working abroad in various fields of science and technology who could, in the future, use their skills for the benefit of Iraq. As noted in my discussion in the previous chapter on technology parks, Iraq should aim at attracting these nationals by creating the right environment, the facilities to encourage them to return permanently or on a visiting basis, and a transparent and flexible labour market. This would help the country to capitalize on its historical endowment of a highly skilled and professional workforce.

Curing a sick system: healthcare

Iraq's formerly thriving healthcare system deteriorated as a result of two wars, the period of sanctions, and mismanagement. By the time Iraq was invaded in 2003, the healthcare system was in serious decline and the public's health suffered as a result. But since that date we have seen no improvement in healthcare: indeed, in many ways, performance has become worse. An exodus of doctors (perhaps up to half of those in the country in 2003), a reduction in the availability of medicines, and hospitals becoming sites of violence themselves are all major concerns. Real improvements can be made only after security is established and once a new Iraq emerges, as this is undoubtedly the core problem for the country's healthcare system.

The health of Iraq's people improved through the 1970s and early 1980s: infant mortality, for example, halved from 1979 to 1989. But with the onset of a period of wars and sanctions, the health service became increasingly starved of investment. Health ministry estimates show that healthcare spending was reduced by 90 per cent during the 1990s. The effects of this decline were severe, with infant mortality rising and life expectancy declining from 65 years in 1987 to 59 years in 1995, before rebounding with the introduction of the UN Oil for Food Programme. In 2002, Iraq's healthcare expenditure was only 1.5 per cent of GDP, far too low to provide a first-world service. Below the aggregate statistics, there is also considerable evidence that healthcare provision was very uneven and heavily politicized.

The US-led occupation has failed to generate any significant improvements in the system and, in several ways, may have made matters worse. Initially, the US reconstruction effort, in the form of the Iraq Relief and Reconstruction Fund, earmarked more than $2 billion for healthcare investment. While around $1 billion has been spent, more than 25 per cent of this has been diverted into security. The result has been a massive reduction in the impact of this investment. In the original plan, for example, 180 new health clinics were due to be opened by the end of 2005. By April 2007, just 15 had been completed.

Far more dramatic than a failed investment programme, however, has been the impact of deteriorating security conditions on the day-to-day operation of the health service. The most obvious problem has been a mass exodus of doctors. The Iraqi ministry of health estimates that 25 per cent of Iraq's 18,000 physicians had left the country by mid-2005, while the medical charity Medact estimated in March 2006 that nearer to 50 per cent of prewar-registered physicians had left. They also estimated that more than 250 doctors had been kidnapped, perhaps because of their perceived wealth – a fact that explains in part the exodus of other physicians. In addition, medical supplies are scarce, leading to a growing black market. There are even reports of hospitals themselves becoming sites for violence. As a consequence, many Iraqis are scared to visit them.

The overall results are that health services are at an all-time low just when health needs are more acute than ever. In emergency care, for example, Iraq is helpless to cope. In the *British Medical Journal*, an experienced Iraqi doctor claimed that half of all deaths from insurgent attacks would have been prevented with the right equipment and staff: 'The reality is, we cannot provide any treatment for many victims.'

An improvement in the security situation would deliver enormous benefits for the Iraqi health system, but this cannot be guaranteed in the short term. Securing existing Iraqi health centres from insurgents, protecting doctors and guarding supplies should be the first priorities. This would help to restore the trust of patients and might help to reduce the flow of doctors out of the country.

A second priority must be a new wave of investment in Iraq's hospitals. It would come from the reconstruction board and would be made direct to hospitals or through local government to cut out the corrupt and inefficient ministry of health. This would help to restore the system of 240 hospitals and 1,200 primary health centres.

Finally, restrictions on publicly employed doctors conducting private work should be lifted. While many of the best doctors have fled due to security concerns, there were, even before the war, 2,000 Iraqi doctors working in British hospitals. Placing unwise restrictions on the incomes of Iraqi doctors just creates another reason to leave.

As in the area of education, every Iraqi must have access and choice if a well-developed healthcare system is to provide widespread benefits. Every Iraqi must be able to choose his or her health insurance plan. Individuals below a certain level of income would receive local government vouchers to pay for their health insurance. Those above this level would pay for their insurance themselves. And all senior citizens above a prescribed age (retired or with a disability) would receive old age healthcare vouchers issued by the local government.

While many of the country's needs will be met by facilities operated by local government, privately owned providers should be encouraged in the longer term. This would offer a major incentive to healthcare professionals to return to Iraq, and would bring much-needed resources into the system. It would also promote healthy competition for healthcare funds between government and private providers, a situation in which the patient will benefit. With regard to privatization, foreign investment could help. Latin America opened up its health sector to international companies in the 1990s and experienced a huge shift towards private healthcare.

Medical tourism could be another way to develop the sector, taking advantage of the reputation in the Arab world of Iraqi doctors as trusted and competent. Medical and dental tourism have become increasing worldwide phenomena in recent years. Patients from the US, Western Europe and elsewhere increasingly travel for medical treatment to places such as Eastern Europe, India, Thailand, South America and some Latin American countries. The cost of surgical procedures in such countries can be a tenth of what the patient would have to pay back home, and in some cases travelling for treatment liberates the new arrival from a long waiting list.

And of course, having treatment abroad means the patient can combine treatment with a holiday in an exotic location.

India has successfully developed medical tourism in hi-tech medical facilities, staffed by doctors who are often Western-trained. There is no reason why Iraq could not become a regional and international medical centre if security and stability are eventually achieved. It has cadres of highly qualified medical professionals scattered over the globe who might be persuaded to return to the country, either permanently or on a visiting basis, to apply their expertise.

Finally, some provision must be made to ensure that all Iraqis have access to the healthcare system. Medical insurance is an important way to keep the population healthy, especially those who are unable to pay for expensive drugs or treatment.

Meeting a basic need: housing

Improving the housing situation in Iraq should also be a top priority for reconstruction. People around the world behave differently if given a stake in the future. There are a few major events in life that make individuals more mature and responsible: getting married, having children and owning their own home.

Iraq's housing situation is in crisis. A UN Development Group/World Bank report on Iraq's housing and urban management needs stated in September 2003 that Iraq had a shortfall of 1.4 million housing units. (The figure had since risen to 1.5 million according to a 2006 study.) The report also found that the quality of the existing housing stock had fallen dramatically due to a lack of investment, overcrowding and inadequate basic services. One result was a deterioration in middle-class housing (in which, the report notes, Iraq had enjoyed conditions comparable to Western standards). Another was the rise of substandard neighbourhoods and unplanned settlements occupied by people living on the poverty line.

As in other sectors, the socialist and political strategies of the past 50 years have left a long trail of ruin. During this period, the government was the major provider of housing, sponsoring 85 per cent of all projects. Saddam's regime intentionally limited the supply of new homes, but also issued below-market loans and subsidized land plots and building materials. Special housing projects were undertaken to advance the government's agenda and to accommodate favoured government officials and supporters.

Since 2003, the situation has worsened as violence and economic collapse have taken their toll, further reducing new building and increasing the need for maintenance. Many small contractors have seen their equipment and materials looted. Very little has been done to improve the situation in this crucial area for winning public support for the government. The US government's IRRF scheme provided nothing for housing. The current Iraqi government has established a National Housing Fund, but the UN-World Bank reports that this has 'not made any significant progress' and that plans to provide state subsidies to develop capacity and rehabilitate the equipment of small contractors 'have stalled'.

The leaders of tomorrow *must* address the housing crisis. First, the government should invest in building new houses for lower income groups. These homes should be sold cheaply so as to give Iraqis a sense of ownership and instant equity. This would also give a massive boost to the construction sector, which is languishing without enough demand.

Second, the government must clarify land ownership. As

noted already, this issue is widespread, and clear title to land is crucial in delivering the investment needed for new building. In addition, the absence of clear title impedes the use of land as collateral and undermines the development of a liquid secondary real estate market.

Finally, the government should restore Iraq's mortgage markets. The UN-World Bank report found that there is 'virtually no formal housing finance available' in Iraq. This may require legal reforms to ensure clear foreclosure procedures, as banks will not make loans if they do not have a way to recover the principal when a borrower defaults on repayments.

Together, these reforms should have the effect of encouraging private-sector involvement. Given the scale of demand and the pressure on public resources for other ends, encouraging the private sector to participate in all aspects of Iraqi housing is crucial. As mentioned before, this will be quite a change from the near-total public provision of the past. The crucial steps are public monies to restart the sector, backed by legal changes.

Central to any attempt to reconstruct the Iraqi state is an improvement in the quality of life of the population. This calls for wise and long-term investment in such areas as education, healthcare and housing. It also demands an institutional environment that provides a flexible labour market that can fulfil the requirements of the private sector. One of the strongest bonds that an individual has with the state is the one created by the state's provision of life's necessities. Thus, the leaders of the Iraq of tomorrow can only build a durable state if their policies ensure that the people receive what they need in the world of tomorrow.

10

Awaiting visionary leaders

There are those who look at things the way they are, and ask 'why?'
I dream of things that never were, and ask 'why not?'
                                                    Robert F. Kennedy, 1968

Vision is the first quality that exemplifies effective leaders. Next, it is their will and resilience to turn that vision into opportunity, prosperity and security for their citizens. Effective leaders are essential for mobilizing human assets, productively and competitively. Throughout history, the most effective leaders have been those with a powerful vision, the ability to communicate that vision and the capacity to mobilize their followers to pursue common goals.

I would like to draw a distinction between leaders and managers. Managers get the job done through others. Good managers focus on cost-effectiveness and quality of output. They organize, motivate, direct and control. Management is one thing. Leadership is quite different. Leaders are the architects who see a concept that others do not see and they transform that vision into an effective plan. Next, they hire the managers – as an architect hires a builder – to carry out the implementation of that plan.

Leadership demands ingenuity, and it is ingenuity that fuels the world's most powerful economies. Leadership demands independence, creativity and initiative.

Iraq is a country of great promise. It is blessed with abundant natural resources. What it needs most is credible and talented leaders who can take advantage of those opportunities. Grand vision and determined leadership is critical to help restore the broken nation.

Building a new Iraq will require expansive dreams tempered by hard reality. Every grand endeavour begins as a vision, when someone sees a thing that is not yet there. But the dream comes to life only when people of energy, imagination and experience perform a sort of magic that turns an ephemeral creation of the mind into something tangible – something possessing substance and meaning and inspiring admiration and pride.

In this chapter, I combine both dreams and reality to show potential leaders of Iraq how one can be transformed into the other; how dreams can give rise to great things.

Three dreams now follow: the first two are mere concepts for future implementation, and the third is my personal dream come true. All three deal with banks, because that area of business has been my speciality for nearly 40 years, but the general lessons they teach can be applied to any project. The first two are banks that I envision for the Iraq of tomorrow, and the third is the bank I established, Investcorp. By telling the story of how my company came to be, I hope to give a concrete example to the future leaders of Iraq that great possibilities stretch out before them, if they allow themselves to have dreams and work hard enough to make them come true.

The optimistic visions of the first two banking concepts were anchored in the real world. They came to me in 2003 when I had hoped that the intention of the US was not to occupy and dismantle Iraq but to liberate it and allow it to be rebuilt. At that time, I was asked by a leader in one of the wealthy

Gulf States to suggest a proposal for a large, meaningful investment in one or two new enterprises that would be viable, but would also have a positive impact on the new Iraq. The aim was to find economically feasible enterprises that could help transform Iraq from a backward nation into one that was dynamic and world-class.

I proposed two ideas. The first was to establish a mega-bank offering comprehensive financial services through a network of branches in every corner of the country. The second was to set up a high-quality, large-scale, real estate development enterprise to play a role in building the new Iraq and placing it on a commercially viable footing.

My counterpart then asked if I myself would be willing to move back to Iraq to assume responsibility for creating these enterprises if he were to pursue my proposals. My response, in view of my age, my international outlook, and my full-time responsibility and commitment to Investcorp, was to politely decline an executive role. Such endeavours would require totally dedicated, full-time leaders. If asked, however, I would be happy to consider serving on an advisory board on a non-compensation basis as one way of helping the country of my birth to move forward.

These ideas interested me to such an extent that I began to explore whether they were commercially viable. Accordingly, I examined the feasibility of the two enterprises for Iraq. Not surprisingly, when the 2003 invasion took a bad turn and the situation in Iraq started deteriorating, the principal contact from the Gulf abandoned his aspirations. With no intention of being personally involved in either of the two projects, my aim is to offer a vision, ready to be realized by any qualified party if and when Iraq emerges as a united, stable, safe and vibrant nation.

When the time is right, whoever picks up the ideas and decides to turn them into reality will certainly need to fill in the necessary details and come up with a realistic financial plan and a well thought-out strategy for implementation. Ideas are not enough. The actual implementation is much more difficult, with many challenges to overcome. At this point, however, the two new banks for Iraq remain no more than dreams.

Bank no. 1: a mega-bank for all Iraqis

Amadeo Giannini was the son of Italian immigrants who established the Bank of Italy in San Francisco in 1904. He displayed the measure of his vision and the scope of his business sense when a massive earthquake and raging fires destroyed vast portions of the city two years later. Salvaging the holdings from his destroyed bank building, he quickly began operating again on a counter made up of a plank laid across two barrels. Unlike other bankers of his day, Giannini was eager to do business with a broad range of the city's population, including working people and small businessmen, often sealing a deal on just a signature and a handshake. He was able to put this philosophy into ever wider practice, beginning in 1928 when his bank merged with the Bank of America, Los Angeles. The Bank of America, as it was later known, became a pioneer in the field, providing blanket coverage of California with branches in every corner of the state.

Giannini's early vision proved successful: to be the preferred banker for every segment of the population and every income group. He wanted to have the largest deposit base and to extend credit to all types of businesses, particularly small ones.

Giannini had the foresight to realize that as small businesses succeeded and grew, their needs for more banking products and services would also increase. Through the scale of his operation, he envisaged making California one of the world's most prosperous economies.

My hope is for someone to apply the same vision to Iraq. Iraq is a large country with widespread population centres of many different sizes. No one has yet attempted to create a pre-eminent, advanced branch-banking system with aggressive marketing and modern technology. There is an urgent need, however, for a first-class financial institution with vision, know-how and a large capital base to combine modern, high-quality corporate banking with a widespread retail network.

Of course, such a bank must have the right environment to work in. As I have noted already in the context of economic development in general, any new economic development would need an Iraq that offers widespread security, political stability, a free-market economy, a stable and freely convertible currency, a world-class legal and regulatory structure, good infrastructure in terms of utilities and transportation, successful privatization, free access to foreign know-how and effective global interaction.

Under these circumstances, establishing such an enterprise could contribute enormously to the recovery of Iraq – my greatest hope and the thrust of this book. Iraq's population of 25 million is highly urbanized, with 36 per cent living in the main metropolitan areas and 66 per cent in the 21 largest cities. Its GDP per capita was $US3,000 to $4,000 in 1980, but had dropped to $US800 by 2003. If and when Iraq is reconstructed along the lines proposed in the previous chapters, its GDP should rebound well beyond these levels.

The mega-bank I envisage would aim to secure a market share of at least 25 per cent, with 1.5 million residential customers, 150,000 small business customers and 5,000 large- and medium-sized business customers. The bank should plan 350 branches covering all major cities and reaching 90 per cent of the population. The bank will differentiate its approach for each customer sector, but will use centralized operation and support systems. This will consist of an efficient, centralized, low-cost back office; a standard, off-the-shelf IT system; and centralized risk management.

The sales and service channels will use dedicated corporate branches with professional relationship managers and online facilities to serve corporate customers. For small businesses and the upper mass retail market, the bank will establish call centres and ATMs. The more attractive customers will be served by a dedicated direct sales force and modern, lean, best-practice retail branches. As for mass and low-income retail customers, the bank will establish low-cost branches and additional mobile units to serve more remote areas.

Catering to a range of clients: corporations to individuals

Inspired by the Bank of America model, I envisage Iraq's new mega-bank serving the entire gamut of the country's varied clientele, from the largest corporation to the average worker. This would involve the establishment of 25 dedicated corporate centres in larger branches, with tellers and about five relationship managers. Iraq has an estimated 15,000 potential corporate customers with an average turnover of $US10 million and about 50 to 100 employees. Of these, the bank should serve at least one-third (i.e. 5,000). These would be offered core banking products including credits, deposits, trade finance, transactions and services. The bank should also offer its corporate customers basic investment banking and financial advice.

Of Iraq's estimated 500,000 small businesses with an average turnover of $US200,000 and 5 to 20 employees, the bank should target 150,000. This would mean establishing 150 modern, lean branches in high-traffic areas and key towns with four to five sales/service-focused employees. These branches would offer a comprehensive range of deposit and lending products, credit cards, mortgages and mutual funds. The emphasis should be on earning trust and providing efficient, good-quality, standardized service.

The mass, low-income market comprises an estimated 4 million people with average annual incomes of $US2,500 to $4,000. Of this total, the bank should serve 1 million living in rural areas and small towns. Products to be offered are basic deposit and lending and limited transactions, priced to ensure profitability. This market sector would require basic service levels at 175 locations, 75 of which should be in larger towns and the rest co-located on mobile units serving smaller towns and rural areas.

Out of a total of 350 locations, 25 would serve large corporate customers, 150 would serve the upper mass/small business sector and the balance of 175 would be low-income branches. In the Baghdad district, for example, I assume five corporate centres, 70 upper mass/small business branches and 40 mass/low income branches.

An organization structured to succeed

The proposed bank would have a total staff of 2,500 to 3,000 people when the organization is in place for full-scale operations. Obviously, this would be achieved over time. The bank should aim for a lean organization with fully centralized risk and back-office functions. Three of its organizational units would serve the client base mentioned above: corporate; small business/upper mass; and mass/low income. The final unit would focus on providing investment banking and private equity services. Product lines would include capital market/project finance, corporate products and retail products.

Underpinning the provision of these services would be units handling operations and information technology (IT), risk management and finance, and administration and human resources. I further propose that there should be a dedicated training centre to develop large numbers of potential employees. The centre would hire young graduates with no banking background and offer them comprehensive, school-like training.

Also essential are a central back office for processing trans-actions and applications; a management information system (MIS) for measuring, reporting and control; an IT system; key banking systems; infrastructure and telecoms. The risk-management group would be responsible for the committees overseeing credit decisions (especially corporate and small busi-ness credit), for scoring models for development and updating, and for the control of credit ratios.

Whoever is chosen to establish and lead this bank should start with a small group of founding experts to translate this vision into a detailed financial and practical implementation plan. This group should hire a talented and experienced professional team with complementary skills who will be secure and trustworthy solution providers.

To operate at full scale, the bank would need equity capital of $US2 billion. Given the equity capital of some of the other banks in the region – $1.4 billion for Qatar National Bank, $1.8 billion for National Bank of Kuwait and $2.4 billion for National Commercial Bank (Saudi Arabia), for example – it should be feasible with such a capital base to create an advanced and comprehensive bank to cover the whole of Iraq.

This bank will begin to succeed if its motivated and highly trained employees offer their customers a number of key services that expand the client base. For example, the bank should become the preferred or only distributor of pensions from the state welfare system and/or wages for civil servants and state employees. This would lock in a customer base that could then be developed for banking and would guarantee a substantial market share.

Second, the bank should offer basic, partially collateralized loans for consumer durables – that could be administered through a network of self-employed sales agents and through shops and traders. This would create, early on, a large customer base for banking and prime risk management capabilities.

Third, the bank should develop and offer simple retail insurance through a low-cost network of self-employed sales agents. In this way it would gain rapid penetration and recognition that could then be leveraged by the bank. An insurance product would also help to educate the people, stimulate entrepreneurship and create jobs.

Fourth, the bank should become the primary conduit for transfers of funds, both domestically and internationally.

Fifth, the bank should develop a full-range, one-stop shop of banking solutions for large and mid-size corporations and for government. It should also provide advisory and professional financial services.

Sixth, the bank should provide the most attractive sector of the Iraqi retail market with fast, reliable, good-quality services. In this way, small businesses would be able to benefit fully from access to modern and cost-effective financial services. The aim should be to be perceived by the customer as the most trusted and convenient banking service provider. Bank employees should help their customers' business to grow and prosper. That should be their mission.

Finally, the bank should provide for the largest sector of Iraqi society – those with lower incomes – financial services offered in a profitable way. It should also fulfil primary banking needs with basic deposit/lending products.

As noted in chapter 7, there are two leading banks serving Iraq and both are in very poor shape. In their favour, however, are their branch locations and brand awareness. While all my proposals are familiar and current in more sophisticated countries, neither one of the services I have described is available in Iraq today. It follows that introducing a major new bank with state-of-the-art capabilities should achieve enormous success. The most important of these capabilities include risk-management by building strong treasury and credit functions. Another capability would be the bank's talented and skilled employees. These would be drawn from around the world by attractive incentives, a highly motivated and performance-driven corporate culture and a leadership that sets aggressive and inspiring targets. Finally, all operations should be adequately monitored and controlled by utilizing high-quality MIS.

Bank no. 2: focused on funding development

If Iraq is ever united, secure and stable, with a free-market economy and a pro-business legal environment, it would greatly benefit from a development bank that specialized in undertaking large-scale projects. Not only would this sort of institution make an enormous impact, it would also have the potential to be highly profitable.

Initially, I envisage this organization focusing on large-scale, highly visible, real estate developments. Eventually, however, it might establish a separate line of business to develop and incubate small and medium-sized industrial projects. Its initial objective should be to build and sell high-quality real estate complexes. These assets would ultimately be sold to businessmen, investors, pension funds and others, either through private placement or through public markets.

I feel that this would be an excellent vehicle to create unique urban developments. Such an enterprise would make a meaningful and tangible contribution to the recovery of Iraq. It would improve the standard of living of Iraq's people and create the necessary infrastructure for Iraqi businesses to get back on their feet. It would contribute to the development of Iraq's urban centres and restore and preserve its historical, cultural and religious heritage. It would also create significant numbers of jobs. My assumption is that demand for high-quality real estate in Iraq would develop in line with the trends observed in other oil-producing countries in the Gulf – Dubai, Abu Dhabi and Doha, for example.

Central business districts, downtown destinations, tourist resorts, tourist pilgrimage networks, retail stores, malls, supermarkets, hotels, housing, office buildings, private hospitals and commercial/logistical/industrial parks would all be needed by the new Iraq. Building a world-class capital with cultural, governmental, educational, residential and conference centres, as discussed in chapter 7, needs a world-class developer capability.

High-quality landmark architecture and high security stand-ards would provide a unique competitive advantage. The organization would need creative master planning along with engineering office capabilities and skills in project management, finance, sales and marketing.

Iraq is the cradle of civilization and needs to build, facilitate and upgrade its unique archaeological and tourist sites, as noted already. Nineveh, Nimrod, Hatra, Ashur, Babylon, Karbala, al-Ukhaidir, Kufah, Najaf, Uruk, Samarra and Ur are sites crying out for attention, attractive accommodation and optimum exposure and utilization. The development bank would develop land and sites, find financial partners and sell the assets as income-generating entities.

In the case of retail operators, the organization might con-sider the feasibility of helping to provide staff, systems, marketing, access to suppliers and a brand. Modern, luxury, first-class hotels are needed in every city in Iraq and the organization should be the premier hotel developer there. Housing would be the single largest potential investment area for the project bank. The organization could make its mark in the affluent market by introducing luxury houses in attractive locations. In addition, the project bank would be the major developer of office space in the biggest cities, distinguishing itself through quality, design and integrity. Finally, for this enterprise to be able to produce world-class real estate, it would need to be significantly capitalized. I therefore suggest an equity base of $US5 billion. Shareholders could be Iraqi citizens, Gulf nationals or international investors.

While I am not laying out any financial plan in this chapter, I hope I have succeeded in introducing the vision, concept and scope of the proposed enterprise. When the time is ripe for implementation, it will not be difficult to fill in the financial details to confirm its feasibility.

Bank no. 3: Investcorp, a vision realized

The third bank I am about to describe also started as a dream, not for Iraq but for an innovative, international, financial institution unlike any other. I was 27 years younger when I came up with the concept in 1980 and committed myself to making it happen. I am presenting it here as an example of how an idea can be transformed into reality.

Established in 1982 and operating out of New York, London and Bahrain, Investcorp has been successful in every single year of its 25-year history. My concept was to establish a highly specialized and sophisticated financial organization, focusing on non-traditional investment opportunities on both sides of the Atlantic. This organization would act as a bridge between the Gulf states and the West, offering selected alternative investments to surplus fund-holders in the Gulf, targeting institutions and high-net-worth individuals.

My story is about how I got involved with an industry that did not yet exist, how I chose a line of business that had no identity and how I started a company that had no precedent, at least to my knowledge. At that time there was no model to emulate or reject. Investcorp arose purely from a concept in my mind.

As background, before I founded Investcorp I began my banking career as a credit lending officer in New York, working for Chase Manhattan, a major international bank now known as JPMorgan Chase. While in that position, I frequently witnessed privately owned family companies facing major challenges. In a typical case, the grandchildren of the founder had inherited the business but did not feel the same passion for continuing the family tradition. In many cases they were eager to sell and cash out. Many of those companies had functioned well in the past as family businesses under the leadership of the founder. They enjoyed recognizable names and strong reputations. But in the hands of their new owners – the grandchildren who wanted to relinquish their ownership – these companies were simply not in a position to be taken public. Many were in decline and would need considerable transformation before being eligible for an initial public offering. The management of those companies was often well aware of what had to be done. They knew that positioning the company for future success would require an injection of additional capital and an ownership able to provide the time and guidance necessary to modernize and transform the business.

In cases where owners were not interested in waiting, and were certainly not willing to inject more capital, the business was left with no way to achieve its potential value. At the time I was beginning to notice this trend as a banker in New York, another trend, altogether different, was emerging half a world away. Energy prices shot up in the mid-1970s. As a result, some of the energy-exporting countries in the Gulf were fast accumulating huge sums of surplus funds that needed to be invested in diversified international assets. The conventional outlets for investments at that time were bank deposits, marketable securities in fixed income and equities and certain direct investments. During this oil boom, the bank I worked for noticed that the tapped reserves of oil were creating untapped reserves of wealth, and transferred me from New York to the Gulf. I was to be responsible for directing and managing Chase Manhattan's activities in the region with the goal of increasing our share of this emerging market.

When my three-year tour of duty in the Gulf came to a successful end, I might have moved to another assignment and possibly a higher position with the bank. Instead, I decided to set out on my own. Having witnessed two emerging trends – the need by many businesses in the West to manage their succession and the growing economic power of the Gulf – I felt there was a place for a financial institution that could meet both needs.

At that time there was no specialized financial institution that operated on both sides of that Atlantic and offered non-traditional investments. So my goal was to build a bridge between opportunities in the West and the surplus funds in the Gulf by offering non-traditional investments to Gulf investors. That was how Investcorp started. I was fully aware, of course, that investors would continue to place a larger portion of their surplus funds in the familiar, traditional investment channels. But by enabling them to allocate a limited segment of their total portfolio to newly introduced, non-traditional investments, Investcorp was, to the best of my knowledge, the first to offer such an opportunity.

I believe that in the Gulf we created the first awareness for non-traditional investments – and, through that awareness, the demand for Western private equity and other alternative investment products. Most private equity firms today operate through a fund. They seek investors and then, once the fund is filled, they go out and pursue acquisitions with no input from the original investors. In order to respond to Gulf market preference, Investcorp devised its own unique approach. Under our model, each investment is offered separately to our clients. The discretion is left entirely to them, on a deal-by-deal basis, to accept or reject participation in any given investment.

If they choose to participate, they also indicate how much they wish to invest in each transaction. In this way the client not only enjoys total discretion, but also has an opportunity to determine the weighting of his participation in each investment. While the economic cost to clients of the Investcorp model is equivalent to traditional fund economics, those two advantages – the discretion and the weighting – have made our products highly attractive in the Gulf.

We are structurally different in another way as well. Since its inception, Investcorp has been publicly listed with full transparency and corporate governance. Its balance sheet is used to acquire all assets and to warehouse each investment before syndicating it to our clients. Investcorp is investment grade rated and has therefore been able to attract long-term international third-party financing of up to 30 years. In the future, especially as more private equity firms choose to go public themselves, greater transparency will become the rule and not the exception.

Our performance has been in the top quartile in all of our lines of business, against any of our competitors worldwide, and our target acquisitions in private equity have been mid-size companies on both sides of the Atlantic – companies that we feel are best suited to our value-enhancement model. Our policy is to remain a highly focused and specialized boutique. I set out to create a bridge, not a behemoth, and am proud of what we have been able to achieve.

Investcorp's mission and culture

From day one, I was determined that Investcorp would be among the very best, pursuing excellence in every field – personnel, premises, board members, law firms, accounting firms and consultants. Our mission is to be our clients' preferred choice in meeting their needs for alternative investment products, namely private equity, hedge funds, real estate, technology investment and Gulf growth capital. In fulfilling this mission, our most important asset is our reputation. Investcorp has earned its status through reliability, transparency, business judgement, value-creation, innovation and superior results.

Today, the Investcorp brand is internationally recognized for its excellent performance in global alternative investments. We are determined to maintain and build on this powerful reputation. To this end, we will ensure that all five of our lines of business continue to generate top-quartile results in their respective sectors. We will also continue to set the standard for superior client service, focusing on our core market of institutional and high-net-worth clients in the Gulf region and growing our franchise with selected new clients. At the same time, we are expanding our focus and serving certain prestigious international institutional clients in the US and Europe as well.

Our objectives have been consistent – to be global in our outlook, organization and operating structure; to create a working, environment that demands integrity, stimulates an entrepreneurial spirit and encourages a deep sense of responsibility to the firm, its shareholders and its clients; to be recognized for our transparency, professionalism and accountability; and to ensure the firm's long-term growth and profitability through the careful yet dynamic management of risks and resources.

Investcorp will continue to be a management-driven organization, institutional in its practices and disciplines but preserving its entrepreneurial spirit and partnership mindset. Our determination to develop, retain and attract talented people, and to provide a distinctive culture in which they can thrive and excel, will remain unchanged.

A quarter-century of accomplishments

Over the past 25 years, Investcorp has earned recognition and respect as a leading financial institution on both sides of the Atlantic and indeed worldwide. Our vision remains clear and our mission unchanged – to excel in every one of our markets, products and lines of business.

A publicly listed and regulated bank since its inception, Investcorp is known for its innovation. It was one of the first alternative asset managers with operations on both sides of the Atlantic; one of the first to focus on multiple asset classes; one of the first to go public; and the first to recognize the need for international alternative investment products among investors in the Gulf and to develop a unique business model to respond to the considerable potential of this market.

By 2008, the firm employed 400 people across 38

nationalities. Almost every member of its senior management team is home-grown, having joined at a more junior level and risen on the basis of merit. Most have been with Investcorp for more than ten years and some for over 20 years.

Our record over the past 25 years speaks for itself. Investcorp has been profitable, and has paid dividends, in every single fiscal year. The average annual return on equity is more than 19 per cent. The original shareholders have received back more than 400 per cent of their initial investment through cash dividends, resulting in an overall return to ordinary shareholders of 20 per cent per annum over 25 years.

The firm has shown consistent ability to grow organically by introducing new products and widening its client base. Established with initial capital of $50 million, Investcorp's market value is now over $2 billion. The firm has transacted investments worth approximately $38 billion, generating top-quartile returns across all lines of business. Total assets under management have grown by 20 per cent per annum over the last ten years and now total $18 billion across multiple alternative asset classes and products. The figure includes over $4 billion managed in a fiduciary capacity on behalf of clients and another $4 billion managed on behalf of shareholders.

For all the achievements of its first 25 years, there is great potential ahead and the prospects are brighter than ever. The firm continues on its path with clarity of vision, financial strength, a prestigious brand name, an impeccable reputation and a rising generation of talented people determined to continue its mission into the future.

Philosophically, I believe every business is, at its heart, a dream. From the smallest restaurant to the largest retailer, each enterprise begins as one person's dream of finding meaning in meeting a need. Investcorp started as a dream – namely, to bridge continents, offer opportunities for investment and build businesses at the same time.

At this stage in my life, I hope to encourage others to fulfil their own dreams. The future of Iraq requires those who are young, energetic and qualified to realize their hopes and aspirations while transforming their country into a world-class nation. That is why, in this chapter, I have presented the story of my dream come true to show that other dreams waiting in the wings can just as well be realized. That is why I have devoted so much time to writing this book.

Conclusion

I would like to conclude by reiterating my reason for writing this book. As indicated earlier, I am not a politician, an academic or a historian. Nor do I plan to go back to Iraq, though I have great affection for the land of my birth. Given its potential to be transformed for the better, I feel the opportunity should not be squandered.

Three times Iraq suffered as a result of military coups taking over the government and replacing legitimate civilian rule. The first in 1936 under Bakr Sidqi and the second by Rashid Ali al-Gailani in 1941 were fortunately reversed and their damage was contained. The third, in July 1958, was the bloodiest of them all and ushered in 45 years of destruction. One lesson is clear. Once Iraq has completed an effective transition, achieved unity and stability and begun making progress towards greater prosperity, it is vital that the military should be subordinated to civilian leadership. The military is there to defend the country against foreign aggression, not as a tool for political advantage or for internal power plays.

Before the tragic overthrow of its constitutional Hashemite monarchy on 14 July 1958, Iraq was a country of enormous promise. In comparison with Taiwan, South Korea, Singapore,

Ireland or Dubai at that time, it was decades ahead and on course for dramatic economic development and a truly bright future. But this violent change of government not only swept away some of the wisest and most visionary, honest and dedicated leaders in the country's history, it also abruptly halted their prescient policies, a non-sectarian political system and a relatively open society. The junta leaders and dictators who followed led Iraq into a dark period of repression, economic regression and despair.

For the next 45 years, Iraqis lived in a country that was being turned into a prison. Saddam, who ruled for 34 of those grievous years, was a tyrant with an aggressive, 'dark ages' warrior mindset. He did not comprehend the advantage of achieving economic power and focused, instead, on building his military might in order to become the leading aggressor in the Middle East. Year after year, Iraqis realized the magnitude of their loss and felt the acute pain of their situation.

Meanwhile the US as the world's single superpower was determined, especially after the attacks of 9/11, to engage militarily in the Middle East. As a result, Iraq was targeted for invasion – the event that brought about Saddam's downfall but dealt untold harm to the prospect of a united, democratic and prosperous Iraq.

Saddam was a monumental and unparalleled evil, destroying Iraq and preventing it from achieving its potential. I therefore applauded Iraq's liberation by force because there was no alternative. This was followed, however, by three grave mistakes. The first was the skipping of a critical prerequisite – a long and constructive transition period, following 45 years of tyranny. The second, in 2003, was the wrong choice of Iraqi individuals to serve on the Governing Council, which then became a platform for promoting these same individuals as the country's future leaders. The third was the rush to hold elections which, contrary to widespread propaganda, were undemocratic and served simply to entrench the choice of those unworthy leaders and legitimize their rule.

There are enormous disparities between the declared principles of the occupation and what has occurred in practice. In this book I have been critical of the direction Iraq has taken since the end of the Saddam regime. I am deeply disappointed that the fall of the tyranny in April 2003 was not followed by a well-managed, extended, effective and necessary transition, as was the case in post-Second World War Germany and Japan.

By 2003 the Iraqi people had two overriding wishes: first, to have the opportunity to get rid of Saddam's tyranny; and second, to replace Saddam with an honest, competent, visionary and dedicated leadership that would move the country forward and make up for time and resources squandered. The invasion of Iraq in 2003, and the way its aftermath was handled, fulfilled the first wish but not the second. Iraqis were initially jubilant to see the end of the Saddam regime. It was not long, however, before disappointment set in and jubilation turned to deep hostility. Since the occupation, Iraq has become more divided, more miserable and less safe than ever before. It has become a symbol of violence, a shattered state, a dysfunctional economy and a society deeply in conflict along ethnic and sectarian lines. The much-touted 'surge' policy has temporarily made the situation merely bad rather than appalling, with tremendous problems left unresolved. Unless drastic measures are taken to address Iraq's current crisis, the downward spiral will continue and will lead towards national disintegration.

There are those who claim that this tragic result is exactly what the neo-conservative architects of the war intended. Their objective, it is argued, was to see Iraq dismembered and destroyed. If this was indeed their aim, one must admit it has succeeded brilliantly.

This claim is supported by a number of arguments:

1 A highly credible and respected source such as Alan Greenspan, who claims that 'oil' was the reason for occupying Iraq.

2 Ambassador L. Paul Bremer losing no time in laying the foundations for divisiveness and corruption in Iraqi society during the occupation.

3 US Senator Joseph Biden tirelessly pushing Congress to formalize the dismantling of Iraq.

4 A stream of incompetent policies and statements of denial of any failure emanating from the White House.

On the other hand, there are others – including, I would venture to say, President George W. Bush himself – who probably did not wish this tragic end. They might have sincerely wanted to see a new, strong and prosperous Iraq, able to set an example and become a symbol of stability, prosperity and peace in the Middle East. Obviously, this ambition has not been realized and the outcome has been a disastrous failure – for no other reason maybe than poor planning and sheer incompetence.

A catalogue of mistakes

A series of tragic errors since the occupation has squandered an unprecedented opportunity to build a prosperous new Iraq.

The first mistake was the dismantling of the established secular and professional civil service, armed forces and administrative machine that had governed Iraq up to April 2003. At the start of the invasion, the US Air Force dropped hundreds of thousands of leaflets addressing the Iraqi armed forces and asking them not to fight back. The US, they promised, was against Saddam and not against the Iraqi army. And yet, when the US invasion succeeded with little Iraqi military resistance, the occupiers reneged on their promise and decided to disband the Iraqi armed forces and fire its members. These were cut off from their salaries but retained their arms.

A second error was the US engagement in the social re-engineering of Iraq and the occupation's choice of leadership to replace Saddam's regime. Ever since the invasion of Kuwait in 1990, certain discredited Iraqi warlords and expatriate politicians had been knocking on the doors of US and European intelligence agencies, asking for financial and political support to establish an opposition front to Saddam's rule. It was one thing for Washington and London to support these individuals in the 1990s in the hope that they might succeed in destabilizing Saddam. It was altogether different when the US itself decided to wage war on Saddam and, on achieving victory, to place the leadership of the new Iraq in such unworthy hands.

If the US had carried out background checks on these individuals, few would have qualified. It is hard to understand how the US administration could have presented the traditionally secular Iraq to a bunch of radical extremists so completely lacking in competence and integrity. Allowing discredited politicians to fill the vacuum and take over the government of Iraq was to have profoundly damaging consequences.

Before long, the newly appointed leaders of Iraq were fighting over the spoils. Realizing that they lacked any worthy credentials of their own, they were desperate to hide behind a cause or a platform, and chose ethnic and religious differences as the most convenient vehicle for arousing emotions and inflaming passion among their potential followers. They formed their own militias and secured funding from external sources to fight, kill and spread terror. Pushing their own ethnic and sectarian claims, they grabbed wealth and power while recruiting and bribing followers and consolidating their positions.

The creation in July 2003 of the Iraq Governing Council based on ethnic and sectarian quotas was a grave mistake, later compounded by the Transition Authority Law, premature and poorly devised elections and a flawed and divisive constitution. When elections were called by the US, the warlords got their followers to vote as they were directed. In this way, they were able to win seats and write a constitution to further their own agendas. Among themselves they continued to quarrel over oil and territory while millions of Iraqis were disenfranchised, disconnected, angry and unemployed. In fact, very few people voted in the elections as Iraqi nationals: most voted as Shias, Sunnis or Kurds. With Iraq set on the path to communal conflict, the premature elections were like throwing gasoline on a fire. All they did was fuel the polarization and destroy the fabric of a previously integrated society.

The situation was made worse by the setting of arbitrary deadlines to enforce the elections and the constitution-drafting process. One reason for taking such hasty steps was to appeal to Western and international public opinion and to show that the invasion had brought so-called 'democracy' to the Iraqi people. But this was an exercise in deception, aimed more at placating the American public than serving the long-term interests of Iraq. Iraq's premature election – badly designed to empower occupation agents – simply served to exacerbate divisions in a country that was once proud to be a single nation. These newly emerged sub-national leaders are exploiting emotion to inspire their followers to fight others. The election process that the Washington spin-machine boasted about so loudly has in fact accelerated the process of division. Empowering tribal warlords and different ethnic and religious groups will ensure further disintegration and produce a failed state. The resulting time-bomb will have dire consequences for the entire Middle East. The future challenge for patriotic Iraqis is to commit themselves to the long, hard task of building a single nation.

Can this be done? Over the last five years, when I have been invited to speak on Iraq by organizations in Washington, New York and London, I have always met the same questions: 'Given the diversity of its people, can Iraq really exist as one nation? Didn't the Sunni minority rule with an iron fist?' I answer the first in the early part of this book by describing how Iraqi nationalism and the rule of law from 1921 to 1958 rose above ethnic and religious diversity. I believe it can do so again. In addressing the second question, I argue that Saddam ruled by spreading fear and terror against Sunnis, Shiites and anyone else whom he did not consider to be loyal. His regime should not therefore be seen as one sect oppressing another.

Yet another monumental mistake was to leave large segments of Iraq's borders unpatrolled, making the country vulnerable to infiltration by foreign terrorists. The death and destruction caused by these terrorists contributed further to Iraq's disintegration. It is often asked why al-Qaeda did not exist in Iraq before 2003 and why it became powerful thereafter. The answer, of course, lies in the dismantling of the central administrative authority and the subsequent security vacuum. In the absence of a credible authority, external gangsters found in Iraq post-2003 a potentially failed state and therefore fertile ground in which to pursue their agendas. The failure to safeguard Iraq's borders was an open invitation to al-Qaeda to carry out its criminal offensives.

The occupation dealt a devastating blow to Iraqi nationalism. It destroyed the fabric of a society that had taken 80 years to weave together. Saddam's brutal regime has been replaced by a reckless government that in turn has led to gross incompetence, unprecedented corruption and a total collapse of security. Iraq is today a deeply fractured society, increasingly beset with animosity and violence and one in which citizens have no choice but to depend on communal solidarity for their survival. Fear, violence and revenge go unchecked. Those who can afford to, particularly among the educated middle class, have left the country in droves.

In the five years since the invasion, hundreds of thousands of Iraqis have been killed and up to 2 million have fled to Jordan and Syria as refugees during the height of the violence. In addition, 1.7 million Iraqis have been displaced within the country. With no security, no jobs, irregular supplies of such necessities as water and electricity, and a rapidly deteriorating economy, the country faces disintegration. Today, most Iraqis have lost hope and are in deep despair. The divisions and alienation caused by the invasion are horrific and devastating.

The damage to Iraq since 2003 has been inflicted by Iraqis, not Americans. Over the past five years you could not have picked up a Middle Eastern newspaper without finding a front-page report on the ongoing atrocities in Iraq: 25 people murdered here, 65 there. Ethnic and sectarian cleansing. Refugees. Displacements. Communities that were once mixed, now pure. Outright corruption. Government officials protected by armies of foreign security troops, and so forth.

It need not have turned out like this. It is frustrating to see how an evil tyrant has been replaced by a handful of crooks, fanatics and thugs; how the US embassy in Baghdad (now the largest in the world) along with 140,000 US men and women in uniform is perceived by millions of Iraqis as protecting an imposed, corrupt government locked in the Green Zone fortress; and how Iraq has ended up as a failed state instead of a model for inspiration and hope.

My proposed solution: a third way

First, in my opinion the US should say clearly and unequivocally that it seeks no permanent military base in Iraq. In much of this book I have presented a blueprint aimed at building a new, independent, united and secular Iraq using ideas from its own past, from my personal experience and from success stories around the world. But these recommendations for political, economic and social transformation cannot be implemented until the present state of catastrophic conflict and political disintegration is altered. It is my view that while the situation is grim, one should not give up hope. There is still a possibility that the downward slide can be halted and reversed.

How? After 45 years of repression and totalitarian rule, followed by five more years of chaos and destruction under the occupation, Iraq needs an extended transition to allow for rehabilitation under a just and benevolent central authoritarian rule. This new regime must eradicate all ethnic and sectarian claims and references. It needs to install law and order, to recognize all Iraqis as equal citizens and to foster a healthy and dynamic civil society. Most important, it needs to focus on massive economic reconstruction and development. All this requires honest, conscientious and dedicated Iraqi nationalists to rise up and join forces to establish a new political order aimed at building a new Iraq with a strong civil society and a solid judicial system.

However it comes about, the new leadership's number one priority should be to impose a curfew and strictly enforce law and order to ensure security and stability and prepare the way for comprehensive economic reconstruction. Once security is established and the people sense that the future holds promise, a great economic and social transformation can take place. Unfortunately, in the current unsettled situation, ambitious and talented Iraqis choose to move abroad until the situation improves.

The new leadership of Iraq must be 100 per cent patriotic, with no previous political links or affiliations and no moral debt or favour to be paid back to any foreign country. Reference to any individual's sectarian or ethnic background should be prohibited. All Iraqis must enjoy equal rights and assume equal responsibilities. The concept of belonging to one nation should be re-established, re-emphasized and reinforced. That is how Iraq operated for 80 years prior to the occupation and that is how it should continue to function in the future.

In this vein, I would like to reiterate the importance of recognizing the achievements of the pre-1958 period in Iraq, and to advocate the need for all Iraqis to embrace these important formative years of the state. While most Iraqis with whom I have spoken confess in private their admiration for the achievements of the leaders during the constitutional Hashemite monarchy, I have yet to hear this sentiment repeated in public, loud and clear. It is high time for all Iraqis to stand up and declare that 14 July 1958 was the moment at which Iraq's long downfall started. Before this date, Iraq was on the right path. The members of the royal family were honest and patriotic, as were the political leaders of the time. The competence and far-sightedness of these leaders set Iraq on a course towards prosperity, unity and social advancement. For 50 years, the shining legacies of these leaders have been belittled and falsified by the country's dictatorial regimes. Now, with history validating their policies, the political leaders of the Hashemite monarchy should at long last be recognized and respected.

Iraq's future leadership should dismantle what the occupation has installed. Its first steps should include abolishing the ill-chosen sectarian parliament, cancelling the divisive constitution and discontinuing the ghetto-minded Green Zone government. It should also reverse the policy of dismantling the pre-2003 government machine that proved so disastrous after the occupation. All civil and military government personnel who served before or after the invasion should be incentivized to return to their jobs, so long as they are competent and have not been convicted of any crimes. In short, the entire de-Baathification process should be discontinued and reversed. Moreover, the 'federalism' that was established in Iraq to disguise ethnic and sectarian autonomy efforts should be abolished. Instead, the devolution of central government power should pass to the regional and local levels based on the country's existing 18 geographic provinces and scores of municipalities, with none of these purely political subdivisions based on ethnic or religious identity.

A new cadre of technocratic, secular and competent government officials should take over to focus primarily on economic reconstruction and development. The criteria for serving in the public sector should be merit, integrity, skill, talent, competence and experience, rather than an affiliation to any majority or minority.

The US should support this new transitional government by gradually pulling its troops out of Iraq while continuing to provide financial and technical assistance to help the country evolve into a stable, prosperous and reliable ally in the Middle East. Instead of shooting each other as they are today, Americans and Iraqis should be working together to build a strong economy that can eventually integrate itself productively and effectively into the global market.

The combination of all these changes will eventually lead to the emergence of a consumer-oriented society and generate a prosperous middle class that will form the backbone for an enduring liberal democracy. A vibrant middle class is the hallmark of any modern, growing economy and a prerequisite for long-term stability. It ensures that a large portion of the population has a clear stake in the future, and generates hope among them that dreams are worth striving for and can be fulfilled. When Iraqis are prosperous, with an increasing, tangible net worth, they will have a real stake in the stability of their nation and will transfer their attention from potentially divisive and narrow tribal, religious or ethnic affiliation. That is when Iraq will contribute to making the Middle East a safer place.

A united Iraq has the ingredients to succeed. It certainly has the potential to become one of the most prosperous countries – no longer threatening its neighbours but instead adding economic depth and strength to the region. But none of this can happen until its potential is unlocked.

What is clear is that the present deterioration in Iraq is a time-bomb that no one can afford to ignore. The consequences of a failed state in Iraq would not only destroy the lives of its 25 million citizens, but would have a profoundly adverse effect on the entire region.

I strongly feel that Iraq's stability and prosperity can only be achieved through a courageous U-turn, one that will halt the downward spiral and ensure the restoration of a secular, united Iraqi nation, hungry to achieve its own economic miracle – an Iraq extending from its borders with Turkey in the north to its borders with Kuwait in the south.

In conclusion, the fatal mistake since the occupation has been the failure to realize that Iraq could not become a healthy and flourishing democracy overnight. Any plan for the country's long-term future had to allow for an effective and stable transition between the fall of the Saddam regime and the eventual desired outcome. The attempt to skip this critical prerequisite has been cause for much of the country's tragic outcome over the last five years. Even now, I believe it is still not too late to acknowledge this horrific error and encourage a competent and authoritative transition – essential as it is to a strong and healthy democracy in the future in Iraq.

The reversal at this late stage will undoubtedly be painful and much more complicated, requiring enormous courage and wisdom. But where there is a will, there must be a way out of this current disaster. The central question among the Iraqi people will be whether any future government could ever restore public trust, respect and confidence. Ever since 1958, every regime that forced itself into power has proved to be much worse than the one it replaced. The proud people of Iraq have suffered far too much. They deserve at long last the kinds of leaders who will offer their children a future filled with hope and promise in a unified, open, peaceful and prosperous Iraq.

For Iraq to be able to reverse the tide, it needs a massive movement. A movement to rise up as a united nation, determined to be reborn, to rebuild and to prosper.

Endnotes

CHAPTER 1: A road of hope becomes a tunnel of despair

[1] See Charles Tripp, *A History of Iraq* (Cambridge University Press, 2007), p. 48.

[2] Phebe Marr, *The Modern History of Iraq* (Oxford, Westview Press, 2004), p. 38.

[3] Lord Salter and S. W. Payton, *The Development of Iraq: A plan of action* (London, Caxton Press for the Iraq Development Board, 1955).

[4] Harold Macmillan, *Riding the Storm* (London, Macmillan, 1971), p. 522.

CHAPTER 2: Lessons and examples from the past

[1] Martin Bunton, 'Developmental nationalism to the end of the nation-state of Iraq?', *Third World Quarterly*, vol. 29, no. 3, April 2008, pp. 631–46.

[2] Charles Tripp, *A History of Iraq*, p. 125.

[3] Phebe Marr, *The Modern History of Iraq*, p. 69.

[4] Stephen Longrigg, *Journal of the Royal Central Asian Society*, vol. 43, no. 3, 1956, pp. 257–79.

[5] William Polk, 'The lesson of Iraq', *Atlantic Monthly*, December 1958, vol. 202, no. 6, p. 49.

[6] Extract from a landmark policy speech delivered on radio to the people of Iraq on 17 December 1956.

CHAPTER 3: A road to a new Iraq not taken
[1] Avi Shlaim, *Lion of Jordan: The life of King Hussein in war and peace*, London, Allen Lane, 2007, p. 609.

CHAPTER 4: The neo-conservative recipe for disaster
[1] Project for the New American Century, 20 September 2001, www.newamericancentury.org/Bushletter.htm
[2] Leaked to various media outlets. The *Sunday Times* published the document on 1 May 2005. It was written by Matthew Raycroft to David Manning, dated 23 July 2002.
[3] Dick Cheney, Speech at the Veterans of Foreign Wars 103rd Convention, Nashville, Tennessee, 26 August 2002.
[4] International Crisis Group, *Governing Iraq*, Middle East Report Number 17, 25 August 2003.
[5] BBC Radio 4 interview with Dr Reinoud Leenders for *File on 4* programme, 1 February 2005.
[6] Asharq Alawsat interview with Dr Ahmad Chalabi, *Al-Hayat*, Issue 9828, 25 October 2005.
[7] John Burns and Kirk Semple, 'US finds Iraq Insurgency has funds to sustain itself', *New York Times*, 26 November 2008.

CHAPTER 5: The neo-conservative recipe for disaster
[1] Thomas E. Ricks, *Fiasco: The American military adventure in Iraq* (London, Penguin, 2007), p. 158.
[2] *Iraq Study Group Report*, based on study co-chaired by James A. Baker III and Lee H. Hamilton, published by United States Institute of Peace on 6 December 2006, p. 10.
[3] 'The Iraqi Public on the US Presence and the Future of Iraq'

opinion poll was conducted by the Program on International Policy Attitudes by WorldPublicOpinion.org between 1 and 4 September 2006 with a nationwide sample of 1,150 Iraqis. The results were published on 27 September 2006.

[4] Steven Simon, 'The Price of the Surge', *Foreign Affairs* (Council on Foreign Relations), May/June 2008.

[5] The President of the Kurdistan Regional Government Masoud Barzani, interview broadcast on *From Iraq* (Min Al-Iraq), Al-Arabiya satellite channel, Sunday 4 June 2006.

[6] James Dobbins, John McGinn, Keith Crane, Seth Jones, Rollie Lal, Andrew Rathmell, Rachel Swanger, Anga Timilsina, *America's Role in Nation-Building: From Germany to Iraq*, Rand Corporation (MR1753-RC) July 2003.

[7] Andrew Rathmell, 'Iraq after Elections: Beyond Resistance', *The World Today* (Chatham House, London), vol. 61, no. 1, January 2005.

[8] Vali Nasr, *The Shia Revival: How conflicts within Islam will shape the future* (Norton, New York, 2007), p. 194.

CHAPTER 7: Fuelling progress with oil

[1] Unclassified summary of SIGIR's review of efforts to increase Iraq's capability to protect its energy infrastructure, SIGIR-06-038, 27 September 2006.

CHAPTER 8: Building a vibrant economy

[1] 'Financial Reconstruction in Iraq', Testimony of John B. Taylor, Undersecretary of the Treasury for International Affairs, before the Senate Banking, Housing and Urban Affairs Committee, 11 February 2004.

[2] For these and other principles of urban design, I am indebted to the *Charter of the Congress for the New Urbanism* (1996).

CHAPTER 9: Developing the greatest resource

[1] *Situation Analysis of Education in Iraq*, UNESCO report, Paris, April 2003.

Acknowledgements

I am deeply grateful for the encouragement, advice and critiques I have received from a number of distinguished friends, associates and experts. These people devoted time, energy and talent in helping me to transform my memories of Iraq's past, and my hopes for its future, into the book you hold in your hands.

At the outset, my dear friends Eugene Rogan and his wife, Ngaire Woods – both professors at Oxford – assembled a team of young scholars and researchers to add further valuable data and analysis of Iraq's history, politics and economy to my early drafts of the book. Two creative and gifted people then worked tirelessly to polish rough chapters until they began to shine. Outstanding economist, Marc Sumerlin, provided the framework for the chapters dealing with Iraq's economy as well as adding depth, insight and rigour to the content. Writer and historian, Anthony Toth, employed his exceptional narrative skills to bring clarity, coherence and consistency to the message I wished to convey.

Another formidable economist, Larry Lindsey, reviewed the manuscript and offered a wealth of advice and a detailed critique. I welcomed his thoughtful suggestions and have incorporated them into the book with much appreciation.

As *Saving Iraq* neared its final form, I shared the manuscript with some fifteen friends and intellectuals. My close friend Ezra Zilkha made important suggestions, as did Bruce Reidel of the Brookings Institution and the organization's esteemed president, Strobe Talbott. Another incisive thinker and one of my best friends, Arnaud de Borchgrave of the *Washington Times*, applied his wide-ranging experience in journalism and foreign affairs to improve the flow and accuracy of the manuscript. Bob Gallucci, Dean of the School of Foreign Service at Georgetown University, was most gracious and generous with his insights and advice. Suzannah Tarbush was a terrific researcher and enormously helpful.

Dr Usameh Al Jamali, an internationally respected economist at the Arab Fund for Economic Development in Kuwait, offered further constructive critique – again much appreciated. Crucial input and comment also came from the brilliant Iraqi journalist, Mina Al Oraibi, and the equally outstanding former Iraqi diplomat, Faruq Ziada – a friend since our schooldays together in Baghdad.

Two other distinguished childhood friends deserve my thanks for their encouragement and constructive feedback – HRH Prince Raad Bin Zaid of the Hashemite royal family of Jordan and Jaffar Al Askari. Another very dear friend, the renowned energy expert Abdullah Ismail, contributed his analysis of the prospects for the oil industry in Iraq. I would also like to thank my old friend, Edward R. M. Kane, whom I met in Baghdad in 1962 when he was serving at the US embassy. Ed, too, provided a wise and realistic perspective on the future of Iraq.

Other friends who read the manuscript and offered their

encouragement include Field Marshal The Lord Inge; former British minister, The Honourable Nicholas Soames MP; President Jack DeGioia of Georgetown University; author and Middle East expert, Henry Siegman; and Ambassador Martin Indyk of the Saban Center for Middle East Policy at the Brookings Institution.

I am also grateful to those who read the manuscript and offered the help of their own institutions once the book was published. Professor Klaus Schwab, founder and Executive Chairman of the World Economic Forum, immediately suggested the formation of a Forum task force with a brief to use the book in helping decision-makers to be better informed. As a result, I am hopeful that the recommendations within the book will contribute to the future rebuilding of Iraq. John Coatsworth, Dean of Columbia University's School of International and Public Affairs, offered to host the book's launch at the school in New York.

Special thanks and appreciation go to Graham Jones, a gifted writer who edits and translates what I want to say and movingly expresses my thoughts through his magical command of the English language.

In my own office, I must pay tribute to that pillar of dependability, Elizabeth Pires, who coordinated the entire process with passion, focus and total dedication. And to Sharon Durkin, Lyn Fiel, Suzie Garas and Susan Shafi who worked tirelessly, typing and retyping one draft after another. Between them as a team, no obstacle was insurmountable and they made sure I did not miss a single deadline.

I must also register my warmest gratitude to Alan Samson, Publisher at Weidenfeld & Nicolson, to Editorial Director Lucinda McNeile and designer Natasha Webber, all of whom have shown enormous enthusiasm and dedication in driving this project to its conclusion.

And, most importantly, special recognition and thanks go to my friend George Weidenfeld, a man of extraordinary vision, wisdom and knowledge who, on reading the manuscript, called and insisted that his firm – one of the most prestigious publishing houses in the world – should publish *Saving Iraq*.

Index

Abd al-Wahhab Mirjan 33
Abdul Ilah, Prince 12–13
Abdul Rahman Al Ateeqi 67
Abdullah, Prince (later King) of
    Jordan 13–14, 72
Abrams, Elliott 86, 92
Abu Dhabi 210, 211, 248
Abu Ghraib prison 144
Afghanistan 103, 122
agricultural development 38, 224
agricultural recovery, proposed
    186–191
  cereal crops 186, 188
  date crops and palms 188, 190–191
  food-rationing programme 189
  irrigation 188, 190
  land, irrigated, upgrading quality
    189–190
  water, fresh 190
agriculture after 1958 coup 187
Ahmad Chalabi, Dr 101–102
Ahmed Hassan al-Bakr 66
Al-Jamali, Dr Mohammed Fadhil
    33, 42, 54–57, 222
Albu Nasir tribe 59
al-Fadhila Party 169

Al-Hayat (pan-Arab newspaper)
    101–102
al-Qaeda 116, 120–121, 122–123, 132,
    265
al-Radhi, Judge Radhi Hamza 104,
    105–106
al-Sadr, Muhammad, 15, 33
Al Ukhaidir 249
al-Zarqawi, Abu Musab 116
Alaska 175, 180–181
Alaska Permanent Fund (APF)
    180–181
Alexandre, Comte de Marenches
    66, 78
Aliyah, Queen of Iraq 13, 22
Allawi, Ayad 134, 170
*America's Role in Nation-building: From
    Germany to Iraq* 134
Anfal campaign (1987) 59
Anglo-Iraqi Treaty 7–8
Ankara 209
Annan, Kofi 81
Arab army 13–14
Arab League 45
Arab nationalists 15, 19
Arab Revolt (1916) 7, 35

Arab Union 20–21, 25, 72, 74
Arab world, Iraq's position as
    integral part of 45
Arabs 12, 122, 128
Arabs, Palestinian 19, 41
archaeological sites 191, 247
Arif, Colonel Abd al-Salam 21, 23,
    24, 25, 26
Aristide, Jean-Bertrand 75
armed forces, abolition of 113, 120,
    168, 262
army, Iraqi 12, 13, 21, 23–24, 35, 57,
    138
  rebuilding of 100
Asharq Alawsat (Arabic newspaper)
    102
Ashur 249
Association of Iraqi Women 141
Assyrian revolt (1933) 35
Australia 209

Baath Party 26, 28, 50, 53, 66, 85,
    130, 131 see also 'De-
    Baathification of Iraq Society'
    archives 114–115
Baathist counter coup (1968) 65–66
Baathist regime 58, 59, 60, 66, 154
  expulsion of 97, 123
Baathists 24, 65, 131
Baban, Ahmed Mukhtar 34
Babylon 191, 249
Baghdad 208–209, 210, 211, 218
  airport 38
  anti-government protests (1956)
    53
  Arab summit (1990) 48
  bank branches, proposed 244
  banks in 197

coup (1958) 16, 17, 21, 23–24,
    34
Dora neighbourhood 121
flooding 38
Frank Lloyd Wright designs for
    193
German embassy 13
Green Zone 131, 137–138
holy sites 192
National Museum 106
occupation by coalition forces 97
population rise 40
revolt (1920) 6
royal palace 21, 23
sandstorms 22
US Embassy 266
violence after invasion and
    collapse of regime 106, 112
Baghdad College 23
Baghdad Pact (1955) 18, 22, 25,
    46–47
Baghdad province, inhabitants of 5
Baghdad Radio 23–24
Bahrain 194
Baker III, James 117
Bakr Sidqi 21, 258
Bangalore 202, 204–205, 212
Bank of America 241, 243
Bank of Italy 241
banking concepts 241–246 see also
    mega-bank for all Iraqis
  real estate development enterprise
    240, 248–251
banking reforms 196–200, 202
Barro, Robert 224–225
Barzani, Masoud 124
Basra 169
Basra port 38

Basra province, inhabitants of 5
BBC 107
BBC Radio 4: 100
Beirut, American University 54
Belgium 13
Biden, Joseph 261
Blackwater security company 101,
143
Blair, Tony 84
Bowen, Stuart 102
Brasília 209, 211
Brazil 209
Brazilinvest 84, 86
Bremer, L. Paul 97, 112–113, 114,
261
Britain, independence from 11, 15
Britain, post-war relationship with
15
Britain's legacy, myth of 40–42
British Joint Intelligence
Committee, head of 95
British 'Mandate' (occupation)
(1920–32) 4, 5–11, 18–19
British Medical Journal 231
Brzezinski, Zbigniew 78
Bunton, Martin 31–32
bureaucrats 85
Bush, George H. W. 70, 76–77, 84,
86, 91
Bush, George W. 84, 94, 261
administration 91, 109, 118–119,
132

Cairo Conference (1921) 7
Cairo radio stations 56
California 202, 203, 204, 205, 206,
241, 242
Cambodia 192

campaign against the rogue regime
69–71
Canberra 209
capital city, proposed new 208–214,
215
Center for Strategic and
International Studies (CSIS)
77, 78
cereal crops 186, 188
Chase Manhattan Bank 251, 252
Cheney, Dick 89, 93, 95
China 213
Christians 12, 32, 33, 122, 128
*Clean Break, A: A New Strategy for
Securing the Realm* paper 91–92
Clinton, Bill 70, 75
administration criticised by
PNAC 92
and Iraq Liberation Act 81–82, 83
policy after First Gulf War 82
return to status quo in Iraq
suggested to 79–81
use of effective force against Iraq
93
Coalition Provisional Authority
(CPA) 112, 114, 115, 134, 136
money controlled by 100–101
Cold War 15, 17, 18, 25, 42, 46
Commission on Public Integrity
(CPI) 104–106
Communist Party, Iraqi (ICP) 14,
21, 24, 50, 131
Congo, Democratic Republic of 103
constitution 8
constitution, new 87, 138–140,
141–142, 154–155
and Kurds 125, 126
Resolution 137: 140

corruption, plague of 99, 100–106
    and Commission on Public
        Integrity 104–106
    Congressional committees 104,
        105
    oil smuggling 102–104
Corruption Perceptions Index 103
Council for Oil Policy 170
coup (1958) 16, 17, 20, 21–22, 23–24,
        34, 51, 60, 258, 268
    lead-up to 17–26
    reasons for 50, 51
coup, counter (1968) 65–66
currency reform 195–196

date crops and palms 188, 190–191
de Borchgrave, Arnaud 77–78
deaths, civilian, after the invasion
        107
'De-Baathification of Iraq Society'
        113, 146, 225, 268
'democratization process' 135,
        149–150
detentions 144
developed world, access to 46–48
Diogenes Laertius 225
disintegration encouraged by US
        policies 129–131
Diwaniyah 24
doctors, shortage of 230
Doha 211, 248
'Downing Street Memo' 95
Dubai 192, 194, 210, 211, 248

Eastman Kodak 203
Ebrahim Yazdi 152–153
economic development 38–39 see also
        agricultural development; oil

industry, development of; oil
        wealth and economic revival
    post-Second World War 15–17,
        20
economy, building a vibrant
        183–216
    agricultural recovery, proposed see
        agricultural recovery, proposed
    banking reforms 196–200, 202
    capital city, proposed new
        208–214, 215
    currency reform 195–196
    financial services, developing
        194–195
    financial system 201–202
    foreign experts, use of 206–207
    growth outlook 198–199
    microfinance 201
    recovery, requirements for
        184–186
    stock market 200–201
    technology, embracing 202–207,
        213
    tourism, development of 191–194
economy, crippled, myth of 36–40
economy, informal 227
education, modern 33–34, 39–40
Education and Technology Board,
        proposed 162, 202–203, 220,
        221
education system, reviving 217–225
    accessibility 223
    benefits 224
    curriculum 221
    exam, baccalaureate 222–223
    management and information
        services 222
    maths and science 222

school buildings, repair of
  220–221
teachers 220
vocational training 221–222, 224
Egypt 18, 20, 56, 192–193
Eisenhower, Dwight D. 25
Eisenhower Exchange Fellowships
  76
elections (2005) 130, 134–138, 258,
  263–264
employees, state 60
Energy Information Administration
  (EIA) 164
ethnic mixing and divisions 28–29
Euphrates, River 45, 47, 190

Fairchild Semiconductor 203
Faisal ibn Hussain I, King of Iraq
  7, 8, 9–10, 11, 12, 33, 35
Faisal II, King of Iraq 13, 21–23, 24,
  72, 73, 193
Falah al-Said 52
federalism 160–161, 268
Feith, Douglas 91–92
financial services, developing
  194–195
Financial Times 153
food-rationing programme 189
Foreign Affairs 121
foreign policy 17–18
foreign policy under Nuri al-Said
  43–48
  access to the developed world
    46–48
  alliances with Iran and Turkey 45
  importance of oil 45–46
  Iraq's position as integral part of
    Arab world 45

Fouad Othman 52, 53
France 13
Freeman, Chas 121
frontiers, international 9
future, lessons for 58–60
Future of Iraq Project 133

Garner, General Jay 112, 133
General Electric 203
Georgetown University, School of
  Foreign Service 79
Germany 133–134
Germany, Nazi 13
Germany, post-war 68
Ghazi, King of Iraq 12
Giannini, Amadeo 241–242
Glubb Pasha, General 14
Governing Iraq 97–98
government,
  dismantled 112–115
  separating religion from 147–153
  structure of 158–161
  transitional 130, 134, 155–158
governments, decentralized 160
Grameen Bank 201
Grasse 78
Greenspan, Alan 261
Guinea 103
Gulf Cooperation Council (GCC)
  countries 194
Gulf War, First (1991) 69, 70, 76–77
Gulf War, Second (2003) 84, 85,
  95–96, 111 *see also* occupation,
  US-led
  march to 90–95
  as most 'spun' conflict 132–134

Haass, Richard 77

Hadid, Zaha 193–194
Haiti 75, 79, 103
Hamilton, Alexander 209
Hamilton, Lee 117
Hanushek, Eric 222
Harrow school 22
Hashemite family 7
    monarchy 8, 9, 17, 24, 26, 29, 32,
        34, 36, 41–42, 130, 268
    option 71–78
Hassan, Prince of Jordan 75
Hatra 192, 249
Health Ministry 107
healthcare system 229–233
    doctors, lifting restrictions on
        231
    doctors, shortage of 230
    emergency care 231
    hospitals, investment in 231
    medical tourism 232–233
Hewlett, William 203
Hewlett-Packard 203
Hikmat Al Mukhailif 52–54
Ho Chi Minh 78
Holland 13
Hong Kong 222
hospitals, investment in 231
housing situation, improving
    233–235
    land ownership, clarification of
        234–235
Hsinchu Science-based Industrial
    Park 202, 204
Hussain bin Ali, Sharif of Mecca 7
Hussein, King of Jordan 21, 52, 67,
    80–81, 84–85
    and Hashemite option for Iraq
        72, 73, 74–75, 76, 79–80

Hussein, Saddam see Saddam
    Hussein
Hussein al-Sharristani 170

'Imna' agricultural project 188
independent nation, building
    (1932–41) 11–14
India 153, 204–205, 206, 213, 214,
    224, 233
Indonesia 172, 213
Industrial Technology Research
    Institute (Taiwan) 204
insurgency inflamed 115–118, 131 see
    also violence, post-invasion
    reign of
Intel 203
International Crisis Group 97–98,
    100
International Institute of Strategic
    Studies 86–87
International Iraqi Oil Company
    (IIOC), proposed 174–175, 178
International Monetary Fund 226
invasion, US-led 95–97, 111, 259, 260
    as most 'spun' conflict 132–134
    financial corruption 99 see also
        corruption, plague of
    installation of political power
        centres 96–97
    reconstruction following 112–113
    support for dubious outsiders
        98–99
Investcorp 52, 71, 76, 239, 240,
    250–257
    accomplishments 255–256
    mission and culture 254–255
Iran 45–46, 47–48
Iran-Iraq War (1980–88) 48, 66, 166

Iranian influence on Shias 117
Iraq before 1958 3–4
Iraq Body Count 107
Iraq Governing Council (IGC) 97,
    98, 113–114, 130, 133, 134, 138,
    140, 259–260, 263
Iraq Liberation Act (1998) 81–82,
    83, 90, 93
Iraq Memory Foundation 114
Iraq National Oil Company
    (INOC) 170, 173
Iraq Relief and Reconstruction
    Fund (IRRF) 188, 230, 234
Iraq Strategy Review 119
'Iraq Study Group', US 117, 138
Iraqi Communist Party (ICP) 14, 21,
    24, 50, 131
Iraqi Development Board (IDB) 16,
    25, 37, 38, 39, 42, 50, 56, 59,
    174, 187, 190, 193, 217
Iraqi National Development Board
    209
Iraqi Oil Law 170
Iraqi Petroleum Company (IPC) 16,
    36, 37, 59, 165, 174
Iraqi Railways 52
Iraqis, ex-patriate 68, 262–263
Ireland 183, 184–185
IRIN (UN humanitarian news
    agency) 108
irrigation 188, 190
Islamic Council, Supreme 139, 169
Israel 15, 19
Issam al-Said 52
Istanbul, Robert College 22, 23
Istanbul, Yesilkoy international
    airport 21–22, 23
Istiqlal Party 14

IT services, proposed 214

Japan 68, 133–134
Jeddah 211
Jews 12, 19, 32, 33, 128
Jordan, Hashemite Kingdom of 13,
    20–21, 25, 72, 73, 74, 79, 80,
    109, 226, 227, 265
Jordanian army 13–14
JPMorgan Chase bank 251, 252
judiciary, independent 9

Karbala 192, 249
Kennebunkport, Maine, Walker's
    Point 76, 77
Kennedy, Robert F. 238
Khomeini, Ayatollah 152–153
Khrushchev, Nikita 25
Kirdar, Nemir 11–12, 17, 21–22, 23,
    30, 42, 63–65, 66
    asked to return to Iraq 240
    brother Fahir 53
    brother Nezir 55, 128
    family 5–6, 20, 53, 56, 73, 128,
        140–141
    father 128
    grandfather 5–6, 73, 128
    great-grandfather 5
    and Hashemite option 71–72,
        73–77, 78
    and invasion of Kuwait 67–68
    and Investcorp 250–251, 252, 254
    mother 22, 140–141
    post-invasion suggestions
        unheeded 84–88
    suggests return to status quo in
        Iraq to Clinton 79–81
    World Bank meetings 52–53

Kirkuk 5, 55, 125, 168–169
  oil field 36
  the question of 128–129
Kissinger, Dr Henry 78
Korea, South 183, 184–185, 222
Kufah 249
Kurd army (Peshmerga) 125
Kurdish areas, separatist
  movements in 41
Kurdistan 123, 124, 125, 126
Kurds 12, 27, 28, 32, 33, 35, 112, 122,
  128–129, 136
  press for autonomy 123–126, 139,
  168
  war of independence, virtual
  59
Kuwait, Emir of 48
Kuwait, invasion of (1990) 48, 60,
  63, 67
Kuwait, liberation of 69, 70, 76–77
Kuwait, threatened again 70

labour markets 225–229
  and population displacement
  226–227
  unemployment 226
Lancet, The 107
land ownership, clarification of
  234–235
land reforms 9
Las Vegas 212
law, Sharia 140, 141, 147, 153
Law Number 80: 165
lawlessness, post-invasion reign of
  106–107, 112 see also insurgency
  inflamed
Lawrence, T. E. 7
leaders, visionary, need for 238–239

League of Nations 5, 9, 11, 41, 50
Lebanon 145
Lee Hsien Loong 207
Lee Kuan Yew 191
Leenders, Dr Reinoud 100
Li, Kwoh-ting 204, 206
liberation, US-led see invasion, US-
  led
Libya 172
Lloyd Wright, Frank 193
Lockheed 203
London, St Paul's Cathedral 80
Longrigg, Stephen 39

MacArthur, General Douglas 133
Macmillan, Harold 25
Mahmud, Nureddin 34
Makiya, Kanan 114
Mandi Army 120
Marenches, Alexandre, Comte de
  66, 78
Marr, Phebe 12, 38–39
marriages, mixed 141
'Marsh Arabs' 71
Marshall Plan 101
McKinsey & Company 198–199
Medact 230
medical tourism 232–233
mega-bank for all Iraqis 240,
  241–247
  clients 243–244
  organization 245–247
'Mesopotamia' 5
microfinance 201
mid-Euphrates revolt 10–11, 41
Middle East, tourism in 191–192
Middle East Economic Digest Special
  Report 197

migration since the invasion
108–109, 111, 226–227, 265
migration to cities 40
ministers, government, selection of
33
Ministry of Health 230
Mohammed Ali Kirdar 5–6, 73,
128
monarchy, constitutional 8, 9, 17,
24, 26, 29, 32, 34, 36, 41–42,
130, 268
monarchy overthrown *see* coup
(1958)
Moqtada al-Sadr 119–120
Moscow radio stations 56
Mosul province 9, 41
holy sites 192
inhabitants of 5
Muhammad al-Sadir 15, 33
Muhammed Yunus 201
Mujahiddeen 122
Muslims worldwide 153
Mustafa Boodai 67
Mustansiriyya University 218
Myanmar 103

Najaf 192, 249
Nasser, Gamal Adbel 18, 19, 20,
21, 25, 47, 48, 50–51, 57,
65
Nasserism, spread of 19–20
Nasserites 24, 35, 40, 48, 50
National Assembly, Transitional
130, 134, 155–158
National Bank of Kuwait 246
National Commercial Bank (Saudi
Arabia) 246
National Democratic Party 14

National Economic Development
Board (NEDB), proposed 162,
175–178, 179, 186
National Education and Technology
Board 162, 202–203, 220,
221
National Housing Fund 234
National Oil Regulatory Board
(NORB), proposed 178–179
National Taiwan University 204
Naziha al-Dulaimi 140
Netanyahu, Binyamin 91–92
New York 251
Columbia University 54
New York Times 102, 103–104
Nijyar Shemdin 53
Nimrod 249
Nineveh 249
Nobel Peace Prize 201
no-fly zones 69–70, 123
Norway 170–171, 181
Norwegian State Petroleum Fund
(NSPF) 181
Nowak, Manfred 107
Nuri al-Maliki 137
Nuri al-Said 13, 14–16, 20, 23, 37,
39, 42–50, 51–52 *see also* foreign
policy under Nuri al-Said
and anti-government protests
(1956) 53–54
daughter-in-law 51
personal qualities 49
philosophy 49–50
wife 51
Nussbaum, David 103

occupation, US-led 58, 64 *see also*
Gulf War, Second

occupation—*contd*
four steps towards disintegration
129–130
mistakes 261–266
O'Donovan, Father Leo J. 79
Office of Reconstruction and
Humanitarian Assistance
(ORHA) 112
oil, importance of 45
oil and Kurds 126
Oil for Food Programme 71, 166,
187, 230
oil industry 4
development of 36–37
end of expansion of 48
expansion of 37–38
oil output, highest 165–166
oil prices, rise in 66
oil production and revenue
(1946–58) 37
oil revenues 37, 42, 50, 59–60, 174
proposed distribution of 179–182,
186
oil smuggling 102–104, 177
oil wealth and economic revival
164–182
challenges facing industry
167–169
company, new, with foreign
participation (IIOC) 174–175,
178
fiscal regime 172–173
institutional framework, new
173–174
legacy of inefficiency 165–167
National Economic Development
Board, proposed 162, 175–178,
179, 186

National Oil Regulatory Board
(NORB), proposed 178–179
oil revenues, proposed
distribution of 179–182, 186
oil stabilization fund, proposed
180
petroleum law, need for 169–173
production-sharing agreements
(PSAs) 171, 179
security, need for 168
Omar, Mullah 78
Omar Ali, General 24–25
opera house design 193
Operation Desert Fox 93
Operation Iraqi Freedom 95–96, 111
see also Gulf War, Second;
invasion, US-led
Operation Provide Comfort 112
opposition leaders outside Iraq after
First Gulf War 83–84, 98–99,
111, 113
Ottoman empire 4, 5, 6 *see also*
Turkey
outsiders, dubious, supported by
occupation authorities 98–99

Packard, David 203
Palestine 19
Palestinian Arabs 19, 41
Palestinians 19, 92
Palm Beach, Florida 211
Palo Alto 203
Paris 152–153
parliament 8–9, 32
Perle, Richard 91–92
Peshmerga (Kurd army) 125
Petra 192–193
Petraeus plan 122

Poland 13

police, Iraqi 138 *see also* armed
forces, abolition of

political settlement, need for
162–163

politics, 'mass' 24

Polk, William 39

population 225–226, 242

Portsmouth, Treaty of (1948) 15

poverty after the invasion 108

prime minister 8, 32–33

professionals, secular Iraqi 99

Program on World Policy Attitudes
117

Project for the New American
Century (PNAC) 92–93, 94

property prices 211

Qasim, Abd al-Karim 23, 24, 26,
58, 59, 165

Qatar 194

Qatar National Bank 246

Qazaz, Said 34

Rabin, Yitzhak 79

Rafidain Bank 104, 196–197

Rasheed Bank 196–197

Rashid Ali al-Gailani 12–13, 14, 21,
258

Rathmell, Andrew 135

real estate prices 211

recovery, requirements for 184–186

Red Crescent, Iraqi 227

religion, separating, from the state
147–153, 158

reserves, foreign exchange 60

Reuters 103

revolt (1920) 6

Rice, Dr Condoleezza 86–87

Ricks, Thomas E. 113

rights, individual, state as guarantor
154–155

Riyadh 211

Rand 134, 135

road-building 38

Rolling Stone 121

Rome 84, 86

Rommel, Field Marshal Erwin 13

Rosen, Mir 121

Rumsfeld, Donald 92

Sabah al-Said 51–52

Saddam Hussein
and Baath Party 130
and Baghdad 209
becomes president 66
after First Gulf War 69, 71, 76,
81–82
and Iran-Iraq War 66–67
Iraq suffers under 26–30, 259, 264
and Kurds 27, 28, 123
and Kuwait 48, 60, 63, 67
loyalty to 27, 31
and Oil for Food Programme 71
and oil revenues 59–60, 166
overthrown 260
plays on sectarian differences 29
reign of terror 59, 71, 259, 264
rise to power of 16, 26
ruling elite 59
and Shias 27, 28
US and British determination to
get rid of 84, 90, 94

Salih Jabir 33

Salter, Lord 17

Samarra 192, 249

San Francisco 241
San Remo, Italy 5
Sandhurst, Royal Military Academy
    15
Sardinia 212
Saudi Arabia 164, 192, 194
school buildings, repair of 220–221
science and technology parks,
    proposed 205–206, 213
Scowcroft, General Brent 77
sectarian mixing and divisions
    28–29
sectarianism, new politics of 95–98
security firms, private 101, 143
semiconductors 203
September 11, 2001, terror attacks
    84, 93–94
Sharia law 140, 141, 147, 153
Shia Muslims 6, 12, 27, 28, 32, 33,
    35, 45, 122, 123, 130–131, 139,
    140
  Iranian influence 117
  ulama 33
Shia region, formation of 139
Shia religious leaders 136
Shiite clerics 9–10
Shiites see Shia Muslims
Shlaim, Professor Avi 80
Shockley, William 203
Silicon Valley 202, 203, 204, 205,
    206
Simon, Steven 121
Singapore 176, 183, 184–185, 191,
    206, 207, 212, 213, 214, 215,
    221–222
social change 40
society, fractious, myth of 32–34
Society of American Archivists 115

Software Technology Parks of India
    (STPI) 204–205
solution, proposed 266–271
Somalia 103
Soviet Union 15, 18, 25, 47, 75
Soviets 46, 50, 122
Special Inspector General for Iraq
    Reconstruction (SIGIR),
    Office of 167
sports facilities, proposed 212–213
Stanford Research Park 203
state, separating religion from
    147–153, 158
state as guarantor of individual
    rights 154–155
stock market 200–202
students, lowest-achieving, joining
    armed forces 57
Suez Canal 19, 41
suggestions, post-invasion,
    unheeded 84–88
Sunni Muslims 6, 12, 27, 28, 31, 32,
    33, 59, 122, 125, 140
  leaders 136
  myth of 34–35
Supreme Council for the Islamic
    Revolution in Iraq 139, 169
'surge' policy, US 118–123, 146, 260
  myths of the 118–123
Syria 20, 92, 109, 190, 226, 227, 265

Taha al-Hashimi 13
Taiwan 183, 184–185, 204, 206, 213,
    214, 222
Tawfiq al-Suwaidi 14
Tawfiq Wahbi, Asiya 141
tax system, fair 161–163
taxation system, lack of 136–137

Taylor, John B. 195–196
teachers 220
technology, embracing 202–207, 213
Tenet, George 95
Terman, Fred 203
terrorists, foreign, post-invasion 117,
264–265
Tharthar, Lake 211
Tharthar Dam 38
Tigris, River 45, 47, 190
'The Isle of Edena' 193
torture reports after the invasion
107
tourism, development of 191–194
tourist sites 191, 249
Transitional National Assembly 130,
134, 155–158
Transparency International 103
Tripp, Charles 9, 37–38
Turkey 45, 47, 153, 190, 192, 209 *see
also* Ottoman Empire
Turkish Petroleum Company 36
Turkomans 12, 32, 33, 122, 128–129

unemployment after the invasion
108, 226
UNESCO (United Nations
Educational Scientific and
Cultural Organization) 219
UNHCR (United Nations High
Commission for Refugees)
108–109, 226–227
United Arab Republic 20
United Kingdom Foreign Office,
Iraq Policy Unit 197
United Nations 82, 184
Development Fund for Iraq 101
Development Group/World

Bank housing report 233, 234,
235
Food and Agriculture
Organization (FAO) 190
IRIN (humanitarian news agency)
108
Oil for Food Programme 71, 166,
187, 230
sanctions 187
Security Council resolutions 70,
132
weapons inspection programme
70, 81, 93
United Nations Charter 55
United States *see also* California;
Washington, DC
administration 64
Agricultural Reconstruction and
Development Program for Iraq
(ARDI) 188
capital city 209–210
Congress 101
covert measures to depose
Saddam 70
investment in Iraq after invasion
101
Iraq Relief and Reconstruction
Fund (IRRF) 188, 230, 234
neo-conservative movement 81,
82, 89–91, 92–95, 260–261
openly embraces regime change
in Iraq 81–84
policies encourage disintegration
129–131
policy based on 'Spin' 132–134
State Department 133
State Department, Oil and
Energy Working Group 170

United States—*contd*
  'surge' policy *see* 'surge' policy,
    US
United States Air Force 262
United States-Iraqi Agreements
  (2008) 142–146
  Article 12 (legal matters) 143
  Article 22 (detentions) 144
  uncertainties 144–145
United States-led occupation 58, 64
  forces, promised withdrawal 144
  four steps towards disintegration
    129–130
  mistakes 261–266
unity, argument for 126–127
uprising (*wathba*) 15
Ur 192, 249
Uruk 192, 249

venture capitalists 201
Vietnam 192
violence, post-invasion reign of
    106–107, 112 *see also* insurgency
  inflamed

Washington, George 210
Washington, DC 52–53, 209–210 *see*
    also White House

water, fresh 190
weapons of mass destruction
    (WMD) 70, 94, 95, 132
West, growth in resentment against
    19–20
wetlands, draining of 71
wheat crops 186, 188
White House 79
  West Wing 86
Wolfowitz, Paul 92–93
women, Iraqi, position of 140–
    141
Woolsey, Jim 78
World Bank 52, 233, 234, 235
World Tourism Organization
    191–192
World War, First (1914–18) 4, 7
World War, Second (1939–45)
    13
  period after 14–17
Wright, Frank Lloyd 193
Wurmser, David 91–92

Zaid Bin Shakir, Field Marshal
    73–74
Zakia Haqqi 140
Zimbabwe 103
Zogby International 228